DANGEROUS
AND
PERSUASIVE
WOMAN

THAT DANGEROUS AND PERSUASIVE WOMAN

VIDA GOLDSTEIN

JANETTE M. BOMFORD

MELBOURNE UNIVERSITY PRESS
1993

First published 1993
Design by Judith Summerfeldt
Typeset in 11/13 point Goudy
by SRM Production Services Sdn. Bhd.
Printed in Malaysia by SRM Production Services Sdn. Bhd.
for Melbourne University Press, Carlton, Victoria 3053
U.S.A. and Canada: International Specialized Book Services, Inc.,
5804 N.E. Hassalo Street, Portland, Oregon 97213-3644
United Kingdom and Europe: University College London Press,
Gower Street, London WC1E 6BT

This book is copyright. Apart from any fair dealing for the purposes of private study, research, criticism or review, as permitted under the Copyright Act, no part may be reproduced by any process without written permission. Enquiries should be made to the publisher.

© Janette Margaret Bomford 1993

National Library of Australia Cataloguing-in-Publication entry

Bomford, Janette M. (Janette Margaret), 1953– .
  That dangerous and persuasive woman.
  Bibliography.
  Includes index.
  ISBN 0 522 84542 8.
  1. Goldstein, Vida, 1869–1949. 2. Suffragists—Australia—Biography. 3. Women social reformers—Australia—Biography. 4. Feminists—Australia—Biography. I. Title.
324.623092

For Nik, my best beloved
This is your book, too

◆

Contents

♦

	Illustrations	ix
	Preface	xiii
	Acknowledgements	xv
	Author's note	xvii
	Abbreviations	xviii
1	Childhood, 1869–1889	1
2	The New Woman, 1890–1901	12
3	To America and back, 1902	33
4	The lady candidate, 1903	51
5	Deep waters, 1904–1908	73
6	Women voters, 1909–1910	93
7	Face to the dawn, 1911	104
8	Campaigns for Kooyong, 1912–1914	120
9	Casualties of war, 1914–1915	143
10	Battles for peace, 1915–1916	159
11	Conscription, strikes and spies, 1916–1918	169
12	The world moves, 1919–1922	191
13	A spiritual woman, 1923–1949	204
	Afterword	218
	Appendix 1: Disposal of Vida's papers	227
	Appendix 2: Chronology of memorials	228
	Notes	230
	Bibliography	252
	Index	257

Illustrations

◆

Illustrations are reproduced courtesy of the La Trobe Collection, State Library of Victoria, unless otherwise stated.

Isabella Hawkins   between 38 and 39

Jacob Goldstein

Vida as a child
National Library of Australia

The Goldstein children
National Library of Australia

Vida c. 1890
Vida Clift

Woman's Sphere, 8 April 1903

The Australian delegate to the International
    Women Suffrage Conference
Isobel Creightmore

Vida, the political candidate between 86 and 87
Vida Clift

'A Senatorial Sister'
Punch, 13 August 1903

With Stella Miles Franklin

Senate campaign, 1910
Age, 8 May 1985

The woman's suffrage executive committee
Leader, 12 December 1908

'Miss Vida Goldstein weeping outside the Senate'
Liberty and Progress, 24 March 1910

Foreign contingent of the 1911
suffragette march between 150 and 151

Selling *Votes for Women*
(Melbourne) *Herald*, 6 August 1912

The great suffragette procession
National Library of Australia

Women's farm
Madeleine Westwood

Campaign meeting, 1913

Collecting clothing
(Melbourne) *Herald*, 18 February 1915

'The blood vote'
Australian War Memorial, photograph no. A4801

Vida, 1930
National Library of Australia

'A little child shall lead them' between 150 and 151
Madeleine Westwood

Enlistment poster
Australian War Memorial, photograph no. A3819

Preface

◆

Vida Goldstein's story is the story of first-wave feminism in Victoria. Two years before her birth, the issue of woman suffrage was first raised in the Victorian Parliament; she was thirty-nine when Victorian women were at last enfranchised. During her lifetime many reforms to improve the lot of women and children were won—and some lost again. By the time of her death in 1949 the women's movement was largely inactive, awaiting its revival in the 1960s and 1970s.

Vida is best known for being the first woman to nominate for the Australian Parliament, but the diversity of her interests and activities defy giving her one identifying label. She was Victoria's foremost suffragist for two decades. She worked tirelessly for the welfare of women, children, the unemployed and poor wage-earners. She sought equality for women before the law, within marriage and in employment. She fought for children's courts and the more humane treatment of juvenile offenders. She was also an ardent peace activist and anti-conscriptionist.

Vida was a trailblazer and therein lay her tragedy: the reforms she advocated were decades ahead of her time. Although in her lifetime she enjoyed national and international recognition, she chose to withdraw from public life and her contribution had been almost forgotten even before she died. The first official honour accorded to her was in 1984 when the federal electorate of Balaclava, which abuts Kooyong, the electorate she stood for twice, was renamed Goldstein.

(Ironically the name is usually mispronounced: Vida always used an 'eye' sound in the pronounciation of both her first name and surname.) This recognition arose partly from the work of second-wave feminists, who sought to reclaim the stories of the pioneer suffragists. As Vida once said, 'They learn nothing, and they forget everything'.[1] It is a sign of subjugation to have lost one's history; it is a sign of growing strength to reclaim it.

The process of rediscovering women's history is hampered by the scarcity of material. Vida's public life is better documented than most of the early suffragists through her newspapers the *Woman's Sphere* and the *Woman Voter*, but she preserved few of her personal records and so her story is concerned with events and facts rather than thoughts and emotions. Other suffragists like Rose Scott and Bessie Rischbieth were great collectors. With the help of their collections and letters which Vida wrote to her friends, we get rare glimpses of Vida's private world with its anxieties and frustrations.

The passage of time also hampers the search for the 'private' Vida. The last of her contemporaries was probably Eileen McLoughlin, a WPA speaker, who died in 1980 aged ninety-six. Unfortunately her death occurred before I started researching this book. I had the privilege of meeting or writing to many of Vida's relatives as well as a few people who had known her, all of whom were much younger than Vida. They recalled her with fondness, admiration and respect.

Vida was not a comfortable person to write about; her commitment and involvement was absolute. A biographer has the rare privilege of coming to know another person well (a fact remarked on with some surprise by one of Vida's relatives: 'You know more about her than we do!') 'Living' with Vida for six years was not always easy, but I would not have had it any other way. Her ideas changed my thinking and therefore subtly changed how I live.

At times Vida seems an idealised figure, consistently committed, brave, strong, virtuous, even good-looking and attractively dressed. There is little evidence of frailties or inner doubts: her conflicts appear to have been external ones. This presents a challenge for the biographer. Nevertheless, her sheer courage, her noble consistency of belief and practice, and the historical significance of her undertakings, make her unique and a worthy subject for biography.

Acknowledgements

◆

One joy of writing this book has been the people who have helped me in so many ways. My grateful thanks to Winifred Anderson, Isobel Creightmore, Diana Creightmore, Meredith Creightmore, Peter Lawson, Bert Gardiner, Alice Gilbert, John Holroyd, Christine Honig and Madeleine Westwood for their time, hospitality and information so willingly given. John Breukel, Vida Clift, David Elder, Helen Hudson, David Maunders, M. Elizabeth Pratt, Shayne Medcalf, Stan Robe, Elizabeth Sharpe, Yvonne Smith, Brian Williams and the League of Women Voters all made valued contributions.

I appreciate the assistance of the staff at the Fawcett Library, City of London Polytechnic; the Mitchell Library; the National Library of Australia; the State Library of Victoria; the University of Melbourne Archives; Monash University; the University of Sydney; the Australian Archives at Canberra and Brighton, the London Museum; the Humanities department, University College of Northern Victoria and Loddon Campaspe College of TAFE, Bendigo.

Many of the above individuals and institutions also kindly granted me permission to use copyright material. I am also grateful for permission to use copyright material from Permanent Trustee Company Limited, trustee of the late Stella Miles Franklin and Don Cooper and Kenneth Barry, trustees of the late Leslie Henderson. Every effort has been made to obtain permission to use copyright material but the publishers would be pleased to hear of any inadvertent errors or omissions.

I also wish to acknowledge the valued assistance of the Victorian Ministry for the Arts through its Project Assistance Grant for the final preparation of the manuscript.

Jan Bassett, John and Nancy Bomford, Jean and Nancy Bomford, Maree and Mick Doherty, Debbie and Peter Knight, Doug and Phyliss Smithson and my friends and students in the General Studies department, Loddon Campaspe College of TAFE, Bendigo, all helped with their enthusiasm and encouragement.

Nicholas Bomford encouraged me to dream of what could be and then helped me do it. His belief in me and that Vida's story should be told, combined with his endless enthusiasm, supportiveness and technical expertise selflessly provided, are greatly valued. To him I give my loving appreciation. Lastly, there is Shima, my faithful companion during the long hours at the computer.

Author's note

◆

Although the Australian Labor Party was spelt as such from 1891, Vida persisted in spelling it 'Labour'. I have maintained her spelling, capitalisation and punctuation within the quotes, even when this does not follow the style I have adopted in the text. Similarly, while I support the use of non-gender-specific language, Vida used the word 'chairman' for either sex, hence my use of the term.

Abbreviations

◆

AWNL	Australian Women's National League
COS	Charity Organisation Society
LBS	Ladies' Benevolent Society
NCW	National Council of Women
THC	Trades Hall Council
UCSS	United Council for State Suffrage
UCWS	United Council for Women's Suffrage
WCTU	Woman's Christian Temperance Union
WFPA	Women's Federal Political Association
WPA	Women's Political Association
WSPU	Women's Social and Political Union

1

Childhood

1869–1889

◆

Vida Jane Mary Goldstein (she never used her middle names) was born at 6.30 p.m. on Tuesday 13 April 1869. She was the first child of Isabella and Jacob Goldstein who had married the previous year, when Isabella was eighteen and Jacob twenty-eight. Isabella Hawkins was Australian-born, but her parents were Scottish. Her father had arrived in Portland, on the south-west coast of Victoria, a few years after the first white settlers and, as a squatter in the rich farming land of the Western District, his wealth had grown with the young colony. Jacob Robert Yannasch Goldstein was born in Ireland and was the only child of a Polish-Jewish father and a Dutch-Irish mother. As a young man of nineteen, he emigrated to Australia as an assisted passenger. When the couple met, Jacob was a businessman in Portland. He also served in the militia for thirty years, attaining the rank of lieutenant-colonel, but he never saw action.[1] Jacob's earnings and Isabella's marriage settlement of 2161 guineas enabled them to live in comfort and to employ domestic staff.[2]

The Goldsteins lived in 'Alma Cottage' in Hurd Street, Portland, which had been owned by Isabella's father and used by the Hawkins family as a town house. Vida was born there. A second daughter, Elsie Belle, was born the following year in 1870. After the family moved to Warrnambool, where Jacob had a wholesale and general store, three more children were born: Lina in 1872, Selwyn in 1873 and Aileen in

1877. Shortly after Aileen was born, the Goldsteins moved to Melbourne.

One constant in Vida's life was Lizzie Kavanagh, who joined the family in 1872 as the cook-general. In the early days, she often threatened, 'I'll leave this day month', but she remained with the Goldsteins until her death in 1941. When finances permitted, a housemaid was also employed, but at other times Lizzie did all the work. If someone did not like a particular dish she served, she would make that person a different meal and consequently they all became 'very pernickety'.[3] When celebrating her diamond jubilee of service to the family, Lizzie recalled the early days when 'even with the best of mistresses, housework meant continuous hard labour ... Gone are all the embroidery and lace-trimmed garments that took such a long time to iron, the starched pinafores, petticoats, and dresses, that made washing-day a nightmare'.[4]

Vida never knew her grandparents; Isabella's parents died before Vida was born and after Jacob emigrated from Ireland he seems to have had no further contact with his family. Vida, however, was proud that her paternal grandfather was a 'Polish Jew, a fighter for Polish liberty, who was ultimately compelled to seek refuge in England'.[5] Perhaps of all her grandparents she was closest in character to this fighter for liberty she never met. In the absence of grandparents, the influence of her parents on Vida's personality was that much greater. Isabella and Jacob had lively inquiring minds and dynamic personalities. Their commitment to their beliefs was absolute. They passed on many of these qualities and values to their eldest daughter.

Both parents were devout Christians and the importance of a spiritual life was deeply instilled in Vida. Isabella was a Presbyterian and Jacob a Unitarian. The children were brought up as Presbyterians. Both parents were also passionately committed to working for the 'scientific amelioration' of the poor. They wrote papers on the topic and no doubt discussed the issue in their home. While helping the less fortunate is part of a Christian's duty, and many middle-class people made a hobby of it, Isabella and Jacob were genuinely compassionate and were motivated by a fundamental sense of justice and equality. It is recorded that even as a young girl Isabella had 'pondered the inequalities of life, contrasting the conditions in the men's quarters and in the lonely shepherds' huts with the luxury of the homestead'.[6] From an early age Vida was made aware of the plight of the poor. She learnt that there was no government assistance for widows, the unemployed, the sick or the aged; nor was there support for unskilled labourers on low wages with large families. The misery of poverty was exacerbated by disease caused by malnutrition, poor sanitation, polluted water supplies, inadequate housing and overcrowding. Isabella and Jacob worked to alleviate this suffering and their commitment, practical example and belief that science could be used to solve social problems were all crucial influences on Vida.

Isabella was also a feminist, pacifist and teetotaller and Vida adopted her mother's convictions. Isabella's motivation may well have stemmed from observing her own mother's life. Her mother bore eight children in fifteen years, one of whom died as an infant. She had to contend with a husband who suffered from depression, drank to excess and was violent. On one occasion, when he assaulted her and attempted to kill himself, it was reported in the local paper. Her mother died at the age of forty, when Isabella was only fourteen. Her father died three years later from 'exhaustion and the effects of alcohol'.[7]

Isabella also opposed the inequitable condition of women. Isabella was an heiress, but when she married her property became her husband's; she could not own or bequeath it. In his will a man could nominate a guardian for his children other than their mother. To gain a divorce, a husband had only to prove his wife had been unfaithful once, whereas a wife had to prove the husband's repeated adultery, as well as cruelty and desertion. Women were barred from higher education and many occupations and could not vote. In the year of Vida's birth, the women of Wyoming in the USA were the first in the world to gain the vote. The same year a letter to the *Argus* called for woman suffrage. Veteran feminist Henrietta Dugdale is credited with writing it.[8] Later, Isabella enthusiastically worked in the early suffrage societies hoping to help eradicate these inequities.

Another important influence on Vida was her parents' involvement in her intellectual development. Isabella and Jacob were intelligent, had broad interests and valued learning. Jacob published scientific papers on esoteric subjects, including 'Notes on Living Polyzoa' and 'The Use of Carbolic Acid in Mounting Microscopic Objects'. Both parents took the 'utmost care' with their children's education.[9] Jacob encouraged his daughters to think for themselves and to expect to contribute to society by working. Jacob's progressive attitudes did not, however, extend as far as supporting woman suffrage and this was later to cause divisions within the family.

Jacob's involvement in his children's instruction is illustrated by Vida's 'Autobiography'.[10] At dinner one night, the ten-year-old Vida remarked casually that she thought she could write her own history. Jacob said that if she did he would give her something and that her autobiography would be very interesting. Vida left the room and went to the nursery where she wrote the first page in about twenty minutes. She was called to go out for a walk, but returned before the others and within half an hour had finished writing three pages of blue foolscap. She proudly showed her father, who perused it carefully, then read it aloud to her mother and aunt. They were all very pleased with it and Jacob gave her two shillings and told her to rewrite it, 'taking more time, and more pains'. He told her to write about eight pages and gave her a fortnight to do it. Jacob recorded Vida's age on the manuscript and how she came to write it. Vida remembered him nodding wisely and saying, 'Yes, yes, it is very good—but now go back to the nursery and re-write every bit of it and strike out every second word!'.[11] It was a lesson she never forgot.

When Elsie saw that Vida had been given two shillings, she too set to work on an autobiography. Writing in the nursery, Elsie complained that the other children were too noisy and that she could not think or write well. She was given a shilling for her efforts. The two autobiographies reflect the different personalities of the girls. Vida's is more structured and has an awareness of an audience and a didactic tone that is absent in Elsie's. Vida refers to 'my little readers' and debates whether to tell them information ('would you like to know what it was[?] Well I think I will tell you'.). She verbosely concludes with an exhortation for self-improvement, which was a characteristic theme of her life:

> Well as I am only a little girl off [sic] ten years old, although I think myself a grown person, I have not a long account to give of myself, as I am only 10 years old. Now my little readers [because] I have nothing more to say of myself I will say Good Bye. Now please follow my example and begin when you are as young to give an account of yourself, so that when you are older and wiser you will be able to write longer and better Autobiographys [sic].

Vida's 'Autobiography' provides a few rare glimpses of her childhood. In it she recalled a holiday to Melbourne when she was four. The family stayed at a boarding house in Fitzroy, just opposite the Carlton Gardens. A man who lived there, a Mr Murray, took Vida to the gardens and made her a wreath of flowers which he put around her neck. Vida thought this 'very nice' until it began to tickle her. The Goldsteins made regular visits to Portland to see family and friends. They enjoyed picnics and Vida particularly remembered one birthday party in Portland because she was given an iced cake. She wrote, 'perhaps some of you my little readers would like to be me, but, I wouldn't like that at all'. Recalling the birth of her youngest sister Aileen, she wrote, 'we all had a great treat... [when] such a dear little baby' was born. When told the news, Vida 'jump[ed] for joy'.

Vida also described the sea voyage when the family moved to Melbourne. 'On a very pleasant evening during the month of November I was put on board the steamship *Nelson* and thence made my voyage to Melbourne. It was lovely and calm and I was not seasick at all.' She adds rather cryptically, 'Before I came to Melbourne I used to try and make myself very oldfashioned'. While their parents were settling in, Vida and Elsie were sent to the 'country' at Gardiner, now a south-eastern suburb of Melbourne. They stayed for a month or so with a Mrs Bird, who was 'very cross' sometimes.[12] They were glad to rejoin their family in Hawthorn. Three or four months later Elsie contracted scarlet fever and then Selwyn became very ill with it. Vida was glad to report that 'neither of them was me'. Both children recovered and the family moved to Carlton. They moved quite frequently from one rented house to another in the inner suburbs.

For the Christmas holidays in 1878 Elsie and Vida visited Dunolly and 'very pleasant it was to [sic]'.

Her parents and then Vida kept and cherished these autobiographies and they are still carefully preserved today by her niece.

Vida was taught at home by a series of governesses. She considered herself fortunate in the teachers selected for her. The most notable was Julia Sutherland, who belonged to an artistic and literary family and was a committed suffragist. A school report on the Goldstein children written by Julia survives. Vida's report said:

Vida is still the same hard-working willing and obedient pupil that I found her at first; spreading a good influence on all around her; and although I noticed that she showed less energy in her work during the last month than formerly, that is only a sign that holidays are necessary. With her music she becomes more and more careful every day and as carelessness was her one great fault before, that is very satisfying to her teacher. Her examination papers which I have shown you are not up to her best I think, but still they give a very fair idea of what she can do. A great deal (but I think not too much) of her time was spent in preparing for the Health Society's Examination. She took great interest in the work and it did her good; for the book was just of the proper difficulty for her, though not for most of the competitors. I need not say that she has made steady improvement in all parts of her work. Anyone with the ability and perseverance that she has must necessarily do that. The subject in which she seems to find least interest is Latin, but even there her distaste has not interfered much with her progress.[13]

The character of this conscientious girl, 'spreading a good influence on all around her', remained essentially the same throughout her life.

Julia compared the other children with Vida. She considered Elsie lazy although there had been 'marked and steady improvement'. She noted that her disposition was not, like Vida's, suited to the classroom; that she had many good points and 'that she is quite different from Vida, but excellent in her way'. Lina in the first quarter had worked and behaved so well that Julia was sure she was 'quite another Vida'. Her attitude, however, had deteriorated, although Julia was unsure if this was owing to ill health. Selwyn was interested in improvement, sometimes even suggesting parts of his work that needed attention which was 'not often found in one so young', but he was not fond of his lessons and his homework always seemed a 'burden' to him. His reading needed improvement and she had decided to make it a 'regular lesson' for Vida and Elsie to hear him read on alternate evenings for a quarter of an hour, and 'if it is not done there must be impositions for it as for any other lesson'.

There had been a sudden crying epidemic where all the children ('Vida of course excepted') were apt to 'burst forth at any moment'. This had arisen when she needed to take a 'firm stand in a few matters'. After the storm had been weathered, life became 'more than usually peaceful and orderly'.

When Vida was fifteen, she became a day pupil at the Presbyterian

Ladies' College. The principal, Andrew Harper, paid a high tribute to Julia's teaching when he said that Vida was one of the most thoroughly grounded pupils he had ever received in the college.[14] By August 1884, Julia was no longer teaching any of the Goldstein children, but she wrote to Isabella that she was most interested to follow Vida's progress. Her only fear was that Vida 'will feel inclined to work too hard. She has a conscience that is not easily satisfied and she is not happy until it is satisfied'. She was pleased that Vida was at the college, adding, 'It has its defects of course, like all other schools, but there is a high tone of enthusiasm there and I think that is a great thing'. She was disappointed that she was not to have Vida as a music pupil, 'but I know from what you said that I would have been fortunate enough to have had her if you could have managed it'.[15]

The Presbyterian Ladies' College was founded in 1875 'to provide for the daughters of our colonists as high an education as their sons are receiving at such institutions as the Scotch College, the Church of England Grammar School and the Wesley College'. The founders believed the school should be large, which would make it cheaper and more efficient to run, and that teachers where possible would teach only one subject which they had 'thoroughly mastered'. Lectures were given for subjects like botany and astronomy and pupils' notes were examined from time to time and short examinations set. The other subjects were taught by class teaching and examinations were only given when necessary and only in the senior years. Fortnightly reports were sent home to parents. A wide range of academic subjects and optional classes was offered.[16]

Vida enjoyed her time at PLC. She was a talented all-rounder and achieved success in her academic studies, music and gymnastics. She also participated in extra-curricular activities at the school. She was a member of the Magpie Club. Amid much secrecy the initiates would meet in the gymnasium and discuss 'with great animation' Thomas Macaulay's essays on Hastings, Milton, Clive and Bunyan. Each girl sustained her opinion with the 'utmost zeal'. Outsiders tried in vain to discover what went on in the meetings. The following year's Magpie Club report asserted that members were not 'giddy school girls', but were anxious to improve their minds and to spend their leisure time profitably. They read essays on Madame D'Arblay, Frederick the Great, Addison and Pitt the Younger. They held several animated debates on 'Who is the greatest living man?'.[17]

The school magazine *Patchwork* was progressive during Vida's time at the college. It reported advances of women in academic fields, recording women's achievements at the University of Melbourne (where women had been first admitted in 1880). It also included information about women's colleges and academic gains overseas. One article asked, 'Should women have a vote?'. The author was afraid most girls were not interested in the issue, but went on to present the arguments used against women voting and then to counter them. Opponents of the suffrage argued that the vote would deprive women of their feminine graces, but the writer attested that 'womanhood is not a type of weakness, but of a different sort of strength'. Another objection was that mixing in politics was out of woman's sphere. The reply was:

> Woman's sphere, it is said, is in the home. Truly; but we cannot consent to have the radius from a vital centre arbitrarily limited; and further, we know that harsh necessity drives multitudes daily from their 'sphere' to outside labour ... The sphere is a circle of chalk which the tide of necessity and the steps of these noble ones are obliterating.[18]

Vida was influenced by these ideas and later called her paper the *Woman's Sphere* and often adopted this technique of stating then countering the opponent's arguments.

Not everyone associated with PLC was progressive. At Vida's first Prize Distribution, the Moderator of the Presbyterian General Assembly, the Reverend J. Clark, told the prize-winners 'to bear their honours meekly, and avoid posing as learned young ladies. They could find other means by which to use their learning and talents than by becoming blue stockings'. This was greeted by cheers.[19] It was an attitude that Vida was to meet often.

The principal, Andrew Harper, was a strong advocate of women's education but he also believed that his pupils should not be overworked. He was proud that the college had 'shown that we can educate girls as thoroughly and on much the same lines as boys, without in any way affecting their health injuriously'.[20] Harper considered that pupils who were well prepared did not need to overwork or cram to succeed. In his 1885 report he recorded that the health of the pupils was good and that 'No one under our control has been permitted to overwork, and if any pupil living at home has done so, it has been in direct opposition to my constantly repeated entreaties and warnings'. Boarders were not permitted to read after 8.45 p.m. because he believed that reading after the brain was tired was a waste of time and harmful. For scholastic success, Harper recommended sufficient sleep, exercise, youthful good spirits and adequate preparation.

Despite Harper's warnings, Vida was 'Heavily handicapped by a physical breakdown, owing to the strain of study', when preparing for her Matriculation in 1886.[21] The roll shows that she was absent on ten days at the end of the year. However, she gained her Matriculation with honours in English and French and passes in Latin, algebra and arithmetic. At PLC she was awarded the second prize for French and the third prize for English. She also won equal first prize for private readings and a first prize for music.[22]

In his 1886 report, Harper summed up his philosophy of education.

> The aim of school education should be to give pupils such a training as will enable them to continue their own education with ease and efficiency, to put into their hands and practice them in the use of instruments of higher culture, and to awaken within them ... an intellectual hunger which will insist upon being satisfied.

Vida retained her 'intellectual hunger' throughout her life.

Vida's religious education was also fundamental, as ultimately her spiritual beliefs would govern her life. Isabella and the children attended the Presbyterian Scots Church in Melbourne. Isabella chose this church because the minister, the Reverend Charles Strong, was a liberal thinker whose ideas were well ahead of their time. His ideas caused dissent and he faced many crises, including criticisms of his decision in 1883 to support the move to have the Public Library and Museum open on Sunday afternoons.[23] His attitude to science and religion caused further controversy. He argued that science need not threaten Christianity; rather it could purify and strengthen it.

> Science (thought of as systematised knowledge applied to religion) ... enabled religion to take a higher and wider flight; to think of God and man and human destiny in a far nobler way and to seek God, not afar off in dim ages of the world's childhood, but here and now, in the very constitution of man's own nature as essential to humanity as science itself.[24]

The Presbytery accused him of heresy. Weary of the continuous agitation, Strong resigned from the Presbyterian Church of Victoria. The case was eventually dropped after he had sailed for England, but it was not resolved.[25]

On his return in 1885, he founded the Australian Church, and many of his former congregation, including Isabella and her daughters, followed him. He formed the Religious Science Club to examine religious questions, including world religions and comparative religions, in a scientific manner.

Vida was still a schoolgirl when the Australian Church was established, but its enlightened attitudes were important in her development: the move away from traditional Presbyterianism exposed her to scientific rationalism and other doctrines. It is very possible that she was first introduced to Christian Science, which would change the course of her life, in Strong's Religious Science Club. Strong was also a practical Christian and his enthusiastic leadership resulted in many schemes to help the poor. Isabella was an active worker and Vida became involved from an early age. Sewing meetings were held in the Goldstein home for Strong's Social Improvement, Friendly Help, and Children's Aid Society. Vida became a committee member while still in her teens, gaining valuable experience for her future work. Long after Vida had left the Australian Church, she continued to work closely with Strong, supporting his charitable work.

◆ ◆ ◆

After gaining her Matriculation, Vida led the light-hearted social life of the debutante, attending balls and parties. She was full of life and high spirits. She was a popular companion and had many suitors. Her self-confidence and a certain independence of spirit distinguished her from other young women. John Monash, a junior officer under her father's command, discovered that she did not succumb to his charms like other young women. Monash, an 'accomplished flirt', recorded in his diary how young women accepted his 'caressing advances', but when he met the 18-year-old Vida for the first time:

> ...having long looked forward to such an opportunity...I was much disappointed for I found her all too self-possessed and affected, and she plainly did not like me; but if I can get an uninterruped half-hour with her, I doubt not I can put myself on a satisfactory footing with her.[26]

It is not known if Monash got his 'uninterrupted half-hour'. Their lives were to take opposing paths; Monash went on to become the first Australian to command the First AIF in World War I, while Vida took a leading part in the Victorian peace movement. Despite these differences, they regarded each other with respect and they remained in touch until Monash's death in 1931.[27]

Vida enjoyed good health and played many sports with vigour and skill. She excelled at lawn tennis and won many prizes. She also played billiards well and was an accomplished horsewoman. Once she drove a coach and five horses from Dean's Marsh to Lorne to test her strength. Her arms ached and were so stiff she 'could not lift them to do her hair for a week'.[28] She was adept at clay pigeon shooting, but refused to shoot live targets, and rode a bicycle for recreation. She appreciated music and played the piano. She 'was the life and soul of every kind of harmless pleasure, and enjoyed it all to the full'.[29] Vida, however, wanted more than the life of the debutante. Her apprenticeship for her life work was about to begin.

2

The New Woman
1890–1901

◆

When Vida turned twenty-one in 1890, Australia was entering an economic depression. Victoria was the State most severely affected as financial institutions went bust and unemployment burgeoned. The Depression had two direct effects on Vida: it forced her to earn her own living, and the suffering which she saw at this time culminated in her decision to dedicate her life to alleviating such distress. Already a committed suffragist, during this decade Vida came to the conclusion that the oppressed could be helped best if women had the vote because women would use their political power to improve social and economic conditions. Vida would serve a long apprenticeship as a suffragist before emerging as the leader of the Victorian suffrage movement by the end of the decade.

Although it was unusual at this time for a young woman of Vida's class and background to embark upon a career, the Goldsteins had brought up their children to expect to contribute to society. The Depression made earning a living an economic necessity, not just a social obligation. The Goldsteins were caught in the financial crash: Jacob was retrenched and had no pension. With the loss of this income, the ongoing dispute with the trustees of Isabella's father's estate became even more important. When Isabella was ill, Vida took on the task of writing about the management of the trust to her Aunt Appie, adding that her mother found it 'very hard writing about this matter'.[1] Ultimately, much of the money was dissipated and little, if any, of the original fortune reached the grandchildren of Samuel Hawkins.

Vida decided to help the family's finances by becoming a teacher, one of the few occupations open to women. She taught at the Toorak College established by Mrs Connolly, who had taught French at PLC when Vida was a student there. Then Vida and her sisters Elsie and Aileen opened a preparatory school for boys and girls in Inkerman Street, St Kilda. In 1892 the school was relocated to the family home 'Ingleton' in Alma Road, East St Kilda. The school faced stiff competition from a plethora of small private schools operating in the area at the time and had to contend with the fact that many people who had lost money in the Depression could no longer afford to send their children to a private school. In the second year, only sixteen pupils were enrolled. In 1896 Vida advertised vacancies for boarders.[2]

The school was co-educational because Vida believed this promoted a more rational relationship between the sexes. She encouraged individuality and 'abhorred standardization in teaching'.[3] The classes were small and each pupil was given individual attention. The classes at PLC had had fifty to sixty pupils, which she considered unsatisfactory because slower workers were left behind and to a certain extent neglected.[4] The sisters were strict and did not tolerate 'nonsense' from their pupils.[5] Years later, Vida said she and her sisters were happy to 'rejoice in the fact that a large number of their pupils of whom they have been able to keep trace are doing brilliantly in the professions they have adopted'.[6]

As the Depression worsened, the Goldsteins' philanthropic work became more pressing. In her free time, Vida accompanied Isabella on her visits to the slums. Vida, having 'tasted all the sweets of society' as a debutante, soon discovered that 'the other side of life was beginning to force itself upon her'.[7]

In 1891 Isabella took the Reverend Charles Strong through the Collingwood slums. He publicly condemned the appalling conditions and began an anti-slum crusade, with Isabella and Vida working closely with him. When the municipal authorities claimed he was exaggerating, a *Herald* reporter went to investigate. Escorted by Isabella, whose 'good deeds are proclaimed by the poor', he was shown dilapidated homes with rats scampering through them. One woman told him the rats 'jump on my bed, run over my face, and often keep me awake all night'. Waste poured through the yards and formed pools under the houses. Typhoid was common. Isabella was obviously well known to the people; one girl ran up to her with a bunch of white chrysanthemums. One chap said he wanted work, not charity, and she replied kindly that she knew that, and would not offer him charity.[8]

This was the attitude of the Charity Organisation Society, which the Goldsteins were associated with for almost thirty years. Jacob was a founding member of the Melbourne branch of the COS, established in 1887, and held various executive positions for almost two decades. Isabella was often on the committee and Vida was a member for many years.[9] The COS philosophy influenced Vida's approach to working with the poor. At the first Australasian Conference on Charity in November 1890, Jacob gave a paper entitled 'Charity Organisation: its Principles and Methods' and he read a paper by Isabella entitled 'United and Systematic Charity'. Both papers reflected COS ideas, which were progressive for the 1890s, that poverty should be controlled through the application of scientific principles, rather than blaming the poor or accepting their suffering as God's will. The possibilities of science excited Jacob, who enthusiastically embraced the new discipline of sociology because it promised scientific solutions to social problems. Vida shared his enthusiasm and later studied sociology and economics in her search for the causes of poverty. In his paper Jacob explained the appeal of sociology:

> Socialism is theoretical, but impracticable—therefore, is misleading, if not wholly untrue. Sociology is scientific, and must be practicable, because, dealing with facts, it arranges and governs them so as to discover the laws that govern society.[10]

Jacob argued that the rich should elevate the poor by their personal influence and practical suggestion, rather than by indiscriminate almsgiving. The aim was to enable the poor to help themselves and to prevent poverty, rather than relieve it; charity should be scientifically organised so that eventually it would be unnecessary. He suggested the idea of 'friendly visitors' who would have responsibility for four families and also a Penny Provident Fund which would collect tiny sums from the poor for use when they were in need.

Isabella's paper called for a united and systematic charity organisation to prevent people obtaining charity from more than one source. She said that if men or women of the 'drinking or loafing order' would not support their children then the government should compel them to do so, adding that it was impossible for good citizens to be reared in such circumstances.[11] This argument, that improvement of the home situation would lead to better citizens in the future, was often used to justify improving living conditions for women.[12]

A precursor of modern casework, the COS 'held that poverty was due largely to the maladaption of the individual to his environment', so it helped individuals deal with specific problems but tended to underestimate the complexities of the problem and the fact that often the causes were beyond the control of the individual.[13] The COS method was to investigate each case and if it were considered 'worthy' then the person was helped. In practice two-thirds of the cases were rejected and the investigation was understandably resented. The COS 'earned itself far more popularity amongst its subscribers than ever it did amongst those to whom it offered aid'.[14] The society had no answer for those who did not want to work or those it considered 'undeserving'. The COS wanted to co-ordinate all the benevolent societies to avoid duplication and possible 'cheating', but this move was resisted by the other charities.

The COS adopted Jacob's idea of friendly visitors. They were usually women of the leisured classes and they became the 'very heart' of the organisation.[15] They advised the poor on health, hygiene, budgeting and employment. Again this was not always done tactfully, but the newspaper account of Isabella's visit to Collingwood shows she was a welcome visitor, as was Vida when she took on the same work. On one visit to the slums, Vida was accompanied by the journalist May Maxwell. Many years later Maxwell recalled the visit:

> She [Vida] was out to help several deserted wives and penniless widows who had young families to feed and clothe.
> The poverty was heartbreaking. To this day I can picture one woman, whose clothes were only rags, balancing herself on a rickety chair in a tiny room with a floor strewn with dead rabbits. She was skinning one on her knees. These skins would be used in the making of bell toppers—men's high silk hats.[16]

The COS believed that handouts were demeaning and only gave money as a last resort. It tried to provide work whenever possible, but this proved difficult to put into practice in the midst of a depression. In 1894, the COS established the Leongatha Labour Colony in co-operation with the Victorian Government. Jacob was appointed honorary superintendent. The men were given some training as labourers and were paid their wages in a lump sum when they left. The colony was less than a success. Jacob and the resident manager, William Squire, had bitter differences of opinion which culminated in Jacob suing Squire for libel. In 1899 the colony's administration was attacked in Parliament. An investigative committee acknowledged Jacob's 'energy and enthusiasm', but recommended that trustees should run the colony.[17] The left-wing paper *Tocsin* supported Squire. It objected to Jacob because 'he bosses Leongatha for nothing, and actually does another man out of the billet'. It pressed for a parliamentary inquiry, asserting there must be some case 'against the superfine amateur farmer who reigns supreme over what he describes as "a feckless lot, the majority of whom are drunkards"'.[18]

In March 1903 members of the COS inspected the labour colony and its books and reported that they were very impressed. It had all been 'cleared to grass, all the timber being dead'.[19] It was closed late in 1903 and when it reopened the following year Jacob did not resume as superintendent. By 1908 the social experiment had been reduced, in Jacob's words, to a 'sort of country benevolent asylum' with seventy-five men who 'pass their time, draw their miserable pay and leave as soon as they can'.[20] Vida, however, remained convinced of the feasibility of the concept and during World War I established a women's farm to train unemployed women.

Vida always maintained that handouts were only stopgap measures. She became increasingly interested in seeking the causes of poverty and looking for practical measures to eradicate the injustice and the misery. She joined various reform societies and worked enthusiastically for them. The campaign to have female officers for female prisoners in Pentridge Gaol was successful in 1894. Vida joined the Criminology Society and the Anti-Sweating League which aimed to improve working conditions. Isabella was a committee member of the league, as was the English socialist Henry Hyde Champion, who was to become her son-in-law. The Factories and Shops Act of 1896 helped alleviate some of the problems of sweated workers. A minimum age of thirteen was set, and a 48-hour week was introduced for women and children under sixteen. Minimum conditions were set for outworkers, and inspectors were appointed to help enforce these conditions. The campaign continued for further improvements in working conditions, including equal pay, and Vida remained actively involved. Isabella also campaigned for women she believed to have been wrongly convicted in the courts. In January 1894 she was prominent in the unsuccessful attempt to save Frances Knorr, a baby farmer (or foster parent), from being hanged for the deaths of three babies.[21] Vida later followed Isabella's example and championed hapless women and children who came before the courts.

◆ ◆ ◆

Running parallel with her social campaigns and philanthropic work was Vida's interest in woman suffrage. Vida always said that she 'could not help becoming a suffragette,[22] being her father's daughter'. Although Jacob opposed the suffrage for women, he had brought up his daughters to 'think and work things out for themselves and not accept ready-made opinions'.[23] Possibly his opposition made her fight harder.

The Victorian Women's Suffrage Society, formed in 1884, was the first woman suffrage society in Australia. Henrietta Dugdale, Annie Lowe and a Mrs Rennick were foundation members. Annette Bear (later Bear-Crawford) and Isabella were early members. In 1889, the first Franchise Bill was introduced in the Victorian Parliament by Dr William Maloney, but was unsuccessful. By 1891 there were three suffrage groups in Victoria. They decided to present a Petition for Women's Suffrage to the Victorian Parliament and were assisted by the Woman's Christian Temperance Union and the Victorian Temperance Alliance. The WCTU involvement meant that country women were also included, but this alliance of temperance and suffrage alienated some supporters who feared women would use the vote to bring in prohibition.

Canvassing door to door, gathering signatures for the petition, was Vida's first work for woman suffrage. It was also excellent training for a future parliamentary candidate. Vida later wrote that the few women who refused to sign were those 'whose interests ended at the garden gate'.[24] It was very rare to be refused by those women who were the wives of working men or who worked for social reform outside the home. These women knew the suffering and hardship of women and recognised the need for women to take part in public affairs. Working men encouraged their wives to sign:

If the husband opened the door, he would call his wife, saying 'Here's a lady who wants to know if you want the vote'. And, invariably, she did. But in the more favoured suburbs, a husband would quite frequently refuse to allow his wife to sign; or a woman would say meekly and wistfully, 'I'd like to sign, but my husband won't let me'.[25]

The suffragists obtained 33 000 signatures. It was the largest petition ever presented to Parliament; several attendants were required to carry it into the chamber. It 'staggered those who had scornfully declared that no self-respecting woman wanted to vote'.[26] The Bill was regularly passed by the Lower House, the Legislative Assembly, which was elected on universal manhood suffrage, but it was invariably rejected by the conservative Upper House, the Legislative Council, which was elected by men who paid more than £100 in annual rates.

In 1894, heartened by the grant of the suffrage to women in South Australia, Annette Bear-Crawford formed the United Council for Women's Suffrage to co-ordinate the parliamentary efforts of the various Victorian suffrage societies. Vida, Isabella and Annette were prominent in the most active society, the Prahran Women's Franchise League. Annette realised the need for good women speakers and used the meetings to train the women. This gave Vida valuable experience in public speaking. She later recalled feeling 'incredibly shy and nervous and [I] only consented to give an address or state the case at a meeting when Mrs Bear-Crawford was in the chair and undertook to answer questions'.[27] Vida's 'quick brain and logical mode of thinking led her into the discussions'.[28] Vida admired Annette enormously. Although Vida was sixteen years younger, the two women had much in common—a ready wit, great energy and total commitment to winning the suffrage and working for the disadvantaged.

This decade was the most intellectually stimulating time of Vida's life. She met many liberal thinkers whose opinions she respected and together they discussed the questions which fascinated them: how could poverty be eradicated? how could a more just society be created? what was the cause of crime? would woman suffrage and women's entry into the public sphere destroy femininity? how could women participate equally in society? Through such discussions and her contact with people like Annette Bear-Crawford, Charles Strong and Hyde Champion, Vida came to formulate her ideas. She attended the

Warawee Club where men and women listened to lectures and joined in debates on such subjects as 'Woman's Dress' and 'The New Woman Defined'.[29] The popular press portrayed the 'New Woman' as masculine and coarse, but progressives argued that she must be more than a poor imitation of a man and more than just a suffragist. She had to find new ways of achieving social, political and economic equity, while preserving the strengths of womanhood. This was Vida's challenge.

Strong addressed this issue in a sermon entitled 'Concerning Women'. The women's movement had not made greater progress because women viewed the movement individually and provincially, rather than as a stage in human evolution; it was too narrowly associated with the suffrage and the right of women to ride bicycles when its concerns should be much broader. Women spent their time on petty things which blinded them to greater issues, but this was the fault of men. Women were degraded and idle, selfish, worldly and frivolous because men encouraged them to be. He advocated a Sisterhood in God which would embrace all women and all classes and work 'unselfishly for uplifting, enriching and spiritualising all human life'.[30] When Vida came to form organisations for her political and suffrage work, she echoed Strong's emphasis on the need for education and organisation. She also tried to include women from all walks of life and political convictions and her fundamental aim was, like Strong's, the 'spiritualising' of human life.

Another powerful influence on Vida was Hyde Champion, a former military officer turned journalist and publisher. Ten years older than Vida, he was urbane, well travelled and intelligent. He actively supported the suffrage cause by including women's issues and reports from the Prahran Woman Suffrage League in his publication *Champion*. In later years he provided many ideas and practical assistance to support Vida's endeavours. In 1895 he published 'The Claim of Women' in which he conveyed a grim picture of the current status of women and the relations of the sexes, especially within marriage. He predicted that women would obtain the vote within months, but they would vote as their menfolk did. However, 'on sex-questions they must ultimately express and enforce a very distinct view' although it was difficult for women to speak publicly on such matters because if the woman were unmarried she was considered shameless, and if married it was assumed she was publishing her own experiences. The pressing issue was to recognise women as human individuals, not just tolerate them as child-producers and the 'satisfiers of a distorted primal appetite'. The socialisation of women sapped their health and prepared them only for marriage and motherhood. Champion deplored the fact that the sexes were kept separate and did not get to know each other as friends. The modern woman did not quarrel with the institution of marriage but with its abuse: enforced maternity; frequent child-bearing and constant ill health; the man's 'raging appetite' turned upon her, when she had looked for 'sacred aspiration'; the realisation that she was not to be a companion to her husband; and her loss of financial and other rights. Champion concluded that women would use their political power to improve their circumstances, but it would take many generations and much educative work. He advocated that the oppressed sex 'must needs make common cause with the oppressed class [the workers]' before the position of both could be improved.[31]

All these ideas had a strong impact on Vida. There was so much to be done, so much that could be achieved. Vida became determined to dedicate her life to working for the betterment of humanity, especially women and children. She refused all offers of marriage. (It is said that one of her suitors was Champion; he married her sister Elsie in 1898.[32]) Vida began her apprenticeship in earnest under the tutelage of Annette Bear-Crawford. She spent long hours at the Public Library, seeking scientific solutions to old problems. She came to the conclusion that the fundamental right was the right of women to vote and this political power would produce improved social and economic conditions. She attended parliamentary debates, whenever they related to women and children, and so gained an understanding of parliamentary procedure. She began to lobby members, urging the woman's point of view and suggesting amendments more favourable to women. As her knowledge and reputation grew, members drew on her expertise. Sir Frederick Sargood kept her busy for a fortnight before the Suffrage Bill came up for debate in the Victorian Parliament in 1899. Almost every day he sent a messenger to Vida requesting facts and figures and she 'practically prepared his speech for him', but it was not delivered. He was not 'going to put himself out by making a stirring speech in favour' of a Bill he knew would be defeated.[33]

Between 1894 and 1900 six suffrage bills and one referendum bill were introduced to the Legislative Assembly; those that passed the

Assembly were rejected in the Legislative Council. The bills produced some fierce debates. Many politicians subscribed to the belief that men should act in the public sphere while women should remain in the private sphere, a belief feminists came to see as fundamental to the patriarchal ordering of society. Some politicians feared that women would vote differently from men—from the heart, not the head, demanding costly welfare reforms. The suffragists agreed that women would vote differently: they would use their vote to improve society by introducing female qualities into the public sphere. One politician grumbled that the opposite would also happen; that the private sphere would be ruined by the intrusion of politics. He feared politics would be discussed at every meal and 'instead of the home being the centre of elevating influences, it will be turned into a bear-garden'.[34]

One example of the more extreme arguments used by parliamentarians against woman suffrage and the suffragists indicates the fears and prejudices of some legislators of the time. Frank Madden, MLA, said in 1895:

> Woman Suffrage would abolish soldiers and war, also racing, hunting, football, cricket, and all such manly games ... Women suffragists are the worst class of socialists. Their idea of freedom is polyandry, free love, lease marriages, and so on. Are these the qualifications for the franchise! Are we going to allow women who would sap the very foundations of a nation to have votes?[35]

Some members believed that the women who so dared to go beyond their sphere to demand political rights must have loose morals. One asserted: 'The women who were asking for the vote did not belong to the respectable classes of society... [They] are a few agitators and extremists, and the unfortunates of the city'.[36] Another member echoed this sentiment: 'The class of women who are now howling about women's suffrage would be at every little dirty corner arguing and quarrelling and fighting. It is in their nature, and they cannot help it'.[37] Even the men who supported woman suffrage were described as 'weak-kneed and weak-headed'.[38] Vida did not take this personally, although she empathised with the calumny the suffrage pioneers had faced and privately was indignant at how women could be so maligned in a Parliament which governed women, but which women had no power to elect.[39]

While such attitudes about suffragists were held by some members of Parliament, campaigning for woman suffrage took courage. A deputation of 300 women attended the Legislative Council in September 1898. One later described what occurred:

> The conduct of some of the honourable members was so disgraceful that it gave one the impression of a den of satyrs, or a 'sexual degenerates' ward of a lunatic asylum rather than of a body of 'elected' legislators ... The deputation was ... crowded into a place reeking with tobacco and grog, and ogled and giggled at by a semi-intoxicated mob of 'superior' legislators.
>
> The weighty, business-like, and earnest speeches of good women voicing the aspirations and heart-wishes of hundreds of thousands were interrupted by low jests and idiotic exclamations, such as 'Who'll mind the babies?' 'New Woman', and others not fit to print. One woman in fact had to reprimand one fellow for his impudence and his laughter, which smelt of liquor and was tinged with indecency...
>
> Another unctuous darling of the National Ass [sic] accosted two of the younger members of the deputation with the following indecent remark that should have been followed by his being consigned to the lock-up. 'You girls, you don't want votes. You want—something else'. His leering pause deserved six months without the option.[40]

In 1898 Annette and Vida published *A Reply to Speech against Women's Suffrage, by Sir Henry Wrixon, K.C.M.G., M.L.C.* This committed to print some of the basic ideas now developed between the two women. They asked how could men legislate for beings different from themselves and emphasised that the Bill only asked for the vote, not for women to enter Parliament. To counter the argument that most women were dependent and therefore could not vote independently, they said that married home-makers worked, and were as independent as working professional women.

> The work done by wives and mothers, is as essential to the State as that of men; and that of the vast majority is far harder than that of the majority of husbands, whose hours of labour are limited, either by law or custom; unpaid domestic work is never finished'.[41]

This is right in the mainstream of feminist thinking; the issues of the endlessness of domestic work became a catchcry of second-wave feminism.

Wrixon had said if all women voted the same way they could outvote men. Annette and Vida challenged this, saying that most women would not disregard the interests of their sons and husbands.

They said that women paid taxes equally with men and while women did not undertake military duties, nor did 'the majority of the Honourable Members of the Legislative Council, but they are not on that account deprived of their vote'.[42] Vida later used a similar retort equally effectively against the conscriptionists.

Another project Annette and Vida worked on together at this time was raising money to extend the Queen Victoria Hospital, which had been established in 1896 by eleven female doctors, under the 'inspired leadership' of Dr Constance Stone, the first woman to register with the Medical Board of Victoria.[43] The hospital was staffed by women and run for women. Vida credited Annette with the idea of the Shilling Fund, whereby every woman in Victoria was asked to donate one shilling to the hospital. Annette put the idea to Dr Stone, Isabella and Vida at the Goldstein home 'Ingleton'. Annette's 'genius of organisation' ensured the success of the fund. While acknowledging Stone's 'splendid work', Vida said honour must be paid where it was due and that the idea was wholly Annette's and 'carried to fruition through her organising, speaking, and writing ability'.[44] It took some women two years to save their shilling, but the new extensions were officially opened in June 1899. When the hospital needed funds for further extensions in 1900, Vida, as secretary of the United Council for Women's Suffrage, was responsible for another Shilling Fund which raised enough money for an extra ward. The first appeal had been associated with Queen Victoria's diamond jubilee. The second coincided with a visit of the Duke and Duchess of York. Vida sent a circular about the appeal to the New South Wales suffragist Rose Scott and wrote, 'I am not pining to give proof of loyal feelings but I do want to help our very own hospital'.[45] In later life she came to admire royalty more.

Vida continued to teach in her school while being involved in many other activities. In her late twenties, she began to serve on the executives of several organisations. She became a vice-president of the Prahran Women's Progressive League and later held office in the Fitzroy branch of the Australian Women's Association, a mutual benefit society for women which was established in 1900 through the Australian Natives' Association.[46] Already a pacifist, she spoke out against the second Boer War, which began in 1899. She later said she was 'held up to public scorn as a pro-Boer, because I dared say what I believed to be correct'.[47]

Vida also led the Try Society's girls' club at Hawksburn from 1898 to 1900. This was probably a paid position. The aim of the Try Society was to 'take such children as we often see at our police courts—wild, wayward, untamed—and train them up to be useful and intelligent members of society'.[48] Some of the children were found employment in the country. Activities were run two to three times a week and the girls were taught elocution, singing, writing, sewing, cooking, scripture, drill and calisthenics (the most popular class). Vida also made home visits to become acquainted with the girls and their parents in their own environments. It was reported that she 'attaches great importance to this branch of her work'. Vida complained about the girls' unpunctuality and arranged that they had to report to her on arrival and were not allowed to leave without written permission. She believed that strict observance of these regulations would enable classes to be conducted smoothly and successfully.[49]

◆ ◆ ◆

At the end of 1898, Vida closed her school to concentrate on her suffrage work. Annette Bear-Crawford was leaving for England early in 1899 and would represent Victorian women at the Women's Congress in London. Vida and her friend Ina Higgins, a horticulturalist and suffragist, agreed to undertake the United Council for Women's Suffrage work in her absence. Annette, however, contracted pneumonia in England and died on 7 June 1899. Her unexpected death at the early age of forty-six was a grievous loss to the women's movement and to Vida, who greatly admired and loved her. Like-minded friends are precious and Vida missed her sorely. Throughout her life, she paid tribute to Annette's achievements for women and children. The memorial service held at St Paul's Church in Melbourne was the first such service in Melbourne for a woman. Later a memorial tablet was placed in Christ Church, South Yarra.[50]

Vida was Annette's logical successor, but some members of the United Council for Women's Suffrage saw her as radical and threatening. The suffragist movement, including the UCWS, was weak and divided, but Vida managed to develop a following by providing strong and intelligent leadership. She was enthusiastic and devoted all her energies to the work. She excelled at public speaking and interviews with the press. She was young, good-looking, well groomed and had an attractive personality. Her audiences appreciated her articulateness and ready wit, and her dignified behaviour commanded respect, even from people who disagreed with her views. Although she now dared to go beyond 'woman's sphere', she retained her femininity. In combining all these qualities, Vida was the prototype of the new suffragist, but she also had an implacable faith in the verity of her beliefs; her refusal to compromise would bring her much difficulty later. Her graceful appearance belied a considerable strength.

Vida's first public speech was at a woman suffrage meeting in Prahran in July 1899. A month later, she addressed a crowded meeting in the Melbourne Town Hall. Alfred Deakin spoke and Annie Lowe, a suffrage pioneer, moved the first motion. She quoted a parliamentary member who had called women 'shrieking cockatoos'. She said that it was the male of the species which did the shrieking. (The phrase was never used again in Parliament.) Lowe was keen to reassure her audience that the vote would reinforce the status quo. The women 'did not seek to destroy home life, but to raise the tone of it. Their first duties were their most important duties, and those lay in the home'. Charles Strong supported the resolution and referred to a letter he had received which described the women leaders as 'women who smoked cigarettes and said "damn" ... wore gem hats, and stood in public places with their arms akimbo'. He assured his audience that the movement 'had not destroyed the womanliness of the women leaders' and that the vote would make women better wives and companions.[51] Vida rose to second the next motion. Her training had not been wasted. Her delivery was described as having 'ease and fluency of speech ... united with a charm of manner essentially womanly, and this, together with the clearness and precision of her arguments, carried the audience irresistibly with her'.[52] Vida's voice had 'clear bell like tones'; it carried well and her thorough knowledge of the subject led to 'an assurance of manner and precision in argument for which she became noted'.[53] Vida's long apprenticeship was over.

Vida was an astute organiser and realised that the best chance of winning the suffrage was by gaining as wide support for it as possible. She fostered good relations with the Trades Hall Council, who donated money to the Women's Franchise League, and in 1899, at

Vida's request, a committee of three men was elected 'to act with the Ladies' to help organise a suffrage conference. In turn, the Women's Franchise League offered to assist the Trades Hall Council to organise women workers;[54] this was Champion's ideal of the oppressed sex and the oppressed class joining forces.

Vida also had to find ways to deal with the people she was now called on to work with, most of whom were considerably older than her. She wrote to Rose Scott:

> We like you have some very ill-advised people to work with. It is often a case of 'save us from our friends' but I am thankful to say we have got them pretty well under control now. They used to be most dangerous.

She had organised the 'friends' into committees to prevent them from 'venting' on their own, adding that 'United action is essential'. Vida praised the 'splendid men' on their committees and Champion in particular was 'a tower of strength. Our success is largely due to him. He is always brimful of ideas and a splendid tactician'.[55] Champion suffered a debilitating stroke at about this time, which left him paralysed down his right side and with speech difficulties, but he continued to assist Vida.[56]

Vida's astuteness in dealing with people is shown in another letter to Rose Scott when they were arranging a suffrage memorial to be presented to the Prime Minister, Edmund Barton. Vida said that the signatures of the president and secretary of each organisation were sufficient, but 'it may be necessary to guard against petty jealousy by having the signatures of Vice Presidents also'.[57]

Vida's ascendancy of the woman suffrage movement in Victoria was confirmed when she was appointed general secretary of the United Council for Women's Suffrage on 1 August 1900. She had previously been the organising secretary. Her salary for ten months, plus postage, petty cash and 'suburban locomotion', totalled £86 8s 9d.[58] She had the responsibility for co-ordinating the UCWS activities and the thirty-two societies affiliated to it. A month later, Vida launched the monthly paper the *Australian Woman's Sphere*. This gave her a voice which none of the other Victorian suffragists had and strengthened her position as leader of the State's suffrage organisations. On the masthead Vida displayed a quotation from Terence (a freed Roman slave who became a comic dramatist): 'I am a human being, and I believe nothing human is outside my sphere'. It is not known how the paper was financed, other than Vida's comment in the first issue that when

> a very generous offer was made to me, to found a monthly periodical, of which I should be registered proprietor, with full editorial control, I could not refuse a position of such tempting possibilities, although it entailed embarrassing responsibility. One condition only was attached to the offer—viz., that definite proof should be given that a number of Victorian women wanted such a paper controlled, as I am told all publications to have any chance of success, must be, by one individual. That condition has been fulfilled, for here I am in the editorial chair, with in my hands that Archimedian lever which moves the world—if only it is wisely worked.[59]

It is not known where the money came from; the estate of Annette Bear-Crawford and/or Isabella Goldstein have been proposed, although the former is more probable. It is unlikely that Isabella had money to spare at this time and Vida would not have written in such humble tones if her mother were her financier. The first front cover featured a full-page portrait of Annette; other suffrage pioneers were featured inside. It could have been funded by a member of the UCWS because the paper was treated as an organ of that body. The first issue included a list of all UCWS affiliates under the heading 'Our Organisation'.

In outlining her hopes for the paper, Vida said that she did not want it to be dull but that it would contain serious reading, and that she would always have time 'to read helpful criticism, however plain-spoken' and suggestions would be received 'with patience, even if impracticable'.[60] While some of the subsequent communications must have been of a dubious nature, Vida dealt with them in light vein. To 'R. L.' of Geelong she responded, 'Do you not know that it is possible to be funny without being vulgar?'.[61] Her response to 'M. L.' of Adelaide was 'Absolutely unprintable',[62] and to 'R. J. J.' of Sea Lake, 'We fear your suggestion would rather startle a sober-minded community'.[63] One can only now wonder what was written. Vida maintained the right to refuse certain advertising and she felt 'compelled' to refuse an advertisement for intoxicating liquor, although the *Woman's Sphere* was not a temperance paper. Later she extended the ban to patent remedies.

Vida was convinced that women could enter any sphere they chose and the *Woman's Sphere* ran a series of articles on women who had succeeded in business and the professions. The first of these featured Elsie Champion and her Book Lovers' Library. This had been started in a tentative way in 1896 by Isabella, possibly with Champion's assistance, and had been built up by Elsie at a time when other book ventures were failing. Elsie praised the work of her women assistants, saying they were quicker and more intelligent than men and that they deserved equal pay for equal work. Her terms of employment were generous: 36-hour weeks with three half-days and a month's holiday each year and a share of the profits, as well as 'about twice' the usual salary. She had no sympathy with men who complained that women were taking their jobs. She said these were 'sedentary "lady like" positions' and men 'ought to be doing the rough open-air work so much needed in a young country'.[64] Later editions suggested that women consider careers as bookbinders, fire and life assurance agents, pharmacists, nurses, and running holiday boarding houses.

Other suffragists from interstate contributed to the *Woman's Sphere*, including Catherine Spence from Adelaide and Rose Scott. There were reports on women's issues from overseas and articles on a wide range of social, political and economic issues of interest and concern to suffragists. The paper did not avoid addressing issues related to sexuality, although in conservative quarters it was considered shameless for women to discuss such matters—even more so, if the women were unmarried and the discussion in public. An early edition addressed 'Dr Barrett's Bogey'. Dr James Barrett, the physiology lecturer at the University of Melbourne, blamed Australia's declining birthrate on the emancipation of women. Women were taking on new careers, doing what men could do, and ignoring what only they could do—have babies. Vida replied that the women's movement did not intend to deter women from motherhood, but wished to make them better mothers through increased education and civic responsibility.[65] The suffragists argued that their work would reinforce traditional values and make better wives and mothers. To argue anything else was too threatening.

Vida seems not to have questioned that a married woman's first duty was to have children, but she also argued that it was the right and duty of all women to contribute to society in the public sphere. Vida denied that suffragists would use artificial means to avoid maternity. Contraception was seen as an attack on the family, blurring the boundaries of sex for reproduction and for pleasure, and with it the psychological distance between a virtuous woman and a prostitute.[66] Although she opposed 'enforced maternity', Vida advocated abstinence as the only means of birth control. Even in 1918 she was to write:

> Although realising that under present conditions it [contraception] is frequently a wife's only protection against unwanted, overworked motherhood, it is just as frequently a misnomer for a sex-indulgence that dares to call itself the expression of 'love'.[67]

While the suffragists have been criticised for failing to break with traditional morality, it is now argued that abstinence, as advocated by early suffragists including Vida, gave women control over childbearing when contraceptives were unreliable and not freely available.[68] Certainly Vida wanted women to have the choice of preventing pregnancy, but she also clung to the notion that the deeper spirituality of women would triumph over the physical natures of men.

Vida never condemned the women who had unwanted pregnancies, and she often helped women who had illegitimate babies. In 1900 the UCWS, led by Vida, was the 'most vocal and persistent advocate'[69] of Maggie Heffernan, a destitute girl who was sentenced to death for drowning her illegitimate baby. The *Woman's Sphere* publicised the case and argued for mitigation because the girl was suffering from puerperal mania at the time.[70] The sentence was eventually commuted to five years, of which only two years were served because of ill health.

◆ ◆ ◆

The first issue of the *Woman's Sphere* also included answers to the anti-suffrage petition. This petition was the result of a letter to the *Argus* on 19 July 1900 by Carrie Reid and Freda Derham asserting that women did not want the vote. It was eagerly taken up by opponents of the suffrage who arranged a ladies' meeting of protest. Women with such delicate sensibilities as the authors of the letter could not possibly speak in public, but they were offered help—by Vida's father. Jacob told a delighted audience that 'He was not the only one of the name interested in the subject, so the meeting could understand why' he had volunteered his services. This was greeted with laughter.[71] A petition was organised and further meetings were held. It was Vida's only public difference of opinion with her father.

The second meeting was just as enthusiastic. One speaker told the appreciative audience:

> Women were constituted by God to be the queen of the affections of the heart and the empress of the household—(applause)—and any artificial means adopted by Parliaments to alter that state of things were contrary to the law of nature and the law of God, and must necessarily result in injury and degradation to women. (Hear, hear.)[72]

The suffragists responded by holding a woman suffrage meeting at the Melbourne Town Hall on 17 September. Vida was one of the speakers. She continued to denounce the petition, which she dubbed the 'Declaration of Dependence', through the pages of the *Woman's Sphere*.

On 25 September the anti-suffrage petition was presented to the Victorian Parliament. In eight weeks, 24 000 signatures had been collected, compared with the 33 000 of 1891. The two groups watched the Suffrage Bill being debated. The Antis sat in the Gallery and the Woman's Suffrage League members sat in the Upper Gallery where, according to the *Argus*, they 'kept up a fire of sotto-voce and uncomplimentary remarks about the opposing speakers'. Vida and her father sat side by side, 'like the lion and the lamb', while behind them Carrie Reid 'watched the battle with the eye of a Kitchener'.[73] The Bill was once more defeated. Vida privately called the rejection 'monstrous',[74] but it had been expected; the suffragists had insufficient numbers in the Upper House.

While the emergence of the Antis was a concern to the suffragists and the fact that it was instigated by women must have been especially galling, the movement disappeared as rapidly as it had arisen. There was, however, one long-lasting effect in the Goldstein household: the breakdown of the marriage of Isabella and Jacob. The relationship had had its difficulties, and as early as 1888 Isabella's sisters were talking of the Goldsteins' 'home troubles' and that 'Goldie' seemed 'quite determined to bring matters to a climax',[75] but it seems that the suffrage issue was the one that finally divided the couple. At about this time Isabella, with Vida, Aileen and the Champions, moved into a large flat at 88 Oxford Chambers, Bourke

Street, in the heart of Melbourne. One of the arguments against woman suffrage was that it would cause dissent in the home, but Vida contended in the *Woman's Sphere* that 'It will not cause dissension except where dissension already exists'.[76] Jacob did eventually rejoin the family, but the rift between Isabella and Jacob was never healed and they rarely spoke to each other.

Vida enjoyed city living with its ready access to lectures, clubs and other entertainments. She always lived in the heart of the city or maintained an office in the city when the family moved to the inner suburbs. After Jacob's death in 1910, Isabella had 'Wyebo' built at 1 Como Avenue, South Yarra. Later they rented large modern flats or whole floors of apartment buildings. They needed this space to accommodate their large household and their various enterprises. Vida, Isabella, Aileen and the Champions all had their own rooms-cum-offices. Later Aileen's friend, Geraldine Rede, joined them. Lizzie Kavanagh, the cook-general, always lived in and sometimes other domestic help lived with them too.

◆ ◆ ◆

Throughout 1901 Vida campaigned for the suffrage, edited the *Woman's Sphere* and worked for the UCWS. In February and March she toured country Victoria to address public meetings on the suffrage. At Gisborne she so impressed an opponent of the suffrage that he seconded a vote of thanks to her and warmly wished her every success in her work. In March 1901 women from South Australia and Western Australia voted in the national election for the first Federal Parliament. Vida was encouraged by the number of petitions being sent seeking the vote for all women. Women had voted and the question was gaining topicality. She resigned as secretary of the UCWS in mid-1901 but continued as secretary of the parliamentary committee.

Vida supported the campaigns for equal pay by the Victorian Lady Teachers' Association and the Public Service Association, through the *Woman's Sphere* and by lobbying. She later recalled that the Federal Public Service Act was

> bristling with discrepancies in pay for men and women doing exactly the same work and all in the man's favour ... to get the principle of equal pay for equal work embodied in the Bill, some of us had to spend days at the House, lobbying members — always hateful work — showing them the

many injustices in the Bill, from the woman's point of view, and endeavouring to get them to see them as we saw them. We had to tramp round, getting petitions signed; we had to write to the press. Had there been women in the House, there would have been no need for such tactics, because the injustices were so obvious to us that they only had to be pointed out and the majority of members readily promised to get them removed.[77]

Equal pay was achieved for public service clerks in 1902, but the provision was removed in 1916, at the peak of wartime patriotism, without protest.

Vida continued her interest in penal reform and campaigned for the establishment of children's courts, but again the rivalry between the various women's groups was evident. In October 1901 the *Woman's Sphere* dismissed 'dilettante' ladies' committees and their efforts for neglected children, saying the WCTU and the various suffrage leagues had been calling for children's courts for years. In July 1901 Vida helped found the Household Economic Association, which aimed to 'promote practical knowledge of household economy among all classes, and good feeling between employers and employees'. The subcommittee included Vida, Charles Strong and Margaret Cuthbertson, the first female factory inspector in Australia. The association wanted domestic service to be raised to the dignity of a profession. This could be seen as self-interest; middle-class women relied on domestic servants to free them to pursue their own interests. Vida, however, argued that it was a means of employment for women—about half the female workforce were still domestics at the turn of the century—and she believed that it would improve their lot if the status of the job were increased.[78]

In November 1901, Vida also attended the formation of the National Council of Women's Victorian branch, an affiliate of the International Council of Women. Janet, Lady Clarke, who had had to take Annette Bear-Crawford's place at the ICW's quinquennial meeting in 1899, called the Victorian NCW's initial meeting and became president. Vida was enthusiastic about the NCW and encouraged women's organisations to join it because being 'practical and broadminded in its aims, [it] will give an impetus to women's work'.[79] Little did she know when she wrote this that within three months she would be representing the NCW in the United States of America.

3

To America and back

1902

◆

Late in 1901, Vida received notification of an International Women Suffrage Conference to be held in Washington DC in February 1902. The conference aimed to establish an International Woman Suffrage Society and bring together workers for women's rights from all parts of the 'civilised world'. Many Australian women's associations were enthusiastic, realising that the conference meant an opportunity to exchange information and ideas and learn about the movement worldwide. Vida was selected as the Australian delegate and an appeal was launched through the *Woman's Sphere* to fund the trip. Each delegate was to write a report on the status of women in her country and Vida was sent a list of twenty-eight questions on which to base the report. She was very impressed with the professionalism of the planning.[1]

Vida, at thirty-two, was now an acknowledged authority in many social welfare areas. When news of her trip was made public, she received several commissions. The Victorian Government commissioned her to study American methods of dealing with neglected and delinquent children and the Criminology Society asked her to report on the American penal system. The Trades Hall Council also commissioned her to study American unions and their effectiveness, but a deputation to a THC meeting protested against Vida being selected to represent the industrial workers at the conference. It was alleged that at 'some time' she had opposed the Factories and Shops

Act. This was disproved and 'hearty approval' was given to her selection as a delegate. It was stressed that the conference related to the suffrage, not industrial questions, and the meeting decided she should be assisted with all information necessary to fulfil the THC's commission. Not content with this vote of confidence in Vida, her detractors in the THC organised a memorial challenging Vida's 'fitness' to represent industrial workers and sent it to the Suffrage Conference in America. On 28 February a deputation of Vida's supporters told the THC of this memorial and stressed that Vida had been fully credentialled and was empowered to speak for the THC on industrial matters. There was considerable debate on the matter for several weeks and then it disappeared from the Minutes book.[2]

Meanwhile, Vida finalised her travel plans and made her farewells to family and friends. A fund set up for her travel expenses was boosted at the last minute by £30 from the Womanhood Suffrage League of New South Wales. Her sister Aileen agreed to act as editor of the *Woman's Sphere* and Vida promised to send detailed reports to her for publication. (These proved so popular that circulation increased dramatically.) On 3 January a reception was held at the Austral Salon to farewell 'Our Delegate'. Vida was presented with a bouquet of flowers and several speeches extolled her virtues and hard work for political, municipal and social reform.[3]

In Sydney Vida stayed with Rose Scott for two days. This was the first time the two women had met. Vida's trip had excited the interest of the Sydney papers and Vida gave three interviews. One reporter called her 'this attractive, but aggressive, young lady', but went on to say that ten minutes into the interview he learned 'what Australian men are' and was astonished to hear of the legal, social and economic inequities there were between men and women in Australia. Vida was convincingly erudite on a wide range of issues and the reporter was sure she would acquit herself well in America.[4]

The New South Wales National Council of Women appointed Vida a delegate to the Conference of the International Council of Women to be held after the Suffrage Conference and donated £5 towards her expenses. The evening before Vida embarked, a large number of women gathered at Rose Scott's home to farewell her. The next day many well-wishers were at the wharf to see her safely aboard the S.S. *Sierra* and wish her Godspeed.

The first port of call was Auckland where Vida met members of the Political League and collected information on the suffrage in New

Zealand which she would present at the conference. After a brief stop at Samoa, the ship reached Honolulu on 21 January. Despite warnings about an outbreak of bubonic plague, Vida joined a party of six which landed and went sightseeing.[5] Her first image of San Francisco's Golden Gate Bridge, as the ship sailed into the harbour early on the morning of 27 January, 'excited me more than I can tell; I could scarcely realise that I had actually reached America'.[6] She was met by three women bearing letters from Carrie Chapman Catt, the president of the National American Woman Suffrage Association and organiser of the conference, outlining Vida's itinerary. She was immediately introduced to the cost of living in America; the charge to have her boxes taken to her hostess's home was triple the Australian price.

During her three days in San Francisco, the president of the local Suffrage Council took her sightseeing. Then she set off by train across America. Her ultimate destination was Washington DC, but she had several stops along the way. The first was Salt Lake City, the capital of Utah, where women had had the vote since 1870. When told she was to stay with Mormons, she experienced a 'horribly gelatinous shivery shaky feeling'. She 'had visions of arriving at the house with my host and two or three dozen wives drawn up in line to receive me'. In fact when she arrived, 'Though I looked in every corner I did not see any more wives about. In one way I felt relieved, in another slightly disappointed. I am always on the *qui vive* for anything in the shape of an experience'.[7]

Vida's impressions of Mormonism were favourable; the people were 'wonderful', their organisation 'simply perfect'. She was impressed by their system of caring for the spiritual and temporal welfare of all members and by the fact that poverty was unknown in their community. She followed a hectic schedule during her two days in the city. Vida was amused to find she was a distinguished visitor and that every club and society wanted to entertain her. She was busy from eight in the morning until eleven at night. She visited Utah State Prison and reported that in many respects—accommodation, diet, privileges for good conduct—it was superior to Victoria's system. She attended a Mormon service, had an interview with the president and his counsellors, gave a lecture on 'Australian Women and their Public Work', enquired into woman suffrage in Utah and attended a reception given in her honour.[8]

In Chicago Vida addressed women teachers. She also visited the state prison at Joliet and found it in most ways superior to the Victorian system. When she attended a sitting of the Juvenile Court, she was accorded a seat on the bench. The presiding judge was

> interested heart and soul in the waifs that come before him. I thought that he dealt with each case in the most tender and sympathetic manner; but when it came to talking [to] girls of about seventeen to eighteen, who were before the court, he seemed rather helpless—he didn't quite know how to treat them.[9]

Vida did not like Chicago. 'My chief recollection will be of its dirt and extreme cold.'[10] She found the 'overwhelming breeziness of Chicagoans' combined with the dirt 'more than the average person can stand' and related how 'Chicagoans tear along the streets like perfect tornadoes and if they send you flying on to the roadway, or bang you up against a lamp post, or through a shop window those are mere details—they're all in the day's work'.[11]

Travelling on to Washington, Vida met several women also bound for the conference. They enjoyed each other's company, which helped pass the time during a lengthy delay caused by severe snowstorms and the breakdown of a freight train ahead of them. When Vida at last reached Riggs House around midnight Carrie Chapman Catt came to her room to greet her. The impact on Vida was profound.

> I can't even begin to tell you what she is like, for nothing that I could say could possibly give you an idea. She is beautiful, and graceful, and seems to be simply adored by every one about her. And to hear her speak! she is not a speaker, she is a born orator. She has a perfectly marvellous executive ability; to see her preside over a great meeting is something not to be forgotten.[12]

It has been said that what we admire in others is what we aspire to in ourselves; this could have been a description of Vida, or the woman she was soon to become.

◆ ◆ ◆

From 12 to 18 February Vida attended the annual convention of the National American Woman Suffrage Association. The foreign delegates to the conference addressed meetings on the state of woman suffrage in their countries. There were 186 American delegates and representatives from eight other countries: Australia, England, Canada, Germany, Norway, Sweden, Turkey and Chile. Reports were read from France, Belgium, Switzerland, China and Japan. The foreign delegates were welcomed in a speech by a Miss Clopton who said, 'Australia, associated in our memory of childhood's geography as the abode of strange beasts and barbarians, sends us a full, up-to-date representative woman, widely awake to all the refinements of life, and fully cognisant of all the rights of her sex'.[13]

Vida gave her address on 13 February. She briefly outlined the history of the suffrage movement in Australia and in particular Victoria. The problem in the unenfranchised States was 'the Lower and representative Houses are in favor, the Upper and unrepresentative Houses are against, and they will never yield except to outside pressure'.

> In New Zealand women have had the vote since 1893. The enemy said the most dreadful things were going to happen; the happy home would no longer exist, women would flock into every public office, and the colony would be completely ruined in three or four years. None of these dreadful things happened. To-day New Zealand occupies a position of prosperity second to no other country in the British dominions.

She then listed the reforms in New Zealand and the enfranchised Australian States she attributed to the women's vote, including equalisation of divorce laws and increases in the age of protection of girls. (Vida's conviction that the suffrage would lead to reforms ignored the fact that many such reforms were being enacted around the world, with or without woman suffrage.) She concluded:

> A federal franchise bill has been drawn up ... and will shortly be introduced. Its success is certain, as four-fifths of the members of both Houses are publicly pledged to give women the suffrage. This will be the greatest step in the direction of political equality that we have yet seen, and must be a splendid object lesson to the world ... Woman suffrage is with us to stay, and that our success may hasten the day when you American women will stand before the world as the political equals of your men folk is the earnest desire of the countries which have sent me here to represent them at this great Conference.[14]

From 19 to 23 February the First International Conference on the Suffrage Question was held to form an International Woman Suffrage

Committee. Susan Anthony was elected president and Vida felt honoured to be elected secretary. Vida described her meeting with Susan Anthony as 'the great memory of my life'.

> I shall never forget the moment of my meeting that wonderful woman, Susan Anthony; she is eighty-two years of age, and for over fifty years one of the foremost in the suffrage fight, and still fighting with wonderful strength and energy.[15]

Susan Anthony attended every meeting and Vida noted that, despite the long hours, she was always down first to breakfast each morning.

Vast audiences attended the public meetings and Susan Anthony's appearances were met by rapturous applause. The marvellous sense of camaraderie created an excited fervour and the delegates worked from 7.30 a.m until at least midnight every day. One committee meeting was held at one o'clock in the morning and 'did excellent work, too!'.[16] Vida was pleased to report that the General Committee found her minutes of proceedings and reports excellent. A subcommittee of Carrie Chapman Catt, Florence Fenwick Miller from England and Vida drew up the constitution and an International Declaration. The first two principles of the latter were:

1. That men and women are born equally free and independent members of the human race: equally endowed with talents and intelligence, and equally entitled to the free exercise of their individual rights and liberty.
2. That the natural relation of the sexes is that of independence and co-operation, and that a repression of the rights of one inevitably works injury to the other and to the whole race.[17]

Vida was very impressed (and a touch envious no doubt) when the financial secretary asked for £1000 to carry on the work for a year. Immediately she saw 'these splendid American women rising one after another and guaranteeing amounts of from £1 to £100, until more than the required amount was raised'.[18] Vida admired the organising skills of the American women and said their conventions were an education in the art of running public meetings. This sowed the seed for her subsequent endeavours in Australia.

Vida compared the American suffrage movement with the Australian one:

Isabella Hawkins married Jacob Goldstein when she was eighteen and had Vida, her first child, a year later.

Jacob Goldstein in the uniform of the Victorian Garrison Artillery.

Vida Mary Jane Goldstein; her characteristic confidence and assurance were apparent even as a small child.

Vida, standing, with her siblings; from left: Selwyn, Aileen, Lina and Elsie.

Vida, in about 1890, had matriculated with honours and was a popular companion at parties, balls and picnics.

The *Woman's Sphere* featured powerful sketches to emphasise the injustice of denying women the right to vote. This one also reflects the racism of the period.

Vida, the Australian delegate to the International Women Suffrage Conference in Washington DC in 1902, adopted this daring Edwardian fashion in which to represent her country overseas.

Here the working people do little, and know little about it. The women suffragists in America come from the well-to-do, educated, middle-class, and the men who support them are of the same. The very wealthy don't bother themselves about politics, and the working class, unfortunately, have no power, but are manipulated by the party machines. Politics are entirely in the hands of unscrupulous men, who have risen from the ranks and made money.[19]

The foreign delegates were received by President Theodore Roosevelt, a proponent of woman suffrage. Vida thought 'his strength of character and purpose [was] writ large all over his face'.[20] The meeting was reported in the *Woman's Journal*:

> To the young lady from Australia, he mentioned that he had several Australians in his regiment. 'And you found them good men?' she asked. He answered, 'Excellent.' He said that Australia was a very interesting country. He asked in which of the Australian Colonies women now had the vote, and seemed particularly struck by the fact that they were so soon to have national suffrage throughout Australia. Miss Goldstein said she thought it would be a great object lesson, and he answered, 'I think so too.'[21]

Vida's speeches were well received and she was so much in demand that she hardly had time to write home. In one day she made four speeches: one to the Committee of the US Senate; one to the Committee of the House of Representatives and two at the Convention. The other suffragists called her 'Little Australia' and delighted in telling her that her speeches were 'olright'. People were interested in Vida and Australia. Vida was an accomplished, entertaining speaker and an inspiring representative of soon-to-be enfranchised women. The Commonwealth Franchise Act which enfranchised all Australian women federally was passed less than two months after the conferences ended. On 24 April, as Vida prepared to go on stage to give a speech, she was told the news. She jubilantly announced the enfranchisement of Australian women to the meeting.

Vida received considerable press coverage, all complimentary though not all accurate. One report described the 33-year-old Vida as the 'dark, alert, slender girl from Australia'.[22] The *Woman's Journal* called her 'Viola' and reported that she was invited to address the local Council of Jewish Women in the belief that she was Jewish.

Vida said she was often mistaken as Jewish, but her name came from a 'remote ancestor' who was a Pole.[23]

Vida wrote pen portraits of the international delegates and some of the notable American suffragists and collected their autographs in her album. Turkey's representative, Florence Fenshaw, was the Dean of the American College for Girls in Constantinople. She wrote in Vida's book, 'In the words of our happy Turkish phrase—"Light to your eyes"—and—success to the cause to which you have committed your life'. All the delegates were lively, literate women and Vida found talking to them immensely stimulating.

The Americans and the foreign delegates also enjoyed meeting Vida. Her autograph book is full of complimentary remarks about her personality and her inspiring speeches. Carrie Chapman Catt wrote: 'The presence among us of "Little Australia" as we have learned to call her in affection, will bind us continually closer'. George Catt wrote: 'By a sort of acquiescence there has come into being a term for the earnest women that I have met and liked—I count Vida, "one of my girls". Come again and welcome'. Susan Anthony wrote: 'We are all delighted with the delegate from Australia—she has won lots of friends wherever she has been'. An anonymous writer penned the somewhat cryptic, 'Kindly remember me who was with you at the "Lone Feast" in 1902'.[24]

After the suffrage conferences Vida attended the informal Conference of the International Council of Women. The president, May Wright Sewell, was very interested in the work of the National Council of Women in Australia and she and Vida met privately on several occasions.

◆ ◆ ◆

Vida left Washington at the end of February and travelled to Philadelphia where she attended a sitting of the Juvenile Court and visited the state prison. Vida thought Philadelphia the 'quietest, primmest, slowest going place imaginable'.[25]

She was unsure of her return date, but said it would be soon because she was running out of money. She had been invited to speak at several meetings and felt obliged to return the favours she had received. Staying a little longer would also enable her to investigate further the treatment of neglected children, the conditions of labour and the American criminal code. The Goldsteins sent Vida money to allow her to fulfil these commitments. Vida may also have earned some money from lecturing—she commented on how well paid American speakers were. In New York she was the guest of the Catts. In eleven days she addressed seven meetings and spoke to the Senate Committee of the State Legislature.

Vida had had three weeks of 'keen excitement and downright hard work' after a tiring journey across the continent and it finally took its toll. She was forced to have a complete rest for several days in New York. When she had recovered she visited the Statue of Liberty. 'What a mockery it is! The statue of Liberty a woman!' she wrote.[26] She was fascinated by New York's cosmopolitanism, its size and liveliness. She visited numerous welfare societies. She found nothing to equal South Australia's system of dealing with neglected children and the authorities she visited were most interested in her account of that State's Children's Council. She believed, however, as she had at Chicago, that the American penal system was far in advance of Victoria's. She particularly favoured the Elmira system in New York where prisoners were given indeterminate sentences and only released when they were cured. Crime was treated 'like the liquor habit as a disease' and prisoners were given 'useful, exhilarating, and stimulating' work to benefit their bodies and minds. She also emphasised the importance attached to those who looked after them: 'With us, any person will do to look after prisoners; whereas the diseases they are suffering from are mental, and require even more scientific care than the physical maladies treated in the hospital'.[27]

After visiting Boston, Baltimore and Philadelphia, Vida travelled west, speaking at cities along the way. People were amazed at her heavy schedule and that she could keep up the pace. She was well received and the papers were enthusiastic and flattering, writing comments such as 'Everyone was fascinated by her personality and her intellectual power'.[28] Nevertheless, Vida concluded that the standard of American journalism was poor and it was 'humanly impossible' for an American reporter to write accurately, adding that 'the frills and furbelows that have been hung round some of my most innocent remarks have amused me, and sometimes vexed me. Some of them have even reported interviews that have never taken place'.[29]

On 18 May Vida visited Elizabeth Cady Stanton, another of the great American suffrage pioneers, in her home at Rochester, in the

State of New York. Now aged eighty-six, she was still mentally alert and writing a history of woman suffrage. Vida recorded that 'In the attics were the records of suffrage work for fifty years... all docketed and arranged chronologically'. She felt it was a great privilege to meet such a woman and 'to feel that she has entertained some friendship for an other-side-of-the-world suffragist like myself'. She was given a copy of Cady Stanton's book *Reminiscences* and was sent other volumes, which she eventually placed in the State Library of Victoria.[30]

The next day she was taken for a walk in the woods by a naturalist, Mr Dobbin. Vida delighted in the opportunity to admire the birdlife and vegetation close at hand, rather than as she flashed past them in the train. She was also taken to Niagara. She admired the falls from several vantage points and then was taken under them. This entailed disrobing and donning a flannel bathing suit, then an oilskin coat, cap and trousers with canvas shoes tied around the ankles. Vida wished she had been photographed in this garb. She had to pluck up her courage to go behind the falling water and found the prospect 'simply appalling'. Once under the falls, however, she felt 'more than repaid for having had to make such a guy of myself'.[31]

When Vida arrived in Indianapolis, she discovered that the German women of the city had arranged a special reception for her under the misapprehension that she was German. Vida said she was very sorry to disappoint them, but thought that with an Irish father and Australian mother she 'could not possibly palm myself off as a German'.[32] Nevertheless she was given a warm welcome.

Vida's interest in education was reflected in many visits to universities, which were 'all characteristic of different phases of American educational methods'.[33] She admired American teaching because it was based on 'scientific educative methods' with continuity from kindergarten to university. She considered Americans better educated than Australians and found them 'delightful conversationalists' because of the oral teaching methods used which were 'a vast improvement on the merely instructive methods, which most of us Australians, have been victims to in our youth'.[34]

On her return to San Francisco in June, she wrote:

> Here I am back in San Francisco, after a triumphal progress through the States. The whole tour really has been a triumph. I have been received everywhere with the utmost kindness—indeed, with enthusiasm...

Although I have had a perfectly delightful visit, it has been real hard work all the time. Travelling on trains, living in one's trunks, speaking everywhere I went, visiting penal establishments, charitable institutions, schools, universities—you can draw a mental picture of what I have been through, and yet I don't think you will be able to form any idea of what the whirl and the rush has been. And you can't imagine what wholly delightful invitations for theatres, concerts and pleasure trips I have had to refuse, because with only a limited stay in each place, I have had to put work first and pleasure second.[35]

She did manage to enjoy a rest as the guest of Theresa Speddy, although while 'resting' she gave speeches at the two receptions in her honour and was the principal speaker at one of the two meetings she attended. One day they went to the Chutes, an amusement popular with San Franciscans. The Speddy children enjoyed it—so did Vida. The party entered a car which took them up a wooden incline to a platform fifty to sixty feet above a lake. Then they transferred to a long flat-bottomed boat and were launched on a 'wild and whizzing descent to the shallow lake at the foot'. The first time they went down, Vida was in the back and did not get such a bump, so she was keen to go down on the front seat. None of the others wanted to go down again, so Vida went alone and because the boat was not heavily loaded 'when the craft struck the water I struck the air, and, at a considerably later stage of the journey, the seat. I need hardly tell you that I shall always have a lively and jarring recollection of shooting The Chutes'.[36] She added that one stepped out of the boat 'feeling that life is the very tamest affair to those who have not shot The Chutes'.[37]

During the final weeks of her visit, Vida met, and was entertained by, many interesting people. She continued her inquiries into industrial conditions and the treatment of neglected children and visited the Fabiola Hospital which was staffed and managed by women, but open to both sexes.

Vida was later criticised for becoming too pro-American as a result of this visit. While she certainly saw much that impressed her, especially in terms of relations between the sexes and welfare activities, she appraised what she saw and was prepared to say what she found unimpressive. She was not impressed with the American political system, having expected more of the birthplace of democracy. She attended what she considered important debates in

Congress (education of Indians and the Philippine question), but both chambers were almost empty and she thought the general tone of proceedings lacked dignity. As well she was 'struck dumb' to see fruit and cake vendors in the corridors. She concluded that politics in America was in a

> perfectly hopeless state. In Australia we only hear a small portion of the corruption practised here. I could never have believed that things were so bad. The better class of men won't interfere in politics, and so they are left entirely in the hands of the unscrupulous.[38]

Vida also took a keen interest in the plight of the coloured people in America and publicly deplored the behaviour of a so-called Christian minister who walked out of his church when a coloured man took the pulpit.[39]

◆ ◆ ◆

Vida left San Francisco on 24 July and arrived in Sydney on 16 August, where she stayed with Rose Scott once more. On 20 August she addressed the New South Wales Woman Suffrage League. Her experiences in America had given her an increased confidence and assurance. One journalist who interviewed her in Sydney described her as a woman with a mission: 'you can see it in her face, behold it in her manner and hear it in her voice'. She airily told him, 'You can "pump" me' and proceeded to tell him about the reforms she had observed in penitentiaries and the work being done with neglected children. When questioned on woman suffrage she said women would not vote hastily and would vote along similar lines as men. She believed men would support a female parliamentary candidate more readily than women, because they had a broader education and realised that the logical outcome of giving women the vote was that women would stand for Parliament. When asked about the possibility of a woman forming a government, Vida replied that if the woman had the talent 'you could not stop her', but she did not support the idea of an 'all-woman cabinet' because she believed the sexes should act together in Parliament and at home.[40]

On her return to Melbourne, Vida was welcomed at a public function on 26 August at the Masonic Hall in Collins Street. Sir William Lyne, the former Premier of New South Wales and now a member of the House of Representatives, presided. A long list of speakers had been arranged, representing the groups associated with Vida's trip, but after the chairman, two senators and Annie Lowe had spoken, Dr William Maloney 'opportunely interfered' and Annie Lowe spoke on behalf of the six remaining speakers. Vida then spoke for an hour. The Melbourne Women's Progressive League, which had formed on 22 July and elected Vida president in her absence, also welcomed her home. She addressed them on the International Women Suffrage Conference.[41]

Vida soon embarked upon a heavy schedule which included giving talks on her experiences in America, preparing reports on her findings and being interviewed by journalists.

Vida gave an address on 'Industrial Conditions in America', at the Trades Hall Pleasant Sunday Afternoon on 21 September. She spoke knowledgeably to an attentive audience on such diverse topics as the methods of American labour organisations, immigration, the Beef Trust, the coal strike in Pennsylvania, the tramway strike in San Francisco, factories legislation, arbitration and child labour. She was not optimistic about the industrial scene in America because Americans were not prepared to be labourers and imported immigrants for this purpose. Americans wanted to climb the social ladder and this made it difficult for unions, because there was not the solidarity of a united body. She feared that a tremendous upheaval between capital and labour was imminent. The female workers were unorganised and unenfranchised and earned pitifully low wages. Child labour was an 'awful curse'. Americans were opposed to compulsory arbitration and conciliation and factory inspections were often a farce, with many inspectors in the pay of the employers.[42]

Vida wrote a report on the George Junior Republic in New York State. Of all the programs for delinquents she had seen, this had impressed her most. From experience she had discovered that even the 'most patient loving care under probation' had no effect on some delinquents. They were not hopeless cases, but the 'roots of their ill deeds go further down than one can reach merely by probationary oversight'. She blamed poverty and foolish or wicked parents, but believed it was possible to help the children. At the George Junior Republic, youngsters between the age of twelve and eighteen were taught the principles of self-government by experience rather than precept. They were 'given charge of their own lives, their own private, their own business, their own public affairs'. On arrival the children had to serve a month without a serious offence before they were made citizens. The republic had a president and other office-bearers, civil and criminal courts, a gaol, post office, general store and board of health. They had their own legislature and held elections with franchise for both sexes. This was all operated by the children and all positions were open to all.

The founder, W. R. George, believed children had a keen sense of justice and that they felt the punishment more keenly if it was meted out by their peers.[43] The motto was 'Nothing without labour', and the children worked for aluminium tokens which were cashed in at the store for all their requirements. They soon learnt that if they were lazy or careless with their money or fined for misdemeanours they would go hungry or without clothing. Vida recommended that a similar scheme should be established in Victoria.[44]

In October, Vida published an 'Open Letter to the Women of the United States'. Since speaking at the suffrage conferences she had been enfranchised federally and she was proud that Australia now led the way on woman suffrage. She believed that American men of public affairs were in favour of woman suffrage, but they lacked support from the rank and file of the working people. Any social reform worth winning had only been achieved through the support of the workers; they suffered most in the present social conditions and so they best understood the need for reform. Convinced that women had won the vote in Australia through the workers, she advised the American women to join with Labor as close allies, because both groups were working for improved conditions.[45]

Vida was interviewed about her American experiences by *New Idea*. The story began, 'If we believed the artist of the illustrated weekly the typical advocate of women's rights is tall, gaunt, goggled, and hideously attired in semi-masculine garments'. The article assured readers that Vida had none of those attributes and the accompanying portrait showed her wearing a dress with a frothy feminine lace collar. It chose to ignore her portrait as delegate to the suffrage conferences in which she sported a tie and a boater with the suffrage colours!

Interviewed in her 'pleasant little rooms at Oxford Chambers', Vida spoke enthusiastically about her visit to America. She said the American women were the freest in the world, despite their lack of the suffrage; that the husband consulted his wife on business matters and relied on her judgement. She said that if it had been up to native-born Americans, women would have had the vote much sooner—it was the more conservative immigrants who were denying women the vote. Socially and educationally she thought the American women were 'far ahead' of Australian women. When asked if it were true that there was a revulsion against higher learning for women in America, she replied that it was because the women were winning all the scholarships. She had found the American women to be very hospitable, receptive, intelligent and good speakers. They were interesting and interested audiences and at some of her meetings she was kept talking for three hours as they 'simply insisted on my continuing'.[46]

Vida also prepared a lecture called 'To America and Back! Cheapest Trip on Record!!!' It cost two shillings first class and one shilling second and was illustrated with fifty-five stereopticon slides which she had brought back with her. Alfred Deakin, then Acting Prime Minister, agreed to preside at its first presentation on 28 October. She gave a brief outline of the trip, then showed the slides and after a five-minute interval she described the manners and customs of the American people. Her lecture was witty and informative and proved very popular. She repeated it in the city and throughout Victoria and attracted large audiences. The proceeds helped offset the cost of the trip.

In the lecture, Vida said that she was surprised that Americans knew so little about Australians and that 'many were astonished to find I was white, others that I spoke English so well'. She said Americans ate breakfast 'terribly early' at 7 or 7.30 a.m. and that 'with only three meals a day and those far apart you can understand they eat heartily'.

She was intrigued by the Americans' attachment to rocking chairs—they were everywhere, even in the bathroom. It was considered cruel to refuse one to a prisoner and a sentence of five years without a rocking chair was reserved for a crime of a very terrible nature. She found the habit was contagious and that after ten minutes she 'was rocking as madly as everyone else'. Even at a Baccalaureate Service she attended, all the dignitaries sat on stage and rocked. An old man sitting next to an empty chair got it rocking in unison too.

She was not so enamoured of two other aspects of American life—

chewing tobacco and spitting. Everywhere she went there were cuspidors and there was always one in each section of the Pullman. Immediately she entered the carriage she would 'kick the hateful thing under the seat, out of sight'. At one stage, to economise, she took an ordinary car because it was only a three-hour trip. It was difficult to find a clean space and with her long dresses she had to inspect the floor carefully.

> How I wish I could give you some idea of the agony I suffered. Men expectorating to the right of me, men expectorating to the left of me, men expectorating all round me, and when finally a *woman* in the opposite section to me followed suit, I nearly expired.

She promptly summoned the conductor and had herself and her luggage removed to the parlour car. She concluded, 'The all-sorts—and conditions—car is a very democratic idea, and I am a thorough going democrat, but—I like a clean democracy'.

The chewing vice was just as irritating:

> I know of nothing more calculated to set all your nerves twanging, than to sit in a street car or elevated train, and watch half a dozen men, women and children opposite you chew, chew, chewing as hard as they can go. After a time it works you up to such a pitch that you feel like committing murder. I remember one day, on a three hour railway journey a bride and bridegroom were sitting in front of me, both chewing vigorously. I couldn't change my seat, and there for three mortal hours, I had to endure that spectacle. When a man and woman marry, it is quite the most desirable thing that their two hearts should beat as one, but it is a little trying for other people, that they should decide to go through life with their jaws working in perfect unison.[47]

Vida also delivered her report to the National Council of Women in which she praised the founders of the American Council of Women for their foresight in omitting woman suffrage from its constitution, because this would have deterred many women from joining. It was essential to get women to work together. A Council of Women 'would do more to break down the barriers of custom and prejudice against the much misunderstood "political woman", than anything else that could be conceived at that time'. The NCW should remain a non-political body because, 'As some one has said "politics are in time of peace what militarism is in a state of war," and true, lasting reform must be brought about by finer and subtler methods'. The International Council's main aim was for international peace, and this appealed to Vida.

In this document the fundamental principles of Vida's life are now apparent: a desire to work for the betterment of humanity in new and scientific ways based on a strong religious foundation; an emphasis on the central importance of peace; an aversion to party politics and a growing awareness that woman suffrage alone would not solve women's problems. Vida now believed that women would achieve the desired changes by bringing their special qualities into the public arena, with or without the vote. She summarised these beliefs in the conclusion of the report:

> In working for the bettermen of humanity we must use many weapons; education is one, suffrage is another, and so on, but all are of little account unless at the back of them lies the finer, subtler, unselfish, spiritual desire to bring about the true brotherhood of man. The International Council represents this grand ideal. Women are better able than men to meet together and consider social betterment; they are more ready than men to sink their private political views in the larger questions they are called upon to deal with, and so it seems probable that it is to women we shall have to look to bring about true Internationalism ... to bring about Peace on Earth, Good-will to Man.[48]

This report is Vida's first public expression of her fundamental belief in spirituality and the brotherhood of man which, through her conversion to Christian Science, now became the core of her life.

Many Christian denominations at this time opposed suffragism because they upheld the doctrine of St Paul, that man is the head of the house, just as God is the head of the Church. In Melbourne many suffragists joined Charles Strong's Australian Church because of his progressive thinking and support for the women's movement. When the First Church of Christ, Scientist, began services in Melbourne in 1898, many progressives and suffragists were attracted to it. In 1902 Vida, with Isabella, Elsie and Aileen Goldstein, joined the Church. Several of Vida's friends also became Christian Scientists, including Ina Higgins and Lilian Locke.

Christian Science attracted progressives because it was a new sect, founded in 1875, which asserted that Christianity was relevant to a scientific age, teaching that 'to be spiritually minded is ... to be scientifically minded'.[49] It also attracted suffragists because it was founded by a woman, Mary Baker Eddy, and women were equally involved in the services and the administration. It even gave authority for considering God feminine.[50]

Christian Science teaches that God or Mind is infinite and that because God is the only cause and source of all things, matter is unreal. It is a positive faith which focuses on good, believing that the discussion of evil invests evil with apparent power. Evil, sin and illness are unreal because they are not procured by God; rather they are the outward expression of mistaken thinking and false thoughts. Its major tenet is a belief in metaphysical healing; that Christian Science is the Holy Ghost through which Christ healed the sick. True knowledge can only be attained through prayer, and this 'mental work' can alone heal the sick. Hospitals are therefore unnecessary, although dental and optical treatment is permitted. Members do not withdraw from worldly involvements and believe their faith promotes their success; it favours expansion of thought and supports education.[51] Christian Science became the mainstay of Vida's life and she 'found it extraordinarily helpful as an anchor and a background for her Social-political work'.[52]

◆ ◆ ◆

The year had been momentous for Vida personally and for Australian women as a whole. The franchise had been won federally and soon, no doubt, the remaining States would follow suit and grant women the vote. Vida had had the experience of a lifetime in America and had become the best known Australian suffragist overseas. She had learned a great deal about organisation from the American women and had come to enjoy public speaking. She returned to Australia with increased personal confidence and a clearer vision of her goals. In addition, she now had a strong religious faith which would sustain and inspire her in the years to come. In the new year, 1903, Vida would draw on all these attributes—and make history.

4

The lady candidate

1903

◆

When Vida returned from her successful American tour she was invigorated and full of new ideas. She hoped her enthusiasm and experience would be the catalyst that would inspire the women's movement in Australia. However, to her dismay, she found that the *Woman's Sphere* was running at a 'dead loss', that the suffrage work was in a 'most unsatisfactory state' and that nothing was achieved unless she was there to plan and see it to fruition. She wrote to Rose Scott, 'I am in most cases leaning on broken reeds'.[1] It was very different from the American movement where so many people were involved and money was readily available for the suffrage cause. Privately she wrote that 'our women seem to be asleep'.[2] Everyone looked to her for leadership but unless the *Woman's Sphere* became self-supporting she would not have the time to lead the movement. She envied Rose her independent means and added, 'I have to work hard for the barest living'.[3] Rose offered to help the *Woman's Sphere* in the future, but Vida declined, assuring her that she had already done far more than her share.[4]

In February 1903 the Victorian Legislative Council rejected the Women's Suffrage Bill for the seventh time. This was especially disappointing because women had been enfranchised federally and suffragists had hoped the remaining States would follow suit. New South Wales had granted women the vote in 1902, but women in Victoria, Tasmania and Queensland were still unenfranchised. A grand suffrage demonstration was held in the Melbourne Town Hall. Vida said that she regretted that the motion she was seconding was not couched in stronger terms, but added that if they had put in all the 'blood and thunder' they wished they would not have been allowed to use that 'respectable' venue.[5]

Vida continued the campaign in the *Woman's Sphere*. The front page of the April edition was a satirical cartoon showing a lovely woman (not unlike Vida) beside a mad woman and a convict, with a sign above them proclaiming, 'Thou shalt not vote womanhood madness criminality'. Below were the enfranchised: fops, dandies, fat gentlemen, other ethnic groups and even a pugilist.

Vida realised that she needed to recruit members and bring the existing groups together for concerted action, so she instituted a new campaign with the catchcry 'Organise and Educate'. In the March editorial she called on women to unite in one association rather than wasting their energies in scattered organisations. The association she presumably favoured was the Melbourne Women's Progressive League which had renamed itself the Melbourne Women's Political Association and had adopted a thirteen-point 'fighting platform'. This included: adult suffrage; equal pay for equal work; legal equality; amendment of laws regarding children; educational and penal reform; uniform federal legislation on working conditions, old-age pensions and food adulteration; municipalisation or nationalisation of coal-mines; a tax on unimproved land values and the extension of local government and federal powers with the object of abolishing State parliaments.[6]

Federal elections were scheduled for December 1903 and it was acknowledged that the newly enfranchised women could have a significant impact on the results. Vida believed that women must be educated to use their vote wisely. A series of meetings was held in co-operation with the Trades Hall Council to establish an association for this purpose. Women could join the Political Labor Leagues or the Progressive Leagues, but there was no organisation for the democratic women. She wrote to Rose Scott, 'I have got a great scheme on for organizing the women's vote in Victoria on democratic lines'.[7] One legacy of her American trip was Vida's commitment to non-party politics. She opposed membership of political parties because they represented the status quo and male domination. She wanted to establish a non-party political association so that women of all political persuasions could join and to prevent women being 'torn in all directions' whenever they wanted to take political action.[8]

A subcommittee of ten men and women, including Vida, drew up the platform. The meeting to form the association was attended by senators and members of Parliament and was chaired by the president of the Australian Natives' Association, Arthur Robinson. There was debate on whether men should be permitted to join. Most of the opposition came from men, who feared men would manipulate the association for political purposes. Women experienced in conducting societies argued for inclusion; Vida said that while it was intended to be mainly a women's association, officered by women, the help and co-operation of men was vital because the association was addressing human interests, not just women's. The women won the day and men were included.[9] A few men appear on the 'Roll of Honour' as foundation members, but the involvement of men in the association was only ever minimal.[10] It was named the Women's Federal Political Association and the platform closely resembled that of Vida's Melbourne Women's Political Association.[11]

On 13 June Vida was elected president and a constitution was adopted. Vida enthusiastically wrote in the *Woman's Sphere* that the association's purpose was solely political and non-party, so it did not overlap with other women's associations. She pleaded for 'In Essentials—Unity; In Non-Essentials—Charity', quoting the wise words of St Augustine of Hippo. Women should sink their differences and join, even if they disagreed with aspects of the platform. Members who paid five shillings annually would be sent free copies of the *Woman's Sphere*, which had become the 'political organ of the organisation'.[12] Already the association had Vida's hallmark; it was non-party political and she—the new political woman—was its prominent identity.

Both sides of politics watched this new organisation warily. In June the idea was mooted to establish a conservative body to educate women politically; the Australian Women's National League came into being the following year. Labor also realised the importance of the women's vote and began to consider establishing women's branches attached to the Political Labor Council. By making the WFPA non-party Vida hoped to prevent women having to choose between women's issues and party issues. However, less than a month after its formation, Lilian Locke resigned as secretary because the WFPA had 'incurred the hostility of certain labour organisations'.[13]

◆ ◆ ◆

Part of the suffrage debate had involved the question of whether women should be allowed to enter Parliament. In 1898 in their *Reply to Speech against Women's Suffrage*, Vida and Annette Bear-Crawford had been non-committal about this issue, but now, five years later, Vida published an article in the August *Review of Reviews* which supported women entering Parliament. She gave historical precedents for women with political power and argued that there was an essential sex difference between men and women and that a woman could best protect the interests of women and children. She said men were often unaware of discriminatory legislation against women until made aware of it by women. She concluded that sooner or later women would be elected to Parliament.[14] This idea that women would make unique contributions based on their more sensitive, nurturing natures also became one of the principal tenets of second-wave feminism.[15]

On 3 August, while Vida was touring Victoria forming WFPA branches, that body's council unanimously voted to ask her to stand as a candidate for the Senate. She later wrote, 'I saw at once what a splendid educational value the campaign would have'.[16] In her reply to the council, Vida said she was highly flattered, but she thought it should be the decision of the association, not just the council, because while the council had the power to invite a candidate to stand, when the clause was written it was 'never contemplated that a woman might be put forward' and that it was 'only fair' that the association be given the chance to express an opinion.[17] Aware of the potential divisiveness of the move, Vida wisely sought wide approval of the members before she committed herself. A meeting was called for this purpose on 14 August.

In the meantime, Vida pressed on with the work of the WFPA. Pamphlets were published to teach women about voting and mock elections were held to demonstrate the process. The meeting to open the Women's Federal Election Campaign was held on 10 August at the Melbourne Town Hall. Vida, moving the first resolution, reminded women that the eyes of the world would be on them when they voted and that they should register a 'thinking vote'.[18] The *Bulletin*'s report of the meeting described Vida's outfit, including her 'bright piece of coquettish millinery. Its dash of scarlet was the oriflamme of the meeting. Speakers beside and behind her were cheered on by the rakish crown-piece'. It concluded that 'the keen and positive Miss will score where a sallow dowd, in specs and unstylish apparel ... would fail signally'.[19]

On 14 August Vida spoke to a crowded meeting at Dandenong, while the WFPA met to discuss her possible candidature. A letter from Vida was read, in which she wrote that if the meeting approved of her candidature she would accede to the council's request, but if it disapproved she would never forget the honour paid to her. After vigorous discussion, the motion was won 29 to 8. Vida was to be the first woman in the British Empire to nominate for a national Parliament. Three women in New South Wales later nominated: Nellie Martel and Mary Ann Moore for the Senate and Selina Anderson for the House of Representatives.

Immediately her candidature was announced, the question was raised if women were in fact eligible to stand for Parliament. The Home Secretary, Sir William Lyne, said that the Act provided that when 'he' was used, it embraced 'she'. This gave rise to many witticisms of dubious quality in the press, including:

> He took her in his arms and said
> 'Now, do not angry be,
> It's constitutional. In fact,
> It's quite according to the Act
> When He embraces She'.[20]

Vida's nomination was seen as a radical move by the newspapers. Some columnists felt cheated that women, so newly entrusted with the vote, now had the audacity to want to sit in Parliament as well. They argued that Vida would bring ridicule upon the woman suffrage movement because she was bound to fail. *Punch* wrote that a small reluctantly given concession was being used for appropriating 'the whole animal'.[21] An *Argus* editorial reminded readers that advocates of woman suffrage had denied they wanted women in Parliament and added:

> But it has long been an established judgment that woman is in our hours of ease uncertain, coy, and hard to please, and variable as the shade by the light quivering aspen made. Therefore, we need not be at all surprised that she has changed her mind, and determined to exercise the full political power conferred upon her by men in their hours of political ease and light-heartedness.[22]

Truth extolled Vida's virtues, describing her as a 'political sunbeam dancing on the Parliamentary arena... the accredited representative of advanced woman in Victoria, a maid with brains', but it issued grim warnings on what Vida could expect when entering the political arena. She would 'find many rebuffs in politics, and many things to try angelic tempers, and she may be rendered unnatural'. She would come to realise that 'a woman can no more than a man touch filth and remain undefiled' and 'will be glad to get back to first principles and baby'.[23]

An *Argus* article was more positive:

> Think it over, ladies. Rows of bonnets and hats, always varying in size, colour, and structure, would be much more pleasant to survey from the gallery than rows of bald heads—which never vary except to grow rapidly balder as the nourishment forsakes the capillary glands in order to feed the overwrought brain.[24]

It added that women would take their seats thoroughly prepared and armed for debate, because the women's associations had been training women 'in the art of talking—an art which cynics say women need no instruction in'. *Punch* said many men would vote for Vida 'just for a lark', in a 'spirit of cussedness and mischief, just to see what would happen'.[25]

The cartoonists had a field day. The *Bulletin* ran an unflattering caricature of a bespectacled woman vaguely resembling Vida. The woman wore trousers and was climbing up a ladder to the top of the poll. The shocked elector asked, 'But where are your qualifications, madam?', to which she replied, 'Why, I've got them on, stupid!'.[26] Another series in *Punch* showed Vida being carried into Parliament by women. She had a chaperone who beat the Whip with her umbrella, drank whisky and was finally removed by the usher, while Vida refereed from the presidential chair with both sides fighting for her support.[27]

More disconcertingly, Vida discovered that her candidature was not uniformly supported by the individuals and groups she had hoped would help her. Catherine Spence, an unsuccessful candidate for the Federal Convention in 1897, doubted the wisdom of Vida's action: 'I am not at all sure that Vida Goldstein is wise in standing for the Senate. Women do not vote as women for women'.[28] The Victorian WCTU's executive voted unanimously not to support a woman candidate. This action was supported by other groups including the Victorian Women's Franchise League. The Victorian WCTU journal, the *White Ribbon Signal*, wrote that while women would be as well or better qualified than the present members, to nominate would cloud the suffrage issue because the time was not yet ripe for a woman parliamentary candidate.[29]

In an effort to counter this opposition, Vida published leaflets quoting prominent people who supported her candidature. These included Rose Scott, Henrietta Johnson (formerly Dugdale) and notable WCTU members.[30] The official organ of the WCTU, *Our Federation*, condemned the Victorian executive's move because it was contrary to the union's motto of 'No sex in citizenship' and added that women had never won improvements by sitting down to wait for them to happen.[31]

One of the major issues of the campaign was protection versus free trade. Vida, though preferring to call herself a fiscal atheist, when pressed called herself a protectionist. The *Age* was pro-protection and initially supported Vida, saying she could be expected to speak forcefully on issues affecting women—marriage and divorce laws, education and the drink question. In a long editorial, it enumerated many historical precedents of women in power and cited the Aristophanes comedy in which the women rose in rebellion, seized control of parliament house and legislated that all the ugly women should at once be provided with husbands. This prompted the *Age* to ask if Vida would support a tax on bachelors.[32] At meetings after this, she was invariably asked this question. She would answer good naturedly that although she did not see the relevance of the question to federal politics, she believed in equality of the sexes and so the tax would have to apply accordingly.

A campaign committee was organised with Beatrice Moore as chairman and Mary Malcolm as secretary. WFPA funds would not be used towards Vida's campaign, so money had to be raised. A busy schedule of engagements was arranged and Vida relinquished the editorship of *Woman's Sphere* during the campaign. Vida spoke at the first political meeting held by the Austral Salon at their 'Monday Tea' on 24 August. Her address was entitled 'Why Women Should Vote' and members were so interested they stayed well past their normal time.[33]

There was great interest in Vida, a woman who had dared go beyond the private sphere, and she received a lot of press coverage. She kept a scrapbook of cuttings and included all the reports, flattering or otherwise. Many reporters had difficulty writing on this new phenomenon. Some were almost perplexed — and certainly relieved — to discover that she was not 'mannish'. One reporter describing Vida wrote that she 'quivers with life and energy, and from her dark head to the tip of her dainty buckled shoes there's not the slightest suggestion of "mannishness", not even that faint aroma of it that clings to the golf girl'.[34] An 'average woman' interviewed Vida for the *Weekly Times* and happily reported that Vida was not the stereotypical 'strong-minded "woman's righter"'. The 'average woman' supported this by telling her readers that Vida was wearing a feminine jacket with pink silk facings and pink bow at the back of her neck and that her room was suitably domestic with pot plants in the window, violets on the table and some interrupted crochet work nearby. Only then did she report what Vida had to say about the WFPA platform.[35] Throughout her campaign, Vida's physical appearance was reported at the expense of her policies, sometimes through an attempt to describe this new phenomenon of a woman entering politics but often merely trivialising her candidature.

In late September Vida travelled to Adelaide for four days where she reported on the Conference of the International Council of Women to the South Australian branch of the National Council of Women. When interviewed, she said she thought her chance of being elected was slender and that her main object was 'to wake up the women' but if she were not elected, her candidature would make it easier for the next woman. The reporter hesitantly asked her age and Vida was happy to tell him. The subheading for this was 'A Delicate Question' and the age reported was thirty-two, although she was two years older. The same article described Vida as a 'dress reformer' because she wore a dress that 'just tipped her ankles'. She thought wearing drawing-room trains in the street was 'simply disgusting' (possibly she was influenced by her American experience!), that useful attire was more becoming and that exaggerated dress was 'reprehensible'.[36]

Vida returned briefly to Melbourne for a speaking engagement and then travelled to Albury where she attended the Albury Debating Society's meeting. The topic was the fiscal issue and Vida said diplomatically that she had gone to get some enlightenment on the tariff question. (Albury was strongly free-trade). The next night she spoke in Wangaratta. So many people came to hear her that many had to be turned away because of insufficient space. Returning to

Melbourne, Vida spoke on 'Woman's Mission' to an estimated audience of 2000 people.

Vida was a popular speaker but she did make mistakes. When she addressed a meeting on 'Woman Suffrage' at Korumburra, she called the Reform League a 'rank Conservative body'.[37] This caused much hilarity as the chairman of the meeting was also the chairman of the local branch. On another occasion she mistook one of Bridgewater's leading male politicians for a female questioner.[38]

◆ ◆ ◆

Vida formally opened her election campaign in the Portland Library Hall on Tuesday 13 October. There was a large audience, with women predominating. As Vida entered the hall, she was met by loud and enthusiastic applause. She said Melburnians had been disappointed that she had not selected Melbourne to open her campaign and some did not know where Portland was, but for her, Portland was the logical choice: she had been born there; her parents were well known there and she had an affection for the place. As well, the step she was taking was history in the making and Portland was most associated with the early white history of Victoria, having been settled by the Hentys a year before Melbourne was founded.

Vida said that it was the duty of woman to take her share in the work to protect her interests; that she was not standing for self-interest or a parliamentary salary, but to fulfil her duty to do her best for her State because only female lawmakers could best protect women. She believed her candidature would help achieve woman suffrage by drawing attention to the injustice of denying women the vote. From the voting, the WFPA would gauge where the lack of support was, so they could focus their educative work there.[39] She acknowledged the difficulties she was facing:

> She had to fight against the prejudice of those who held that women in entering the political arena were leaving their home duties, and she was also meeting with the opposition of some of her womanhood suffrage workers, which she felt very keenly. The latter were afraid that her candidature at the present juncture would prevent women from getting the franchise for the State Parliament, but she thought their contention was wrong. Indeed, if she felt there was the slightest foundation for that fear she would withdraw.[40]

Vida then outlined her policies; she would be non-party, a protectionist, in favour of White Australia but opposed to the deportation of Kanakas. She was 'wobbly' on assisted migration because she had witnessed migrants being dumped in New York to swell the labour market and cheapen labour. While she believed in the brotherhood of man, at the same time charity had to begin at home. She supported arbitration and conciliation and lessening of state powers and was opposed to establishing a federal capital and a transcontinental railway because of the expense. She answered questions knowledgeably on these and other issues and skilfully deflected questions like should there be bibles in state schools, saying she did not wish to bring sectarianism into the debate.[41]

Two days later when Vida gave a similar address in Hamilton, the hall was so crowded that latecomers had to stand on the platform. The reporter commented on Vida's good presence, her fluency of speech and her talent for turning a phrase well. She frequently relieved her speech with 'a play of facetious or caustic humour' while successfully conveying her earnestness. She stressed that she 'has not undertaken the leviathan task from any motive of self aggrandisement or notoriety hunting'.

> People asked, Why go to all this rampage? Well, for her own peace of mind she would sooner be in her own home than going into public life, but she believed people should go into public life from a sense of duty.
>
> She was a suffragist first and would use the campaign to promote the woman suffrage movement. If elected she would concentrate on the 'political questions which affected the home, industrial and social questions, questions on which the opinion of a woman, given at first hand on the floor of the House, might not be altogether valueless'.

There was a 'touch of genuine pathos in her reference to the sacrifice of social ties and domestic relations which she was making' and the difficulties that beset a young woman travelling alone around the countryside. She handled political questions with 'all the cautiousness of a veteran campaigner'. When asked the usual bachelor question, her quip that 'there were some men to whom she would give no encouragement to get married', was greeted with appreciative laughter.[42]

Vida was not afraid to admonish her audiences. Disappointed by the lack of questions she was asked at Hamilton and again at Ararat, she introduced a 'departure': she would ask the audience questions, so that if elected she could speak authoritatively for the electors. When Vida asked those in favour of the fiscal question to raise their right hand:

> Mr Dawson (rising quickly)—Excuse me, but the chairman must put the questions. (Loud laughter.)
> Miss Goldstein—I think with your permission I'll manage this myself. (Laughter and cheers.)
> ...only 13 voted for free trade and 21 for protection. The result was announced amidst much merriment.
> Miss Goldstein—Those who do not think the fiscal question a vital one—like myself—please vote.
> There was no response and the candidate said rather despairingly 'Do you think this a good thing or not?'
> [Conciliation and arbitration won 35 to 1, then she asked about a national capital.] Two persons had the temerity to declare in favor, whilst a perfect shoal of hands were held up in the negative amidst much laughter and applause.
> Miss Goldstein—Is that the subject you feel most strongly about then?
> A voice—It touches the pocket.
> Miss Goldstein—That's what is to be deplored; when it touches the pocket you respond immediately, but when it concerns social misery you are apathetic.

Nevertheless, Vida decided to repeat the experiment at other meetings.[43]

Vida was to have spoken in Horsham on 19 October and Stawell the next day, but 'due to the dereliction of duty on the part of a cabman' she missed the train from Ararat. The Horsham night meeting was abandoned, but a meeting was held the next morning and another that night, where the front of the hall was reserved for women and the rear for men. This division of the sexes was resented by several people who 'apparently saw in it the relegation at no distant date of the men to the background and the advancement of women to the forefront as far as politics are concerned.' The *Western Star* reported:

> Many of the ladies who went to scoff remained to pray, and Miss Goldstein may confidently rely upon good support from the female electors here—that is if they do not exercise their prerogative of changing

their minds between now and the election day. By her charming manner, excellent command of language, and her selection of subjects that always appeal to women, Miss Goldstein succeeded in enlisting the support of the majority of the gentler sex.[44]

However, the *Horsham Times* concluded that, if elected, Vida would soon regret it because she would find herself 'voiceless and powerless against the overwhelming numbers of the sterner sex.'[45]

When Vida arrived in Avoca she made her way to Host Gregory's Avoca Hotel, somehow missing the local ladies who had arranged a welcoming party at the station for her. The *Ararat Advertiser*'s report by 'Man' was most flattering about Vida but not her opinions.

> Miss Goldstein presented a very pleasing appearance on the platform at Avoca. She was graceful, prettily gowned, and wore a most becoming hat. During her address she toyed prettily with a beautiful La France rose—a move that added much to the effect.
>
> The lady became a favorite with all present almost at once. Her easy delivery of speech, charming voice, modest manner, and absence of anything masculine, being the chief factors in her favor.

'Man' included his objections to her policies: Vida wanted equal pay for equal work, but she had not proved to him that women could do equal work. For instance, it was a 'fact' a 'woman cannot be placed in charge of an important telegraph office where several lines junction, because she is not constitutionally strong enough to stand the constant strain on the nerves'. He added that Vida had not allowed for the strain parliamentary work would place on a woman's 'delicate nature'.[46]

As Vida continued her country campaign tour, she received mostly favourable reports in the country newspapers. The *Yarrawonga Chronicle* analysed her policies and concluded:

> A large percentage of the electors (men and women) will say:—'We will give this woman a vote. Her political creed is healthy, and we shall have an opportunity of studying woman in active political life. If she justifies her election, so much the better; if she fails ... well that will be the end of it all for a time. Better elect a Vida Goldstein as an experiment ... and as the experiment must be tried sooner or later, well, here goes for Miss Goldstein!'[47]

On 13 November, Vida addressed a meeting at Prahran in Melbourne. Even though she was now charging a silver coin admittance (she said she was only a 'poor woman who had to work hard for her living' and that she refused to go into debt) there was a large audience, at least three-quarters of whom were women. She used the motto 'Vote for three men—and one woman'. She said rumours had been circulated to prejudice her chances, including that she had become an out-and-out conservative and that she was a believer in free love. She said she was opposed to easy divorce and that she was not a conservative. She said that free trade was not free and protection did not protect.[48] This alienated the *Age*, which dubbed her 'fiscally unsound' and an 'opportunist'.[49] In its editorial five days later, the *Age* attacked Vida:

> She has no political grasp of the grave questions which must confront the next Parliament; and she asks women and others to vote for her, not on account of any political opinions she holds, or any high cause she would serve, but simply on account of her sex. That is certainly unworthy of the platform of any candidate, and mere euphonious speech and a pretty face are not substitutes for solid opinions and definite principles in the battle of life. Miss Goldstein owed it to her sex as the first lady candidate to have fortified herself with at least enough knowledge to enable her to take sides.[50]

The *Woman's Sphere* also printed denials of rumours that she was a disciple of Tom Mann, the English socialist, saying her opinions were fully formed and publicised before he arrived in Australia. There were also rumours that Vida held 'extraordinary opinions on marriage and family life'. This was an unscrupulous means of seeking to discredit a female candidate, probably fuelled by the fact that Victoria Woodhull, America's first female presidential candidate, was a free love proponent and practised what she preached. The *Woman's Sphere* told readers:

> We had hoped that the time was long past when, because a woman chooses to interest herself in the bettering of her fellow beings, politically and socially, she must be supposed to hold all sorts of heterodox and abnormal views. To those who know her best, and as the Americans quickly discovered, Miss Goldstein is one of the most home-loving and womanly of women.[51]

The rumours upset Isabella, who wrote to Rose Scott at this time saying she felt 'distressed' about women going into party politics, adding 'hasn't my own little Vida suffered—no one has been more cruelly misrepresented—you do not know half'.[52]

Vida set off on another country tour, this time to Gippsland and north-eastern Victoria. The *Bairnsdale Courier* reported her meeting favourably, writing that it was probably the largest political meeting ever held in the town and that 'Goldstein stock' had increased.[53] The *Bairnsdale Advertiser*, however, argued strongly against the wisdom of her candidature; if Vida were foolish enough to carry through to the poll, it would be best if she lost her deposit, so she would suffer the 'discouragement of a monetary penalty'. It illustrates some of the diatribes her candidature unleashed from papers reacting with sexist prejudice to her temerity in standing; they were incapable of even contemplating women entering the public domain. It claimed Vida's aims for social improvements would be sooner achieved by women 'retaining their natural place in the domestic and social scheme of things than by their thrusting themselves immodestly into the turmoil of a strenuous public life for which they are utterly unfitted, physically, whatever their mental equipment for the struggle may be'. The male members would view her—and thus her opinions—with disfavour and scorn. The franchise did not give women a moral entitlement to enter Parliament and Vida's actions would make the chance of woman suffrage being enacted in Victoria more remote. It said Parliament was no place for a woman and Vida would have to 'sacrifice every attribute of modesty and womanliness or court early defeat and disgrace'. She would have to endure 'unblushingly and composedly taunts, jibes and bitter personal attacks that few women could endure and live ... In short, the woman who would succeed in politics must throw aside her womanhood and be a man, or as much a man as she can'. The final objection was that Vida's candidature would

> logically make possible a parliament of women. Can we, as sane people, subscribe to such a preposterous possibility as that of being governed by a legislature and a Cabinet of females—most of them women who had failed in the pursuit of women's great object in life—man—and whose intellectual attainments and individual attractiveness would not, as a matter of course, be of a high order?[54]

With great strength of character, Vida ignored these insults and continued her tour, drawing large crowds in each town she visited. Her Warragul meeting was the largest political meeting ever held there, with 800 people present. Even if most attended out of curiosity, Vida was achieving her aim of increasing people's interest in politics. Her speaking conditions were not always ideal. At Korumburra she had to compete with the local Philharmonic Society practising the 'Hallelujah Chorus' in the next room.[55]

In Benalla on 30 November she won more fans. The reporter acknowledged that no one remarks on a male politician's attire, but a 'lady politician is a very different person'. Vida was described yet again as a 'womanly woman'.

> Dark hair, dressed low upon her forehead, but not absurdly low, merely becoming; sparkling dark eyes, which are very much on the alert, especially when an elector ventures upon a question; prettily flushed face, nicely featured, and a very attractive smile. She wore a black skirt, simply made, and a light cool-looking blouse, a lace collar—not at all an elaborate one—grey kid gloves, a small steel-beaded bag hanging from her waist, and one of those bronzy white straw hats generally called burnt straw, thickly lined underneath with bright red silk and trimmed with a wreath of red roses. A red band of silk round her neck completed the toilet of the only lady candidate, one of the most daring certainly of her sex... She is nice to look at, and absolutely delightful to listen to. The quick, eager way she has of rising to answer questions has its charms, for you see there the enthusiast; her smartness at repartee is a rare gift; her composure when signs of disturbance appear and the way she has of getting off a slap at the other side without in the least descending from the pedestal she as a lady stands on are worth seeing and hearing. Her voice is alert, pleasant, feminine; her delivery could hardly be better; her magnetism—well, those who go to scoff at future meetings will remain to admire.[56]

When Vida spoke in Ballarat on 7 December many people, clutching their silver coins, had to be turned away for want of room. The local paper archly said the people came to see the phenomenon of a lady candidate rather than to hear new truths and that they got what they came for and nothing more.[57] However, an ex-president of the Trades Hall was heard to say, 'I believe Vida Goldstein will head the poll'.[58]

Some papers tipped a Goldstein win,[59] while some thought Vida had a chance, but begrudged the thought of her success. The *Bulletin* wrote, 'Vida may thank her sprightly garb as well as her sprightly wits for a lot of it. A woman who is smart, a good democrat and *not* dowdy has a lot of influences fighting on her side'.[60] However, as Vida's chance of election increased, so did the rumours against her. Just before election day, her committee felt compelled to advertise denials of these rumours in the *Age* and the *Argus*. It was rumoured that women were ineligible for Parliament, so a vote for Vida would be wasted, and that her association had disbanded and given its funds to the Labor Party. Other rumours were that Vida supported easy divorce and free love. The committee assured voters 'Miss Goldstein's views on marriage are quite normal, and she has protested both with voice and pen against easy divorce as being directly antagonistic to the stability and purity of the home'.[61] 'One who Knows' wrote to the papers saying Vida was a Christian Scientist.[62] The committee advertised that 'Miss Goldstein was brought up, and is, a Protestant, and a regular Church attendant'.[63] (Church records show she had joined the Christian Science church the previous year, but if this is correct, it is odd that Vida promised to give any profits from her entrance monies to the Queen Victoria Hospital because Christian Scientists believe hospitals are unnecessary. Vida may have thought her connection with Christian Science might harm her electorally because it was not one of the established churches, but it is out of character for her to lie. Possibly she had begun attending the church in 1902, but she might not have considered herself a convert until later.)

Labor feared if electors deviated from their ticket to vote for Vida, all four Labor candidates could be affected. The word went out that Vida was to be shunned as 'the high priestess of the Victorian Women's no-party movement'.[64] Labor published a pamphlet warning its voters not to split their vote. It said that if the electors wanted to vote for a woman they should vote for the Labor Party, which was 'fighting humanity's battle for all women and all men'. It concluded, 'One vote for Vida Goldstein is as effectual against Labor as one vote for any of the *Argus* Four'.[65] This pamphlet may have been written by Vida's friend Lilian Locke, the former secretary of the WFPA who was now the organising secretary of the women's branch of the Political Labor Council. The two women, however, remained friends and privately Isabella wrote sympathetically about Lilian's position, saying 'to rub shoulders *only* with the uncultured must be very trying'.[66] Vida later wrote:

> Although I regret that the broad basis of the Women's Federal Political Association is not acceptable to Labour women, I rejoice to see women organising on any lines, even on Conservative lines, for organisation means education and enlarged interests, and I would sooner see women educated in views diametrically opposed to mine than not educated at all, and displaying the too prevalent apathy and indifference to important social and political questions.[67]

In the last week of the campaign, the *Argus* appealed to women to vote and to fight against socialism. As women were new to the process of voting, it 'helpfully' published facsimiles of ballot papers so women could have a male member of the household fill them in and then use them to copy from in the polling booth. It insultingly warned women to make sure they did not hand in the newspaper instead of the ballot and included how to vote for its candidates, the 'Victorian Four'.[68]

The December *Woman's Sphere* was an election issue and featured portraits of the suffrage pioneers. It attempted to counter the opposition to Vida's election and exhorted the women of Victoria to 'Close up the ranks', to find out about the candidates and to vote for those who were honest in advocacy of reform and progress. Vida expressed fears that women would not support her and that she had to fight this as well as the 'prejudice of sex'.[69] She believed men were more broad-minded because they were better educated and therefore more amenable to the idea of a woman in Parliament. It was understandable that women 'just freed from servitude are bound to be timid at first'.[70]

As the campaign drew to a close, Vida campaigned in northern Victoria and attracted large audiences. A weedy-looking man followed her, interrupting her meetings with interjections. When Vida declared that men had the advantage over women, he called out from the rear of the hall, 'Don't you wish you were a man?'. She replied cuttingly, 'Yes, and don't you wish that you were one?'.[71]

The only unpleasant incident of the whole campaign occurred at Fitzroy Town Hall, two days before the poll, when a man handed up some written questions. Vida read them and then announced calmly to the audience, 'There are three questions on this paper, and each of them is an insult; I refuse to answer them'. Immediately the men present wanted to throw the perpetrator out. The situation threatened to get out of hand until Vida stepped to the edge of the platform, raised her hand for order and said the man should stay because it might do him some good. This saved the situation—and the hapless man who had handed the note to Vida; he had merely passed it on, at the request of the person behind him. Vida concluded the writer was 'not only an insulter of a woman, but a coward to boot'.[72]

◆ ◆ ◆

On polling day, Wednesday 16 December 1903, Vida was determined to exercise her hard-won right to vote as early as possible. She was waiting in the pouring rain when the presiding clerk, Cr Jeffries, arrived at 7.20 a.m. When the booth opened at 8 a.m. Vida, the first woman candidate, was the first person to register a vote at that booth. Cr Jeffries was so impressed by the historic occasion he decided to preserve the plain white pine ballot box for posterity. The *Age* credited Vida with being the first Victorian woman to vote under the Commonwealth Franchise Act.[73] The *Bulletin* said her enthusiasm was 'appalling' and that the 'average married woman doesn't take her first baby more seriously than Vida took her first vote'.[74]

Vida was then seen 'buzzing cheerily' around town in a 'heel-tipping grey frock with bright pink decorations. A horseshoe of cornflowers was placed, in poetic fashion and an, unhappily, not-justified optimism, over the heart locality'. She said she was not nervous and thought she would poll well.[75]

The papers reported this phenomenon of women voting for the first time, noting that husbands and wives frequently showed each other their ballot papers, but that overall the women acted with good sense and intelligence. One incident occurred where a husband and wife showed their votes to each other and the mouth of the woman hardened. The man had broken their bargain of voting for her two choices if she voted for his two. She was heard to say, 'I'll tell Katie to come down this afternoon and vote for Vida Goldstein, just to spite you. There now! See if I don't'.[76] It was reported that an elderly woman when asked to vote for Vida said, 'Vote for her? Not me. A person who could go and get photo'd with only her stays on, will get no vote from me'.[77] It seems she had confused Vida's name with a brand of corsets called Zita.

The next night, Vida knew she had lost, but undeterred she attended a concert. The *Bulletin* wrote she 'didn't blink an eyelash. Few women are such good losers'.[78] Vida had come fifteenth out of eighteen candidates. She had polled 51 497 votes, half the votes of the top-polling candidate. The *Age* said her vote was 'an astonishingly large one'.[79] She had done better than many had expected and probably no worse than she had dreaded. She did not suffer the ignominy of losing her deposit. She had collected £131 in silver coins and £46 in donations. Her costs including travelling were £187 3s 11d, leaving her with a £10 deficit.[80]

Vida held a meeting where she reflected on the lessons learned from her candidature. She said she was 'beaten but not disgraced', and the audience applauded her warmly.

> Her record of 51,279 votes[81] was a veritable triumph for the women's cause. (Loud applause.) She had overwhelming odds against her in the opposition of the press, the lack of means, the prejudice of sex, and silence with regard to her splendid meetings in the country.[82]

What she did not say was that many papers did support her[83] and that in fact, while some people may have been prejudiced against a woman candidate, she would have gained some votes because she was a woman. Vida had polled much better than the other female candidates. The *Bulletin* attributed this to Vida's 'superior energy and business management'.[84] It said her mistake was to 'urge women's rights so persistently during her campaign' and advised her in future campaigns to 'not mention that she is a woman, just as the male candidate recognises that there is no need to mention that he is a man. She will be simply a candidate'.[85] Vida ignored this advice and always insisted she was a woman's candidate who would represent the female point of view in Parliament.

Vida had travelled throughout the State alone and addressed more than thirty meetings. She had proven that women were physically capable of campaigning. She emphasised this in her assessment of the campaign in *Review of Reviews*.

> As soon as my candidature was announced the enemy prophesied a physical breakdown, and humiliating insults from men at my meetings. From all accounts I stood the racket of the campaign better than most of the candidates. After one month's work the voices of many were tattered and torn; mine was as fresh and clear the night before the battle as it was

when I started skirmishing three months previously. As for insults, I had not the semblance of one offered me until two nights before the election [at Fitzroy when she had been handed the offensive questions]... I have mentioned this incident simply to prove to those who fear that women will be insulted when they aspire to enter the political arena that a body of men can always be trusted to protect women against insult.

The great lesson she had learned was the importance of organisation.

The Labour Party was the best organised party, and their success proves what enthusiasm for a cause will accomplish. To my mind the woman's cause — and after all 'the woman's cause is man's' — is deserving of as much enthusiasm as the labour cause. Indeed, I believe the two are closely allied. The labour cause in its widest sense is the cause of humanity, so is the woman's cause; but labour seeks to reach the goal mainly by material means; women, having due regard for the material, place a higher value on the spiritual.[86]

Vida's refusal to ally herself with a major political party was her biggest handicap, although she always refused to acknowledge this. Her non-party policy and opposition to what she called 'the vicious system of machine politics'[87] cost her votes and denied her a substantial organisation to provide back-up support. The *Worker* declared that if she had stood on the Labor ticket she would have polled twice as well 'and lived in history as the first woman in the world to sit in a national Parliament'.[88] Vida had chosen to concentrate her electioneering in the country to further her 'educative work', but again this was not electorally wise because although she polled better in the country than the city, there were fewer voters in the country. Her campaign had attracted new members to the WFPA; membership increased from 300 to more than 700 and two new branches and eight auxiliary committees were formed. Her candidature had encouraged women to go to political meetings and to take an interest in politics. She wrote, 'I believed that people would come to my meetings out of curiosity, to see the wild woman who sought to enter parliament. They came, they saw, I conquered; that is my arguments did'.[89]

There was considerable debate over how the women's vote had affected the outcome generally and Vida's case in particular. Some claimed the women had voted for her while others, including Vida, asserted that she had won the men's vote.

From the men I had the most kind, the most courteous treatment and warm support—in fact, I have good reason to believe, from the mass of correspondence I received, that in the districts where I did not speak I was more warmly supported by men than by women.[90]

The composition of both houses remained basically unchanged, with the Protectionist Deakin Government retaining power. As Champion had predicted, the women had voted on similar lines to the men and not caused a radical change. Only 52 per cent of electors had voted. Vida argued in *Review of Reviews* that this was hardly surprising because women were so newly enfranchised and it would take time for women to learn the duties of citizenship and then rear children who understood these duties and were sufficiently informed to vote. 'The people of a country are just what the mothers make them, and mothers who have no civic responsibilities cannot be expected to teach the political idea.' She said Australians lacked public spirit and a true national spirit and that 'the mothers of Australia have a huge task ahead of them in endeavouring to teach their children, the citizens of the future, that national welfare means individual welfare, and is a nobler ideal than personal welfare'. She ended with what was to be her catchcry in later years, that 'it is righteousness alone that exalteth a nation'.[91]

One of the letters of commiseration which was printed in the *Woman's Sphere* summed up the feelings of her supporters:

You are a little ahead of your time, and you have to pay the penalty. Considering the circumstances, you did well—more than well ... While unsuccessful personally, you have done much to educate the public, and, for the present, that must be your reward.[92]

The campaign was summed up in a ditty:

> She was pretty
> She was fair,
> Tailor-made and
> Debonair.
>
> She was clever,
> She was bright,
> And her politics
> Were right.

> She was gifted
> In her speech;
> She had mighty
> Truths to teach.
>
> But one thing she had a-missing,
>   Which the legislator wants,
> And I almost blush to name it,
>   But she really hadn't — pants.
>   No she hadn't
>   Really hadn't
>   Poor Vida hadn't pants.
>
> For the great Australian nation,
>   Though it loves to woo and flirt,
> Will never bend its noddle
>   To unmitigated skirt.[93]

Vida herself took heart from the experience. She wrote, '"The world moves slowly, my masters!" woman's world especially; but it does move, and that's something to be thankful for'.[94]

5

Deep waters
1904–1908

◆

Vida spent the Christmas holidays of 1903–04 resting in the country with members of her family. In February Vida resumed the editorship of the *Woman's Sphere*. The question now was: What next? Vida had polled well, but not well enough, and Victorian women were still denied the vote. The lesson to be learnt was organisation and preparedness. In the March edition, Vida reiterated the Women's Federal Political Association platform and asked:

> Is there anything in this platform that the most pronounced member of the Labour Party would object to? ... Joining the W.F.P.A. need not preclude them from joining a Labour League as well ... Conservatives, Democrats, Labourites—the W.F.P.A. wants all within its ranks.

In a period of growth and increasing polarisation of the political parties, this was wishful thinking. The Labor women were joining the Ladies' Committees of the Labor Party, and in April the conservative Australian Women's National League was founded. If the suggestion is correct that this league was established to counter the potential threats to conservatism posed by Vida,[1] then Vida had unleashed a formidable opponent. Anti-socialist and loyal to the throne and the home, the league was immediately successful. Within five years it had a membership of about 16 000 with more than one hundred branches throughout Victoria. There was now little middle ground for Vida's non-party political association and the WFPA probably never had more than 1000 members at any time.

The postponed half-yearly meeting of the WFPA was held in early March. The report noted some successes that might be weighed against electoral defeat. Despite heavy involvement in Vida's campaign, the WFPA had been able to inquire into cases of injustice to women. Petitions against unfair discrimination in the naturalisation rights of married women and proposed reductions in pension rights of public servants had been successful. The WFPA and Woman's Christian Temperance Union had also opposed proposals for the compulsory medical examination of prostitutes. At this meeting, the WFPA was renamed the Women's Political Association of Victoria so that it could be involved in municipal, State and federal politics. Even though women could not vote in the forthcoming State elections, the WPA encouraged them to take an interest in the campaign and to canvass for those who satisfactorily answered its questionnaire. A WPA badge was produced—silver and blue and bearing the WPA initials and the words 'Home, Liberty, Country, Equality'. As part of the WPA's educative work, a model parliament was organised. It was conducted on parliamentary lines with a ministry and political parties. It provided valuable training in public speaking and parliamentary procedure for WPA members.[2]

◆ ◆ ◆

The year 1904 was full of frustrations for Vida and Isabella. The *Woman's Sphere* was running at a loss, but Vida's faith sustained her. She admitted to Stella Miles Franklin:

> I am passing through deep waters with the *Sphere*, but I hope to come out alright though at this precise moment things don't look too promising. [Christian] Science, however, makes one look at the troubles of this life from an entirely new viewpoint and one realizes the beautiful truth in those lines by Henley, 'I am the master of my fate, I am the captain of my soul'. So no matter what, the testimony of the senses is 'all's right with the world' and with me and you and all of us.[3]

Isabella also wrote to Stella of her own 'dark hours of mental anguish'. She felt discouraged when sympathy from her 'near and dear ones seems lacking', but Christian Science had been her solace and taught her to:

go on your own if you conscientiously believe you are right ... Half our effort in this ... is wasted by allowing ourselves to be wasted hither and thither by this and that *opinion* ...

Vida has been through deep waters in her efforts to establish a paper with some *principle* behind it ... yet there will be much uphill work ahead to make it pay its way.[4]

Stella offered the *Woman's Sphere* a serial, but Isabella wrote that although the offer was 'absurdly cheap', they could not afford it at present.[5] Stella then probably offered a story for free because Vida replied:

You are a real brick, and I feel torn in two—with the desire to have a story of yours in my paper and a great unwillingness to take advantage of your generosity. However, I have an inward conviction that I shall yield ignominiously to the first feeling.[6]

In May, the format of the *Woman's Sphere* was altered, in an attempt to broaden its appeal: if the paper paid for itself, Vida could devote more time to other ways of campaigning for the suffrage in Victoria. Isabella was 'not in love with the "up-to-date" cover' and its 'red, white and blue dress'[7] and in November the format was altered again. Vida said the new garb was less glaring and admitted that the experiment of 'cheap but fashionable poster costumes' had given her a 'pang' every time she used it and she hoped the issues would be consigned to a 'fiery furnace'.[8] Vida may have achieved this objective; copies for this period could not be found, so it is uncertain if one of Stella's stories was published at this time. Despite the revised format, the paper continued to run at a loss and Vida's financial plight grew worse.

The state of federal politics was also deteriorating. The newly elected government had been dissolved in April and three ministries would be formed in fifteen months at the invitation of the Governor-General, Lord Northcote. In the scramble for office, principles were sacrificed. Isabella wrote to Stella that political life was 'corrupt to the core' and she 'detest[ed]' the party system because 'we have no statesmen, no principles'. She added that 'all is *self* interest' and 'I'm sick of the whole show and wish Vida was out of it'.[9]

While renovation work in their flat made life 'abominable', Aileen went to stay with her married sister, Lina Henderson, and her family for a few months. Lina had not converted to Christian Science, but Isabella wrote that Aileen had 'unravelled a good deal of the unharmony of that home' and Lina had ceased to 'antagonise' Christian Science.[10] Lina's daughter, Leslie Henderson (who was later to write a history of the Goldstein and Hawkins families), reminisced that as a girl she had little contact with her Goldstein relatives because of friction between them and her parents. She blamed her parents, particularly her father, who she described as a 'hidebound Tory' who 'thoroughly disapproved of Vida's political activities, and probably of all her other activities too', adding that he could not be objective 'once his hostility was aroused'. The differences were eventually overcome and Lina 'swung to Vida's side' and took Leslie to hear Vida speak during her 1910 election campaign.[11]

◆ ◆ ◆

On 11 August 1904, the women of New South Wales voted in State elections for the first time. Vida, writing to Rose Scott, told how she spent the day, 'with you in spirit ... wondering, envying, rejoicing'.[12] Tasmanian women had been granted the vote in 1903, so now Queensland and Victorian women were the only ones denied the right to vote. Since the federal election, there had been three more attempts to introduce woman suffrage bills in the Victorian Parliament, but with the advent of the Bent Government the bills were not even being passed in the Legislative Assembly. Bent and his supporters prided themselves on their conservatism and blamed the female vote for the federal success of Labor, which held office briefly in 1904.

Later in the year, Vida travelled to Sydney to represent Victoria at the first congress of the National Council of Women of New South Wales. Rose Scott's paper aroused the greatest interest. Entitled 'The Laws Affecting Women and Children', it highlighted penalties for crimes against property, which were harsher than penalties for crimes against women and children.

Vida was Rose's guest for the five weeks of her visit. She was made an honorary member of the Women's Club and received much hospitality. The press coverage of her visit was flattering and one reporter wrote that she would probably get into the Senate 'in her own good time'.[13]

She also lectured. The papers described the audiences as large, but

Vida ruefully remarked, 'The paid lecturer is not rushed by the residents of beautiful Sydney'.[14] Privately, she admitted that the trip, which she had hoped would 'bring in some grist to the mill',[15] was a financial disaster. She had arranged it on 'wholly professional lines'[16] and had employed an agent, a 'dear little woman',[17] named Mrs Hillyar. Unfortunately the agent relied too much on Vida's name to draw audiences and the lectures were the 'most ghastly failure'.[18] Vida, being the guest of Rose Scott, had unwittingly 'put all the fat in the fire',[19] because of the intense and bitter rivalry between the Sydney women's groups, especially Rose Scott's Women's Political Educational League and Annie Golding's Women's Progressive Association. Vida knew of the enmity but underestimated its effect. In May Isabella had described the Sydney women as a 'squabbling lot'[20] and in July she wrote of Rose Scott, 'Isn't it curious how that little lady *suffers* so. I have to work hard to feel justly towards her—it *jars* so that she is so jealous of the other women workers in NSW but then what business is that of mine?'.[21] Indirectly, Vida was drawn into the fray. The veteran feminist Louisa Lawson (who was on the council of the Women's Progressive Association) later wrote: 'At a meeting organized by Miss Scott I was standing outside the door when the whole house rose and called for me. Miss Goldstein from Melbourne was speaking and totally ignoring me'.[22] Above all, Vida blamed herself for the financial loss. She told Stella:

> Also the fault is really mine, because I had not done my Christian Science work on this Sydney business, and if a Scientist is not working on right lines discord results instead of harmony. This will, no doubt, seem Greek to you, but it is true.[23]

The same reasons were given by Isabella when she became ill in November. She wrote to Stella that her collapse was 'most unscientific'. Isabella had neglected her spiritual life—the 'mental work' that alone heals sickness—because she had taken on extra work for the *Woman's Sphere* while Vida and Aileen were away. Aileen was travelling in England and Europe as a companion to a 'woman who is *determined* to let her have a good time'. She wanted to stay in London for a few years, but while it was 'never desirable of parents to stand in the way of their children', Isabella would prefer it if Aileen were closer.[24]

◆ ◆ ◆

Vida spent the Christmas holiday reviewing the year. It had been arduous but ineffective. The newspaper was losing money and Victorian suffrage seemed no closer. Vida concluded that working for State suffrage must be her goal and that the United Council for Women's Suffrage (renamed United Council for State Suffrage in 1903) had lost its right to be the suffrage spearhead. She announced her decision in the January edition of the *Woman's Sphere*:

> The Council accomplished nothing last year; there is no evidence that there is likely to be any vitality this year, and I for one am not willing to let this policy of drift continue. The U.C.S.S. having been given every opportunity to lead the suffrage army, has failed. I think, therefore, that the Women's Political Association is now justified in entering the field and assuming control of the suffrage forces throughout Victoria.[25]

Vida later wrote she had been reluctant to disparage the association founded by her friend Annette Bear-Crawford, but the 'younger spirits in the movement chafed at the drift in the United Council'.[26]

Commenting on the likelihood that Victoria would be the last State to grant the franchise to women, Vida wrote:

> I feel the humiliation of the position bitterly, and I would urge the women of Victoria not to leave one stone unturned in an attempt to carry woman suffrage into law this year ...
>
> For over four years I have attempted the almost impossible task of engineering the woman movement in Victoria, keeping it in close touch with the movement in other countries, and of running a paper to help the cause everywhere. I have not done either to my satisfaction. Because of the time that I have had to give to the political field, my paper has suffered severely; because of the time I have had to give to the paper with all its business ramifications, my political work has suffered equally ... so fully seized am I of the necessity for a Herculean struggle to secure State suffrage that I am ready to make every possible sacrifice for it.[27]

One sacrifice was her decision to limit the *Woman's Sphere* to an eight-page pamphlet for one year. It would remain as the WPA organ, but interstate and international news would be curtailed.

On 24 January 1905 the Queensland women were enfranchised. Vida sent a telegram: 'Sincere congratulations from the envious women of Victoria, the first Australian colony to have woman suffrage organisation, the last state to enfranchise its women'.[28] Writing of 'Victoria's humiliation', she asked:

Photo: AP/AAP

Please show you care

CARE AUSTRALIA

A.C.N 003 380 890

FREEPHONE 008 020 046
You can also post a donation to
GPO Box 9977 in your capital city

Commonwealth Bank

QANTAS
THE AUSTRALIAN AIRLINE

bout it? Sit still and say
east will have nothing to
es and make an earnest
29

paign, but desperately
hapman Catt's idea of
ay a sum to be a year,
ed with many notable
aths (in fact, her year
on.
y to secure financial
Sphere. In February she
to fund her suffrage
her attempts to raise
e or no opposition to
any professed friends
noted a 'characteristic'

he women who want it
toria you stand as the
ains to be seen whether
ey will not, why should

on.
time in March 1905.
ublished if there were
ation that it was to be
iled to improve, Vida
on her primary goal

ration of the suffrage
s. In July, Vida told a
as six years since she
hat women were still
e practice of quoting
l's dictum, 'Wives, be
he audience shouted
imagined that the

gentleman, like Paul, was a bachelor. This was greeted with laughter and she continued:

> If he had been [married], he might have learned that married happiness, based on subjection, was insecure. Perhaps, they would say she as an unmarried woman, had no more right than Paul to lay down the law. (Laughter). But even admitting Paul was right was that any reason why married women should be in subjection to all the bachelors in the country (Laughter), or to other women's husbands?[30]

The Premier, Thomas Bent, remained implacably opposed to the suffrage. He had said he would rather take the ladies to the opera than give them the vote.[31] In September, the suffragists invited Bent to attend a suffrage meeting being held in his electorate. The *Age* reported this event as 'Daniel in the Lionesses' Den'. It said the admission charge of a silver coin had deterred the 'rowdy element' from attending. Bent sat in the front row, but 'the voices of the female orators had a soothing effect upon the fagged Premier, and he was soon apparently in dreamland'. Vida said that the women who wanted the vote were those who worked, the 'thoughtful women' who did social and philanthropic work and the 'politically enlightened public spirited women'. When she invited Bent to speak, he did not respond. He was roused from his slumbers and bluntly refused to speak.[32]

◆ ◆ ◆

The Victorian Employers' Federation journal, *Liberty and Progress*, which prided itself on being the 'Only Purely Anti-Socialistic Newspaper in the Commonwealth', reported a public lecture Vida gave on socialism in 1905. Adopting the style often used against Vida in her political campaign, it dismissed her ideas while focusing on her personality and appearance. It said she was speaking 'socialistic claptrap', but she was a 'young lady of charming personality (vide portrait)'. Although antagonistic, it conveys something of her style of public speaking and the conditions under which she worked.

> 'It makes me mad', said the lady socialist, as she stamped her little foot upon the platform, and looked with straining eyes, not at the seekers after truth, who sat at her feet in a dingy suburban hall, but out beyond at the world, the flesh, and the capitalistic devil that therein so much rages. Why did the lady madden so? She was young, she was pretty, she was elegantly

attired, she was armed with a formidable manuscript which contained some beautifully sage-like thoughts on what socialism would be if it were not what it is, and the admission money at the door must have totalled fully twenty five shillings.[33]

The reporter said Vida charged sixpence for a talk on socialism, but used tuppence-halfpenny's worth criticising the AWNL. Vida responded in the next issue that 'A fair-minded critic ... would admit that I evidenced no such pettiness'. Only eight of the sixty-five pages of her speech related to the AWNL. She had denied the charges made by some AWNL members at their meetings that she was 'an out-and-out socialist holding peculiar views on marriage and family life'.[34]

The report said she then quoted from Huxley, Spencer and Carlyle, gave examples of the 'iniquity of the capitalist system' and talked about the cost of living and the wages needed by a working man to enjoy the bare necessities of life. The reporter disagreed, contending that people were better off than in the past and it depended on the way people spent and saved their money. The report continued: 'Socialism will not be a success ... only an improvement on individualism ... its "non-religion" ... will in her opinion prevent its success'. Every so often Vida gave an 'expressive nod, which said as plain as words could, "I, Vida Goldstein, say so, and it is so". There was no gainsaying it. One just had to hear, and to believe'.[35]

Vida responded that her quotes were not

> my 'socialistic clap-trap'. They are the statements of those anti-socialists Alfred Russell Wallace and Huxley relative to 'vast masses of the people in every large manufacturing city', and I gave them as such. [She had not condemned employers as a class but had] asked very successful businessmen, 'Can a man be strictly honest in business and prosper?'... They all confessed, some excusing the fact, others deploring it, that it is impossible to be strictly honest in business. I gave many instances, taken from authorised reports, of trade adulteration and dishonesties, and quoted Herbert Spencer's dictum — 'as the law of the animal creation is "eat or be eaten", so of the trading community it may be said its motto is "cheat or be cheated"'.[36]

This speech was published as 'Socialism of Today—An Australian View' in *The Nineteenth Century and After* in 1907. A well-written article drawing on a wide range of economic theories, it illustrates her intelligent analysis of the subject.

> No-one, unless absolutely blinded by ignorance, prejudice or self-interest, can defend our present system. I cannot. I know too much, *from personal observation* of how the poor live, of how the working classes live, to be satisfied with a system which makes their lives one unceasing round of toil, deprivation and anxiety ... some years ago I began studying the various schemes propounded for social and industrial betterment—co-operation, land nationalisation, single tax, and Socialism—hoping that if I could not find the whole truth in any one of them, I might find something that would minimise the misery I saw wherever I turned. My conclusion was [that] Socialism, with all its faults and dangers, came nearest to my ideal of human brotherhood.

She quoted Huxley's 'indictment of modern conditions' and then focused on living conditions under capitalism in Australia. She listed the weekly expenses for a married man with five children, totalling £2 18s 6d. The £1 10s which was considered a fair wage did not allow the man to belong to a union, take a daily paper or have any amusement, nor to save for his old age. She stressed that modern economists were concerned with the distribution, rather than the accumulation, of wealth, recognising 'that national wealth does not mean national well-being'.

Throughout history the working man had been taught to 'produce wealth for other people' but now he had begun to question these tenets.

> He sees that they come into conflict with God's laws of order, harmony, progress, justice, love. An educated man, he can now *think* for the first time in history; a voter, he can now *act* for the first time in history, and, instead of being content to produce unlimited wealth for other people, he wishes to get for himself a fairer share of what he produces by his own labour.

This passage clearly shows the importance Vida placed on education and the vote and their ability to effect change—and she believed the current capitalist system desperately needed changing.

> The employing class reaps as it sows; it gives as low wages as it possibly can, it shows no regard for the employés' interests. The employés give in return as little work as they possibly can and no regard for the employers' interests. Both ... are victims of a vicious system.

Finally she argued against land ownership and landowners, 'many of whom neither toil nor spin ... [yet] the rent is theirs for ever and ever'.

There is no argument in favour of absolute private ownership of land which would not also hold in favour of absolute private ownership of the air or the waters of the earth. What would be thought of a system which allowed private individuals to own the air, the rivers, the sea, and only allowed the people to use them by paying rent for them? The idea could not be entertained for a minute.[37]

The listing of living costs in this article was part of the Charity Organisation Society tradition of 'scientifically' analysing poverty (Isabella's paper at the 1890 Charity Conference had listed living expenses), and is a notable forerunner of the systematic analysis of poverty done later by sociologists, feminists and government agencies. The Harvester Judgment of 1907, which established the principle of a basic wage for a family man, was influenced by such costings and it is said that Vida's article gave Henry Higgins, who made the ruling, the idea of calling working men and women as witnesses.[38] Higgins decided that a man with a household of about five people needed £2 2s a week, which was in line with Vida's estimates. While establishing a minimum wage for men, it enshrined the concept of a family wage which 'was to bar the progress of women's pay rates for over half a century' because women were not acknowledged as breadwinners.[39]

Vida was still actively involved with the COS and her expertise was often called on. Here, as elsewhere, Vida's perception of social issues was far ahead of her time. In one address to COS members, she said she believed that prevention was better than cure, but it was not possible to solve unemployment unless the economic causes of it could be controlled. She advocated a chair of charity at the University of Melbourne to 'get at the causes of evils' because the 'majority of our University people are very self centred, they do not take a very keen interest in things outside'.[40]

Vida was also prominent among the individuals and groups lobbying for a Children's Court Act. Under the Victorian system, child offenders as young as eight were thrown into Black Marias and locked in police cells with drunk and disorderly adults. Vida had publicised such incidents in the *Woman's Sphere*, 'hammering away at the barbarity' of this treatment of children.[41] She proposed the adoption of American methods, which aimed to change attitudes rather than punish, and used the George Junior Republic as a model.[42] She wanted the Act written 'in a liberal spirit, as it is not desired that the Court shall be an instrument for meting out punishment, but a means for supplying each child with influences he has missed in the past'.[43] The public sector would compensate for the child's deprived environment. Vida drafted the manifesto that formed the basis of the Children's Court Act of 1906.[44]

When the Act was drawn up, lobbyists were not satisfied with some aspects of it. They mounted a campaign to urge amendments and Vida spoke at many of the meetings. She called for a special children's judge and argued that one of the paid probation officers should be a woman. This woman would not necessarily have to deal solely with the girls, because success could be achieved with working with the opposite sex. The detention house should be like a home, run by a married couple who could teach the children. The amended Act was passed in December 1906. Vida was responsible for the removal of the 'iniquitous clause ... rendering it possible to imprison a child *seven years of age*'.[45] Other undesirable clauses remained, however, including whipping, fining and imprisonment of children. From 1907 children were tried under the new Act and when the children's court was opened in 1908, Vida was present to help celebrate the culmination of a great reform in child welfare.

At a Children's Court Conference held on 25 February 1907, Vida successfully moved that a paid female probation officer be appointed. Probation officers were vital to the success of the children's court and most were volunteers appointed by the government. Vida was among the first group appointed in 1907.[46] By 1908 there were 200 voluntary probation officers, each responsible for regularly visiting the children in their care, acting as a friend to individual children and ensuring that they attended school and Sunday school. They were also required to submit reports to the court.

◆ ◆ ◆

Another source of satisfaction for Vida at this time was the enactment of the Federal Marriage and Divorce Bill in 1906, which improved the status of women, although it failed to guarantee women guardianship of their children on the death of the husband. (This was achieved in 1912.) Vida wrote jubilantly to Prime Minister Alfred Deakin that she thought the Bill would 'give us a chance with the women electors—of rousing their interest apart from the class anti-socialist nonsense that is forced down their throats'.[47]

In November 1906, Vida wrote to Rose Scott, 'I really believe we are going to get the suffrage this time!',[48] but once more her hopes were dashed when the Bill was ruled out of order. For the 1907 State elections, Vida, as president of the WPA, and Annie Lowe, president of the UCSS, published a joint leaflet entitled *Women's Appeal to the Men of Victoria*, in which they conceded that women had 'exhausted every constitutional means of self-help possible to an unenfranchised class'. Woman suffrage bills had been before the Legislative Assembly seventeen times and the members there were committed to the bills, but the Legislative Council refused to co-operate. They urged men to demand that the Council pass a woman suffrage bill.[49]

In March 1907, in a new bid to win the vote, twenty societies formed the Woman Suffrage Declaration Committee which aimed to collect forms signed by people supporting their cause. Vida was the secretary and helped organise a women's demonstration in November. A series of tableaux showed women at work in the home and the workplace. Vida provided 'bright and purposeful explanations' for each one of the 'living pictures'. One depicted the women of Victoria kneeling shackled at the feet of Premier Bent, while unbound representatives of the other States looked scornfully at him.[50]

As 1908 dawned, Vida wrote an article reviewing the state of the suffrage in Victoria. She asserted that the Premier lacked enough character to compel the Council to bend to the popular will. Bent's response was that Vida was 'a very nice young lady' and her 'manner, language and style of argument were nice', but he ignored her assertion. Vida later said she was referring to previous premiers, adding, 'I respect an honest opponent like Mr Bent. He does not believe in woman suffrage and there is an end to the question as far as he is personally concerned'.[51] Vida always remained objective and refrained from personal attacks in public, even when she was being patronised or ridiculed, but this is a remarkably bland response to the reprobate Bent, who was well known for his scandalous land dealings.

◆ ◆ ◆

Vida probably kept an engagements diary all her life, but the only one she thought worth preserving was for 1908, the year Victorian women were enfranchised. The diary (without Sundays) is a rare record of her working methods and the amount of work she did for a wide range of causes. She regularly attended Christian Science meetings (including those for Sunday school teachers), the Women's Political Association, the Woman Suffrage Declaration Committee, the National Council of Women, the Criminology Society and the Women's Writers' Club (which she had helped found in 1902).[52]

The diary shows that she spent a considerable time writing letters and reports. She sent a report to the International Suffrage Conference in Amsterdam and wrote to Count Leo Tolstoy for his eightieth birthday because 'Though not friendly to [the] women movement he has done much for humanity'. She wrote to Rose Scott about the Contagious Diseases Bill. When asked to judge a beauty contest, she declined 'in humorous vein!', but she did consent to distribute the prizes to the Coldstream Ladies' Cricket Club. She attended the first anniversary celebration of the Collingwood Free Kindergarten. Charles Strong had established it and Vida enthusiastically supported it because it benefited mothers and children. She also started working on the establishment of a 'sensible club' where 'thinking men and women can meet'. She attended the farewell to Lady Northcote, the Governor-General's wife, and on behalf of the WPA, wrote to thank her for her 'untold help' to the movement, 'which aims at impressing upon men and women that woman has public as well as home and philanthropic duties, that her sphere does not end at the garden gate but reaches here, there, everywhere'.[53] Vida even recorded that she had sent her niece Leslie a postcard of a cat and had written on the back a verse she had adapted from the Boston *Woman's Journal*:

> What is the difference, tell me that,
> Betwixt Aunt Vida and this cat?
> 'Tis summed up in a single clause:
> The pussy runs on all four paws,
> But when she starts on woman's cause,
> Aunt Vida runs on with no pause.[54]

The diary contains newspaper cuttings about woman suffrage. There are reports from England where the Pankhursts' militant Women's Social and Political Union was gathering strength, after the 1907 split over tactics. The Pankhursts had adopted law-breaking measures and were making headlines as mounted police broke up

Vida used this photograph for her publicity for her history-making first political campaign in 1903. She was proudly conscious of her status as the first woman in the British Empire to nominate for a national parliament.

Vida's nomination provoked many satirical cartoons, including this one from *Punch*, 13 August 1903.

Vida with Stella Miles Franklin

SENATE ELECTION.
Vote for the Woman Candidate
WHO POLLED 51,497 VOTES IN 1903.

VIDA GOLDSTEIN

Every woman of every political party should endeavour to secure the return of the Woman Candidate, as All the Men in Parliament cannot represent One Woman as adequately as One Woman can represent All Women.

In her second campaign, Vida made a powerful plea to women to vote for a woman.

Jubilant suffragists gathered in the Botanic Gardens to celebrate their enfranchisement in Victoria—the last state to grant women the vote; standing from left: Mrs Henderson, Miss Smart, Mrs Hunter, Mrs Veitch, Catherine Kilkelly, Mrs Turnbull, Mrs Abbott; sitting: Mrs Davis, Mrs Davidson, Vida Goldstein, Mrs Hobbs, Annie Lowe, Clara Weekes, Mrs Lloyd

MISS VIDA GOLDSTEIN WEEPING OUTSIDE THE SENATE

> One morn a Peri at the gate of Eden
> Stood disconsolate.
> —*Moore.*

Vida's old foe, the anti-socialist *Liberty and Progress*, refused to countenance the possibility of a female parliamentarian—especially an Independent who could split the conservative vote—during the 1910 campaign.

their demonstrations and many suffragettes were fined and imprisoned. Vida wrote to Emmeline Pankhurst, asking for illustrations of the WSPU's banners for an exhibition she was planning, and ordering bound copies of the WSPU's paper *Votes for Women*. This is Vida's first recorded contact with the Pankhursts. The Victorian women were still campaigning within the law, but there was some pressure to change their tactics in line with the English suffragettes. Vida noted it without comment when a Mr Crouch wrote to ask her 'When are you going to smash the windows of the Legislative Councillors?'.[55] She understood the English women's ploy of informing reporters when a raid was to take place: 'Polite propaganda counts for nothing w[ith] newspapers; sensationalism is everything, and so the suffragists have had to make sensationalism the chief motif of their educational work'.[56]

Occasionally she recorded her exasperations.

> Rang up the Prime Minister (Mr Deakin) at his private house to ask if he could help us and the women of Eng[land] by calling re *Times* statements as to women voting in *some* of the Australasian States... He said he would be delighted to help us, and w[oul]d endeavour to get an Eng. newspaper correspondent to cable. He said also 'all but two of the Aust[ralian] states have women suffrage'!!! I asked what *two*. Replied, '*Tasmania* and Victoria!' Shows how even our best men friends can be nearly quite ignorant about the pol[itical] status of women even in Aust[ralia].

Vida was now campaigning on the grounds of 'electoral uniformity'. Victoria would need two electoral rolls—one for federal elections where women could vote and one for the State where they could not vote.

> Letter fr[om] Prime Minister re request for pressure about Electoral Uniformity. Says he has no inf[luence] upon the Premier or State Cabinet on this matter or any other of State Concern. Did not suppose he had, but he c[ou]ld urge the desirability of Electoral Uniformity without mentioning State suffrage. Written him as to that effect.[57]

A deputation from the Woman Suffrage Declaration Committee visited the *Age* seeking its support. They were astounded when the editor informed them that his father had started the suffrage movement in Victoria. He agreed to do all he could to help and to publish as much material as they provided. The *Herald* was similarly supportive and published an article on the suffrage by Vida under the pseudonym 'M. E.' It was encouraging to have the support of the daily papers.

The suffragists were having difficulty collecting the declarations. The campaign had been long and people were becoming weary. In March, a 'bad precedent' was set when the St Kilda council refused permission for the women to solicit signatures.[58] Opposition still existed within some women's groups, including members of the AWNL, who opposed State suffrage because there was so much work and financial outlay involved in organising the federal vote.

In May, Bent stated it was foolish to give Victorian women the vote. The Declaration Committee passed a resolution calling on him to resign because of his derogatory comments. Committee members began to attend Bent's public meetings, but he ignored the women's questions when they related to the suffrage. Vida wrote to Bent, asking him to face a public meeting on the issue. At Bent's next meeting he forbade any questions.

On 2 July the parliamentary leader of the Labor Party, George Prendergast, gave notice that he would introduce the Adult Suffrage Bill as a private Bill. Vida asked him to delay it to the end of the session as a safeguard but hoped that the Bent Government would make it government policy, which would give it more chance of success. In Parliament, Bent remained obdurate, ignoring the pleas to enact woman suffrage from members of all political persuasions including Vida's cousin Harry Lawson, a 'discriminating' Liberal first elected to the Assembly in 1904 and who became the Nationalist Premier in 1918.[59] In England suffragettes were being imprisoned and newspapers noted that militant methods in New York had increased membership from 2000 to 20 000 in six weeks.

Support also came from unexpected sources. James Marion, a travelling 'social reform lecturer', offered to put woman suffrage resolutions at his open-air meetings. He visited Vida to discuss ways of helping the movement. Inspired by a recent march in England, which had drawn 10 000 participants, he urged Vida to organise a similar march. Instead, Vida suggested he send deputations of men to the government and form a Men's League for Woman Suffrage. Marion took up this idea and the Men's League for Woman Suffrage held its first meeting on 20 July, with Charles Strong in the chair.

On 4 August yet another suffrage deputation waited on Bent. He said he could not go back on his decision, as it would seem weak, and he could not go against his old friend Campbell. Vida noted with irony, 'It is argued that women should not have the vote because they will always regard public questions from a personal standpoint'. The Premier did however make a promise, which Vida underlined twice, that 'he would do a thing he had not done before in regard to woman suffrage, he would think over it'. It was decided to visit Campbell to ask him to withdraw his opposition.[60] There were chinks appearing in Bent's armour.

Vida was writing a lot of articles for the newspapers at this time, usually under pseudonyms. They covered a wide range of topics (including one called 'How New Zealand Women Save the Babies') and were probably a source of sorely needed income. She used this medium to keep up the pressure for the suffrage. Under the pseudonym of 'Athena' in the *Herald*, Vida justified the English suffragette's militancy. When the suffrage question was not put, as promised, at a meeting in Manchester:

> Miss [Christabel] Pankhurst and Miss Kenn[e]ly now realised that the drastic action, so long contemplated, was necessary. The kid glove methods of seventy years had only resulted in giving them a useless majority in Parliament and the persistent boycott of the unfriendly Press. It was evident that neither Parliament nor the Press would respond to reason, logic or argument. Therefore, nothing remained but a policy of disturbance, of rebellion against the silence and indifference of their opponents and false friends.[61]

There were fears that the militancy might spread to Victoria and this article led to a 'boom in *Heralds*'.[62]

On 18 August 1908 Vida wrote to Rose Scott that both political parties were content to play with State suffrage and that 'they don't want us to get it'. She had chosen the pacifist's path and had withdrawn from all other public activities so that she did not offend any suffrage supporters. All her endeavours were now pared down to the single fight for the suffrage. She confided, 'at last we have got a great move on'.[63]

On the day that Vida wrote this letter, a deputation from the Men's League waited on Bent. The *Herald* that evening ran the headline 'Premier Coming Around'. There was a vacancy in the Legislative Council and Vida 'interrogated' all three aspirants. They were all 'sound', so the women would gain another vote whoever won; woman suffrage would then need only one more vote in the Council.[64]

On the second reading of the Suffrage Bill introduced by the Opposition, Bent spoke cryptically in reply; it sounded as if his government would make it policy. If this happened, it would go to the Council as a government bill and thus secure the necessary votes. Vida recorded in her diary on 18 September that a minister had told her 'under pledge of secrecy' that this was to happen. Three days later, she wrote that the suffrage seemed sure, but the Bent Government did not want the Labor Party to get the credit for it. Early in October, Vida was at Talma's to be photographed with fifteen members of the Old Collegians of the Presbyterian Ladies' College. By coincidence, Bent was there having his photo taken too. As he passed the women on his way to the dressing room, Vida leant over and asked him, 'What about that Suffrage Bill?'. He started as if shot, and then said, 'Humph! It's *you*, is it?' and passed on. Then he came back and said, 'You ought to get your photograph taken with a copy of the Bill in your hand'. She replied, 'You give it to me, Sir Thomas, and I'll be delighted to do so!'. He laughed and said, 'Oh, I'll let you know on Thursday—I've been trying to get old Pitt round'.[65] Although it was a chance encounter, it was fitting that Vida should be one of the first to be told of his change of heart.

Bent capitulated on 7 October and announced that his government would introduce woman suffrage the following week. Vida was at the National Council of Women Congress when the news came through. With 'evident jubilation', she made the 'most important [announcement] of her life'. It was greeted with resounding cheers.[66] The long battle for the franchise was over. Forty-one years after the issue had been first raised in the Victorian Parliament, Victorian women had finally achieved the vote.[67]

Vida could not resist writing to Bent, asking for a copy of the Bill signed by him, so she could have her photo taken with it. He does not seem to have replied. The first reading of the Bill was on 14 October. Vida's request, that the galleries be open to women during debate, was denied; women could only enter if they had a note of admission from a member.[68] Bent had backed down, but his Bill was mean and restrictive: automatic suffrage was granted to female ratepayers only, while every other woman had to make a special application to vote. This also applied to men and was intended to deter poorer pro-Labor people from voting. It was removed in 1910 before women voted for the first time in Victoria. Women were also debarred from standing for Parliament and this was not amended until 1923, Victoria again being the last State to enact this right.

The suffragists sat in the Speaker's Gallery to watch the Bill pass the second reading on 20 October, after which it was read for the first time in the Legislative Council. They presented the suffrage petition with its 21 000 signatures to the Legislative Council. The Bill was passed in its second reading in the Council on 18 November. Vida was in the gallery and did her own bit of 'suffragetting' by writing (against the rules) the names of the five men who voted against it.[69] She recorded their names in her diary: Austin, Campbell, Embling, Harwood and White. Vida leant forward to congratulate Annie Lowe on achieving this success after so many years. The old campaigner replied, 'I hope, Miss Goldstein, that you will be the first woman elected to Parliament'.[70] Vida later proudly claimed to be the first woman in Victoria to take out an elector's right for the Assembly and she 'also got in first with one for the Council ... on an educational qualification'.[71]

A commemoration *conversazione* was organised to celebrate the victory, and the members of the Woman Suffrage Declaration Committee were photographed in the Botanic Gardens. Ideas were mooted for a memorial. Vida favoured a kindergarten fund or a fund for an office and staff to organise the women's vote, but was no doubt amused by one suggestion of 'A statue of your noble self (rampant) with your fairy foot poised on the prostrate form of Thomas Aldophus Bent! Your form should be white marble, his *black*'.[72]

◆ ◆ ◆

It is ironic that Victoria, which had the first suffrage activity, should have been the last State to achieve woman suffrage. It has been argued that where the suffragist campaigns were strong, victory was delayed because it made the conservatives fight harder to prevent it.[73] The Victorian suffragists were unfortunate that at a time when the rest of the parliaments in Australia were prepared to grant the vote, Victoria had a conservative Upper House, and then the reactionary Bent Government denied women the vote for four more years. While most of Bent's supporters were suffragists, they 'forsook the woman's cause for the sake of office and political patronage'.[74] Instead of being swept along with modern thinking, they prided themselves on their obduracy and conservatism. Vida's election campaign of 1903 cannot have made them feel safer in their parliamentary seats.

Vida always gave much of the credit to the men who had helped support the fight for woman suffrage.

> One feature in the Suffrage Campaign in Australia makes it radically different from that in any other country—the readiness of our men to admit that our cause was a just one, and entitled to immediate recognition. We never had any difficulty in winning the men of Australia to our side.[75]

She said the Men's League provided 'chivalrous assistance'[76] to the movement, but in fact it was formed too late in the battle to have had any real influence. Its main action was the deputation to Bent, and he had realised by then he could not hold out indefinitely. The men themselves did not claim the credit. The *Socialist* wrote:

> Great credit is due to the women who have so long borne the brunt of the struggle. Chief among them is one of our own members, Miss Vida Goldstein, who has worked for nothing else during the past seven years. Now she will be free for other work, after she has had a good long rest.[77]

Another successful tactic Vida identified was the policy of concentration; the suffrage was the vital foundation stone on which all other reforms could be achieved and retained and women had only themselves to blame if they did not give it this priority. 'It is not to be expected that politicians will put Woman Suffrage first, when so many of the women who ask for it put it last on their own programmes.'[78]

Vida was not the only woman to fight for the vote, nor had she done so for the longest time, but she had laboured long and hard, with wit, intelligence and courage. Several valuable years of the most productive time of her life had been spent gaining the vote. Now she believed the women must be organised and educated to use their vote wisely. She wrote to Rose Scott that she wished they could 'patent a flying machine' so they could discuss ideas together.[79] Vida's thoughts turned once more to the idea of a newspaper. In 1909 she launched the *Woman Voter*.

6

Women voters

1909–1910

◆

Vida's new paper, the *Woman Voter*, was published as the monthly newsletter of the Women's Political Association. The first issue was in August 1909. It sold for one penny and had a similar format to the *Woman's Sphere*. It covered women's issues within Australia and overseas, reviewed feminist books and plays, and reported WPA activities. By 1911 it had 800 prepaid subscribers.[1]

Late in 1909, Vida once again accepted the nomination of the Women's Political Association to stand for the Senate. The election was called for 13 April 1910 and Vida vowed to 'use her utmost endeavour to succeed'.[2] On 11 February 1910, at a meeting to champion her, Vida was presented with a WPA banner. The colours adopted by the WPA were the same as the Women's Social and Political Union colours chosen by one of its leaders, Emmeline Pethick-Lawrence. Vida considered the shades 'soft, and truly expressive of the dignity of enfranchised women',

> lavender, [representing] fragrance of all that is good in the past; green, growth, the unfolding and development of all that makes life rich in purpose and achievement; [and] purple, the royalty of justice, the equal sovereignty of men and women.[3]

Vida opened her campaign in Casterton on 14 February. Conscious of the historical significance of the step she was once more taking, Vida wrote to Rose Scott: 'Before opening my campaign tonight, I wish to acknowledge the debt I owe all suffrage pioneers whose work has made my candidature possible'.[4] Her slogan this time was 'All the Men in Parliament cannot represent *One Woman* as adequately as *One Woman* can represent *All Women*'.

Vida's manifesto showed an increased political sophistication and she tried to capitalise on her previous campaign experience. She outlined her platform more confidently and clearly, calling herself a democratic progressive who protected the interests of women, children and workers of both sexes; these were the people who suffered most from bad legislation or administration. She reiterated that Parliament should reflect the opinions of women as well as men and that no man could represent 'Home, Children and Women Workers' as a woman could. She opposed the ticket system, 'which has proved such a corrupt influence in America', supported elective ministries, federal equal marriage and divorce laws, protection and the Commonwealth taking over State debts. She now supported a transcontinental railway so that inland Australia could 'blossom like the rose, and thus prevent the congestion of the population on the coastal fringe'.[5]

She also attempted, not always convincingly, to counter possible objections to her candidature. To the objection that she would split the party tickets, she agreed that she would 'certainly obtain one of the three votes to be cast by the justice-loving voters of both parties', which was hardly reassuring for party-loyal electors.[6]

Another of the objections was that she supported the militant English suffragettes. In November the previous year, Vida and Agnes Murphy (Dame Nellie Melba's secretary) had addressed a large audience on 'The Truth About the Suffragettes'. Vida graphically described the forcible feeding which was being perpetrated on the suffragettes and declared that it was time to choose between submission or rebellion. Agnes Murphy described the suffragettes she had met as women of 'real delicacy, culture and refinement'.[7] Vida argued that the suffragettes had been misrepresented in the press and that they were working for the working women of England, who earned less than a penny an hour. Those who did not know what it was to work for such an amount 'have not earned the right to criticise the Suffragettes'.[8]

Vida embarked on a hectic election campaign, spending the first week in the Western District, the second in Gippsland and the third in Melbourne. She charged admission of a silver coin because she lacked independent means or the financial backing of a party. This does not seem to have deterred her audiences because she continued to attract full attendances; often people had to be turned away. A new feature of this campaign was that she had other women to speak on her behalf and a group of WPA members who canvassed for her. Some meetings were addressed by the chairman of the Central Committee, Mabel Singleton and the secretary, Mary Fullerton, while a Miss Lambrick spoke in the suburbs. Vida was unable to revisit all the country towns from her 1903 campaign, but asked her supporters in the country to form committees to help her candidature. This seems to have happened in many places. Once more, Vida called on women to 'demonstrate the loyalty of women to women', reminding them that female electors were in the majority and if they all voted for their sex, she would be elected. They could disprove the statement that 'woman's worst enemy is woman'.[9]

At a meeting at Carlton, Vida explained why it was necessary to have a woman in Parliament and described how she was forced to work to protect the interests of women:

> Well I may say I am practically in the House now. The only difference is that I am outside the barriers. When a member proposes something that is against the interest of women, I have to signal frantically to a friendly member to come out from the Chamber and see me. Sometimes I don't catch a friendly eye, and then I write a note, and send it in to a member.
>
> I have often written the speeches of members ... and I could sit down and cry in the gallery sometimes, because I hear a member mutilate every point in the speech.[10]

When she spoke at Malvern on 7 March, the hall was crowded. Vida dealt with the marriage and divorce laws and the protection of women workers. An idea of her platform manner can be gained from the report of this meeting. She contended that:

> The present legislative chaos was due to the fact that woman's voice had so far remained unheard in Parliament. (Laughter.) She promised that at least one woman, if she got the chance, would raise her voice in the Senate. (Applause.) All sorts of happenings to her had been predicted if she should gain a seat. (Laughter.) She was not afraid — (renewed laughter) — for she had spent half her lifetime looking after bills. (Loud laughter.) But she did long for a comfortable seat.

A Male Voice: And £600 a year? (Laughter.)
The Candidate: That is a secondary consideration; in fact, no consideration at all. (Hear, hear.) It is said that it will be dreadful for me to sit amongst 35 men. (Laughter.) But the prospect does not terrify me. (More laughter.) I have worked amongst men for years—
An Old Lady: Oh! (Laughter.)
The Candidate: On committees. (Laughter.) People have asked, 'What will Miss Goldstein do at an all night sitting?' (Laughter.) In 99 cases out of 100 all night sittings are unnecessary. (Hear, hear.) If I thought an all night sitting was fixed up for party purposes I would go home to bed.
A Male Voice: Sensible woman! (Laughter.)
The Candidate: If the business was of national importance I would sit it out with the rest. (Applause.) Why! I've been up all night at a ball, and surely I could keep awake as a duty to the country. (Hear, hear and laughter.)[11]

She also told the audience that 'although it is rude to ask for presents, it is my birthday on April 13', the day of the election. This was greeted with laughter and applause. At question time, a woman asked if she favoured a tax on bachelors and Vida replied to the old question, 'I love my sex, and do you think I would advocate anything likely to precipitate them into the troubled sea of matrimony?'.[12]

As in the 1903 campaign, Vida had to contend with being a female candidate and an Independent. *Liberty and Progress* called her an 'acknowledged Socialist' and said that she been 'very properly placed towards the bottom of the poll' in 1903. It questioned the constitutional right of a woman to be elected and claimed Vida was an 'Unconstitutional Candidate'.[13] On 14 March, 'Vesta' (Mrs E. F. Allen) started her column to female electors in the *Argus*. She advised women to 'select one man' for the Senate and said that Independents 'exaggerate their own importance and refuse allegiance to any party'. The editorial the next day also condemned Independents. 'Vesta' advised women to vote Fusion, the party of Protectionists, Free Traders and Tariff Reformers led by Alfred Deakin. This combined grouping against the Labor Party led to 'the fiercest and bitterest party fight Australia has seen'. The WPA recorded that it was a 'marvel that the one non-party candidate, and that a woman, was not mutilated beyond recognition'.[14]

In a campaign remarkable for its vituperative meetings,[15] Vida's were notably dignified and free of interjection and harassment. Other women, particularly members of the Australian Women's National League, were heckled and often drowned out because of their unskilled oratory and anti-Labor ideology.

At a meeting in Brunswick, a questioner asked Vida if she believed that the hand which rocked the cradle ruled the world. Vida responded that the questioner was not acquainted with the modern ways of bringing up babies. She was again asked about a tax on bachelors and replied that men should be prevented from marrying 'before they reached the years of discretion'.[16] She campaigned in Gippsland and Central Victoria and rested for four days during Easter.

As the *Argus* progressively promoted the Fusion ticket, Vida's meetings received less coverage. None of her meetings was reported from 16 March to 6 April, although the paper managed to report Fusion candidates' country meetings. The report of Vida's meeting at Prahran carried the provocative headline 'Men's Evil Ways'. This referred to a statement she had made, in response to a question, that scouting was preferable to cadets as an activity for boys, because the latter aped men who 'smoke and drink and gamble and swear'.[17] This was a precursor of later campaigns to present Vida as a man-hater.

Vida's election committee organised canvassers and the *Woman Voter* ran an amusing account by one of the women who discovered the joys and trials of such work. Some people met her with the old cry that 'Woman's place is in the home'. A 'much befrizzed, golden haired lady' laughed at the idea of voting for a woman, saying she was married, 'as if that statement was quite sufficient to account for her stupidity. Presumably she left her brains at the altar!'. One old lady said she would gladly vote for Vida only she had not applied for her ' "electric" right' and an elderly gentleman said he was doing all he could for Vida by going to all her meetings. He elaborated, 'You see, I go to protect her. I know if there was any disturbance, I could quell it!'. The writer thought to herself, 'More power to you ... The age of chivalry is not dead'. Other women wanted someone to talk to, and one old lady said she would happily vote for Vida for her hard work for the children's courts: 'the pathetic note in the mother's voice told without words of many anxious days and nights passed in fear for her boys, and, perhaps, a personal acquaintance with the Children's Courts'.[18]

Vida held a successful meeting at the Melbourne Town Hall on 7 April. The hall was full twenty minutes before the advertised starting time and Vida, the sole speaker, held the audience's attention for two hours. The *Woman Voter* said she showed an excellent grasp of issues and was well qualified for a seat in Parliament.[19] The *Argus*, however, described the audience as 'attentive but undemonstrative'. Vida was heckled at this meeting by an elderly woman. To illustrate why a woman was needed in Parliament, Vida said that men were unable to design sensible perambulators, let alone adequately represent children in Parliament. The old lady interjected, 'If they were all like you there would be no perambulators in the world'. Vida ignored this, and went on to say she had been misrepresented by the *Argus* and that she did not oppose cadets. A collection was taken up and the old lady started to read a speech she had prepared: 'As one who fought for the enfranchisement of women, I am sorry to see we are making a great mess of it'. When a constable failed to persuade her to desist, she was removed from the hall. Vida was presented with flowers and the meeting closed with cheers.[20]

On 11 April, two days before polling day, the *Argus* published a letter supporting the Fusion Party by Eva Hughes of the AWNL, who wrote, 'I cannot believe that there is any chance of Miss Goldstein being elected; but there is grave danger that she will embarrass our side. Every vote given to Miss Goldstein is a vote given to Labor'. She also challenged Vida's entitlement to speak for the women of Australia. That night Vida spoke at Essendon to a full house. Her arrival was greeted with cheers and cries of 'Good boy, Vida' from a crowd of admiring girls in one corner, perhaps expressing the fact that politics was a man's world. Vida spoke out against Eva Hughes's letter and, defending her goal to represent all women in the Parliament, asserted that a woman had more in common with all women than any political faction could have. She believed her opponents were 'deadly frightened that I shall head the poll' and that this time, women were supporting her.[21] Vida's belief that women should have a primary loyalty to their sex above all other interests was echoed by the second-wave feminists. It is only in recent years that feminists have confronted the problem of accommodating the diversity of women— in political affiliation, sexual preference, ethnicity and class—within a women's movement.[22]

Vida wound up her campaign at Hawthorn on 12 April. There were more women than men present and the crowd spilled on to the roadway. She was well received and called on voters to split the ticket and vote for her, as a protest against the ticket system. The *Argus* had republished Eva Hughes's letter and Vida concluded that the paper feared she would win.[23]

The *Argus* did publish a letter to the editor which extolled Vida, but added an editor's note which said, 'This is the sort of gush relied upon by Miss Goldstein to secure her votes'. It told readers that Vida's politics were 'Labor's politics' and her views were 'opposed to the views of every patriotic man and woman in Australia'. 'Vesta' instructed women not to split their vote and to vote solidly for the Fusion candidates.[24]

Once more Vida was defeated, although she slightly improved her 1903 vote. Reviewing her campaign, Vida said it was remarkable that 54 000 were prepared to 'split the ticket' in a two-party contest to vote for a non-party candidate. She said that, given the circumstances, it had 'required unusual courage and sincerity of purpose to leave the beaten track of masculinity in politics and open up another which men and women shall tread together'. She believed that her 1903 campaign had not been taken seriously, but this time 'prophecies of [her] success were universal'. This had frightened her opponents who had, at every opportunity, drilled their followers 'that if they voted for the woman candidate they would annihilate their party'. While women could have elected her, she understood that they were so ignorant politically that they had not yet learned that it was impossible to get the necessary reforms from men, not because men were unjust but because they did not know how to be just to women. Nevertheless she had succeeded in consolidating the Women's Political Association: she had attracted new members and increased people's political awareness. She accepted that:

> It may be that I am never to have a place in that august body [the Senate]; if so, I am quite content to be a pioneer, to blaze the track for other women. That I have made the pathway easier for them is my rich reward.[25]

Vida denied that she was attempting to gratify personal goals, arguing that if this were her motivation she would have joined a party and probably been elected. Instead she had chosen to stand for principle.

> I don't say that I was officially approached, but I was informed by those I regarded as representatives of both parties that if I joined their party... my

entry into Parliament was assured, but I despise party Government, and I would not join one body or the other.[26]

She acknowledged that it would take many years to educate women to vote for other women, but that she was not discouraged and would try again.

◆ ◆ ◆

In April 1910, two pioneers of the women's movement died: Annie Lowe and Catherine Spence. Annie died shortly after the election; 'the last time she took a pen in her hand was on April 12th when she was just able to sign her postal ballot'. Illness would not stop the old suffragist exercising the right she had sought for so long.[27]

Catherine Spence died on 3 April, her autobiography unfinished. In it Spence recorded that there was 'none I admired more for her public spiritedness than Miss Vida Goldstein ... Her life is practically spent in battling for her sex'.[28] Jeanne Young, who completed the autobiography, wrote that Spence 'had always admired the fearless attitude of Miss Goldstein in her non-party work, and she was glad to associate herself with her when in 1909 she came to Adelaide to found the Women's Non Party Association of this State'. Young wrote of Vida's election campaigns:

> We always watched with the intensest interest Miss Vida Goldstein's election contests, invariably regretting her non-success. This was due, not to any shortcoming in Miss Goldstein, for she is not only a charming woman, but a very fine and courageous platform speaker, but to an innate Conservatism and prejudice against women in public life, which is much more noticeable in Australia than in either America or Great Britain.[29]

The conservative Jessie Ackermann, who was responsible for founding many WCTU branches, was less kind in her assessment of Vida. In reviewing the role of women in Australian politics, she wrote that women could hold the balance of power if they stood together, but there was no national leader who 'could carry the women out of the dense "anti" atmosphere' and unite them regardless of party or religion in the cause of securing just laws for women and children.

> There is not one [woman] with the genius of organisation and the ability of generalship in the entire Commonwealth who could direct the women ...

> The nearest approach to such an one I found in the charming personality of Miss Vida Goldstein ... [who] is widely known, has the reputation of being a good speaker, and certainly possesses a breadth of view which should enable her to command a great national following.

Ackermann believed that while a lack of funds and rumours about Vida's strong political leanings had hampered Vida's election campaigns, 'there must be a weak point in her ability to present the cause in a manner which forces it as a vital issue upon the consciences of men and women'. Also, many women objected to a woman thrusting herself into the 'filthy cesspool' of politics. Ackermann concluded that 'until a clear-brained, all-round woman springs into being, there is not likely to be a united national movement on the lines indicated'.[30]

◆ ◆ ◆

After the election, Vida resumed her WPA activities, including working for equal pay for female teachers and campaigning to have police matrons for women at lock-ups. Another campaign, to raise the age of consent to twenty-one, was a continuation of Annette Bear-Crawford's work—her Vigilant Society had succeeded in having the age raised from fourteen to sixteen in 1891. Vida argued that a girl's money or land was protected by law until she was twenty-one, so surely the girl should be too.[31]

Vida fully supported the suffragettes and was outraged at the way they were being treated. In June, Muriel Matters, an Australian campaigner for the English suffragettes, arrived in Melbourne to address meetings on the fight for the vote in England. The WPA arranged Muriel's reception and the *Woman Voter* publicised her visit and illustrated it with a poignant photo of her dressed in prison garb. Muriel had been imprisoned after she chained herself to an iron grille in the House of Commons and demanded votes for women. The grille —in the ladies' gallery—was a hated symbol of women's oppression, which Vida was to observe and condemn less than a year later. Vida and Muriel arranged a resolution supporting the beneficial effects of woman suffrage which was passed unanimously in the Senate and sent to the British Prime Minister, Henry Asquith.[32] This shows Vida's influence, even though she remained 'outside the barriers' of Parliament.

Vida had much to be pleased about. The WPA was flourishing, invigorated by the increased membership gained during the election campaign. In July, its club rooms were opened in the Block in Collins Street. The facilities consisted of a large room, a furnished dressing room, kitchen, piano, writing and tea tables, electric light and a gas stove. Some of the younger members set up an operatic and dramatic company and performed *The Runaway Girl* in November, which was a great success. The *Woman Voter* was paying its way. In August it published a story by Stella Miles Franklin entitled 'Jilted', and later in the year, a story by Mary Fullerton was published. Possibly now that the paper was making a profit, Vida could pay for these stories and so encourage female writers.

Vida turned down the opportunity to stand for the by-election for the House of Representatives seat of Kooyong, because she believed voters were not ready to give their only vote to a woman. The women's parliament resumed and Vida usually took the part of the Governor-General or the Speaker. One topic discussed was domestics. The wealthier classes were finding it increasingly difficult to find good domestics because girls preferred to work in factories, where they were paid more, for shorter hours. The women's parliament called for training for domestic workers, a minimum age and ten-hour shifts with a three-hour break. When it was suggested the eight-hour principle should apply, the women's Prime Minister dismissed this as 'not practicable'.[33]

In September, the WPA organised a promotional tent at the Royal Melbourne Show. Close by, members of the AWNL set up their display and handed out their paper for free. Vida and the WPA refused to give the *Woman Voter* away, 'thinking it too good to be thrown away after a careless glance from the unthinking, indifferent citizen'. Vida said she wanted '*quality* not mere *quantity* of membership'.[34] To win elections, however, she needed numbers, and with the limited WPA membership and meagre finances she could not hope to compete with the AWNL.

The WPA women found their male neighbours at the show most helpful; they secured their tent against high winds and gave them cups of tea—a refreshing change of role! Several male passers-by were antagonistic. Vida wrote how these men 'hurled the Bible at my head', quoting the second and third chapters of Genesis wherein Eve is placed under the dominion of Adam. Vida retorted that according to the first chapter of Genesis Adam and Eve were created simultaneously and both were given dominion over the world. Vida also identified another type of man:

> Then there were the fatherly old men, who were really hurt at the thought of the angel, woman, coming out of the sweet security of home to take part in the hurly-burly of industrial and political life. They bungled in expressing their inmost feeling, but managed quite unconsciously to convey their idea that women should marry, and if they didn't, it was because they hadn't been lucky enough to find a man who would take care of them. These men always assume that if a woman does not marry it is because she has not had the chance to do so.

Vida believed men who 'engaged in hard, manual labour were the broadest-minded and most enlightened politically'. She said that at first she was inclined to 'fume' at the 'callous indifference' of some of the women, but then 'a wave of compassion swept over me' and she realised that 'they have been so long in bondage to tradition and custom that their poor enslaved minds cannot grasp the meaning of freedom and justice for themselves, let alone others'. Vida concluded that they had done good propaganda work and it was decided to repeat the venture the following year.[35]

Another activity interesting Vida at this time was a women's congress being organised for the following year by a committee of Old Collegians of the Presbyterian Ladies' College. Topics to be discussed included 'The Development of the Girl—Physical, Mental and Moral', 'The Social Effects of the Minimum Wage' and 'Women and Citizenship'.[36] Vida contributed to the organisation of the congress and it proved highly successful, with enthusiastic press coverage, but she did not see the result of her efforts. A more pressing call had come—from the Pankhursts in England. By the time the congress took place, Vida was 10 000 miles away, working for woman suffrage once more.

7

Face to the dawn

1911

♦

Early in 1911, Vida accepted the invitation of the Pankhursts to visit England as a guest of the Women's Social and Political Union. As a suffragist and a representative of enfranchised women, she would, it was hoped, be able 'to help the woman's cause at the heart of the action'.[1] Women in England were still denied the vote and imprisoned suffragettes who went on hunger strike were forcibly fed, which often led to horrific injuries.

Vida sailed from Port Melbourne on 14 February. She stood on the deck of the S.S. *Malwa* clutching bouquets of flowers tied with lavender, green and purple ribbons. She was excited by what lay ahead, but also aware that she would be away from family and friends for more than a year.

Extracts of Vida's letters were published in the *Woman Voter* but, unlike her American visit, only one letter from the voyage was published. Vida wrote from Colombo:

> The fact that women are 'the burden-bearers of the world' is strongly emphasised in Colombo, where women shuffle along bearing huge baskets, bundles of grass on their heads, and possibly a baby on their hip, while the men walking by their side or behind them look on as if it were the greatest trouble to carry themselves to their destination.
>
> Every time I used a rickshaw I had a feeling of self-contempt. I could never get used to treating even the most degraded type of black man as an animal.

I left Colombo believing more firmly than ever in the wisdom of a White Australia. At this stage of our civilisation the black and white cannot dwell together without both deteriorating—in spite of American experience. The coloured man takes all the vices of the white man, and the white man becomes dehumanised. He is so accustomed to being waited on hand and foot that he never does a thing for himself when he can get a coloured man to do it, and he is so full of contempt for the coloured man that he sees everything out of focus, and his tendency is to live only for himself and in himself.[2]

After a 'wretched' Channel crossing, she arrived at Victoria Station in London at 7.40 p.m on 19 March. To her surprise an enormous crowd of WSPU members was waiting to greet her. The first person she recognised was Muriel Matters. The WSPU leaders, including Emmeline Pankhurst and Emmeline Pethick-Lawrence, were also there. 'What a reception!' Vida wrote home, 'a delightful welcome... Cheer upon cheer! Cheer upon cheer!'.[3] The size of the crowd was even more remarkable because there had been great uncertainty as to which station she would arrive at. This rousing reception recognised Vida's international importance as a suffragist. In America she had been one of the youngest delegates and had had to find her own funds for the trip. Now women who were her own age and her peers were paying her to visit because of the unique contribution she would make.

Vida was taken to the Inns of Court Hotel, where Emmeline Pankhurst lived, and immediately the reporters arrived. The next day Vida stayed in bed till 2 p.m. She attended a WSPU meeting, then went to dinner with the Pethick-Lawrences. Another guest, Ethel Smyth, sang three suffrage choruses she had composed. Vida said Miss Smyth was a 'great musical genius. If she were a man she would be acclaimed all over England'.[4] (She was later made a Dame.)

The following day, Vida was escorted by Keir Hardy, the first leader of the Labour Party in the House of Commons and a dedicated socialist, pacifist and chief adviser to the suffragettes, on a tour of the Houses of Parliament. She described the buildings as:

Beautiful, majestic. *Great* and yet *small*, for in the heart of them is embodied the smallness of the English mind. The Grille behind which women visitors are concealed reveals the true English conception of Woman, the mother of the race.[5]

She watched the Speaker's Procession, then they took tea on the terrace. Vida observed with amusement the 'fleet', which was stationed there to protect parliamentary members from possible suffragette raids from the Thames. It consisted of a boat and three policemen.

Vida made her first speech at the Albert Hall on 23 March 1911. Even though the suffragettes were prohibited from advertising their meetings, 10 000 people were present, all informed of the meeting 'merely through individual effort'. Vida must have had a sense of *déjà vu* to be once more campaigning for woman suffrage. She asserted that the women's vote in Australia had brought forward many measures for domestic legislation, including the principle of equal pay for equal work, and assured the 'anti' stalwarts that it had not led to dissension in the home because the women voted as their men voted. At the end of the meeting, £6000 was collected for the suffrage cause.

Vida described her reception as 'magnificent'. She was pleased everyone could hear her and she could see people applauding her from the balcony 'where they looked like flies'.[6] The WSPU paper, *Votes for Women*, devoted a page to Vida's speech and described her as 'a speaker of great power, as well as an active and keen worker'.[7] In a congratulatory letter, Florence Rankin wrote that she had had 'misgivings about the acoustic properties of that huge place for anyone unaccustomed to it but to my astonishment you were more easily heard than anyone I have ever heard there either man or woman'. She also praised Vida's 'freshness and confidence which the Cabinet has tried so hard to stifle in our wonderful leaders'.[8] It was at one of the Albert Hall meetings that Edith Gardiner first heard Vida speak. She was so impressed that when the Gardiner family emigrated to Australia, Edith immediately contacted Vida and joined the WPA. She became a stalwart vice-president in the difficult years of World War I.[9]

After her Albert Hall triumph Vida set out on a 'most successful' lecture tour of the big manufacturing towns of England and Scotland, followed by ten days in the south of England, 'every minute of which was perfectly delightful, both as to companionship and the glory of the surroundings'.[10]

Vida returned to London in mid-April and remained 'a fixture' there to the end of June, attending functions, some in her honour, giving lectures and receiving the generous hospitality of many people.

At the Men's League for Woman Suffrage dinner, given in Vida's honour, many people prominent in the movement were present, including Charlotte Despard and Millicent Garrett Fawcett representing the non-militants of the Women's Freedom League and Emmeline Pethick-Lawrence and Emmeline Pankhurst representing the WSPU. Vida hoped it was a 'happy augury' that this was the first time the Constitutionalists and the Militants had met together since their split in 1907.[11]

Vida was sent a card for the Speaker's private gallery which she thought would enable her to avoid the indignity of having to sit behind the 'hateful grille'.[12] When she arrived, however, she found a grille in the private gallery too. 'Only woman suffrage', she wrote, 'would ever have persuaded me to sit behind it. It is beyond my comprehension that women have tolerated it for so long'.[13] She was there to witness the introduction of the Conciliation Bill which would enfranchise one million women. The debate was not of a high standard, but she hoped that success was near.

> The debate showed the utter hollowness of the assertion that the militants have 'put the clock back'. Before militancy was started a woman suffrage debate was the signal for ribaldry and ridicule; now the subject is tackled seriously, and everyone knows the battle is won. [14]

Early in May, Vida spoke at Swiss Cottage and visited Kew Gardens. The 'gloriously perfect English spring' was something never to be forgotten.[15] When she spoke at the Pavilion with Christabel Pankhurst, she wrote laconically, 'Magnificent audience. Packed from floor to ceiling. I always receive most delightful receptions'.[16] She visited the Ramsay MacDonalds. He was the chairman of the parliamentary Labour Party and while he supported woman suffrage, both he and his wife were 'rabid opponents of the suffragettes'. A sewing party was in progress, so there was not much opportunity for Vida to discuss the issue with them.[17]

Vida joined the crowd of WSPU members and supporters at Euston Station to meet the Lord Mayor of Dublin on 11 May. He had been sent to use his right of petition to the House of Commons (unexercised for twenty-three years) for the Conciliation Bill to be passed. The train was two hours late and did not arrive until midnight. Vida was impressed that no one left early, even though many would not get home till 2 a.m. On their way to the refreshment rooms for supper:

> We saw dozens of policemen hiding under a stairway. What they expected from the suffragettes goodness only knows. When the train arrived there they were asserting the authority of the law in a most provocative fashion, trying to keep the crowds back ... What I saw of the behaviour of some of the police that night was sufficient to convince me of the brutality they can be capable of when there was something on [sic] which they might consider militant.[18]

The next day Vida witnessed the presentation of the petition to Parliament, a 'most picturesque ceremony', before motoring with the Pethick-Lawrences to the opening of the Festival of Empire at the Crystal Palace. Vida wrote home that they had seats near the royal box and they were also seated near the royal family at the reception which followed at the Dominions Club. Then they rushed home to dress for the Lord Mayor's dinner, where Vida was seated next to the Japanese artist Yoshio Markino. She thought he was a curious mixture of the 'ideal and practical' who understood the 'true inwardness of the movement'.[19] She preserved the cards for the Speaker's private gallery and the Mayoral dinner in her album.[20]

Vida attended the at-home of the Writers' Suffrage League and the dinner for the Australian Prime Minister, Andrew Fisher, given by the Labour Party. Margaret Fisher agreed to join the woman suffrage procession being planned for June. Vida also met Olive Schreiner, a South African author and feminist, and George Bernard Shaw, who signed Vida's autograph book under his wife's signature, adding 'husband of the above'.

In the weekends Vida visited the countryside, 'surrounded by nature's luxuriant growth of brilliant colouring'. Her constant travels led to gentle jests about 'Miss Goldstein and her suit-case'.[21] Vida felt humbled by the kindness showered upon her. One weekend she stayed with the Balfours at Woking. (He was a former Conservative Prime Minister.) While there, Vida wrote that she saw an aeroplane for the first time and heard a cuckoo and several nightingales.[22]

Vida also took the opportunity to spend time with her brother Selwyn and his family, who were now living in England. Selwyn, an engineer, had worked in Western Australia until 1908. The family then lived in Mexico for two years, surviving a revolution—Selwyn dined with the rebel bandits—and the torpedoing of their ship, before moving to England.[23]

Vida attended the Imperial Conference and wrote a paper, 'Women and the Imperial Conference', for *Votes for Women*. She said that women in New Zealand and Australia had the vote 'because it is easier to overcome the anti-suffrage forces, ignorance, tradition, and prejudice in a young unfettered country'. She spoke on naturalisation (under the English Act, a married woman took her husband's nationality and could not regain her own, even if divorced or widowed) and the loss of political status for Australian women who came to England.[24] She also formed the Australian and New Zealand Women Voters' Association of London (later renamed the Woman Suffrage Union of Dominions Overseas) and became their 'inspirer and guide'.

A Great Suffrage Procession was being organised for 17 June 1911 and Vida's task was to organise the women from other lands who were to join it. She was so busy that when George Bernard Shaw invited her to lunch he had to use his persuasive talents to encourage her to spare the time. He wrote, 'No matter how much you may be occupied with the Procession, you must eat, unless you wish it to be your funeral procession'.[25] On the day of the procession Vida and Margaret Fisher led the Australian women, who carried a banner bearing the Australian coat of arms and another, painted in 1908 by Dora Meeson Coates, depicting the young girl of Australia instructing Mother England to 'Trust the women Mother as I have done'. Vida wore the suffrage ribbons pinned over her heart. This march was the WSPU's largest so far. The women marched five abreast and their route was lined with crowds ten people deep. The most moving sight was the contingent of 1000 women who had been imprisoned. They were dressed in white and each carried a silver pennant. In their midst a huge banner proclaimed 'From prison to citizenship'.[26] An elated Vida told the Albert Hall meeting that night the 'wonderful' procession 'will melt even the heart of Mr Asquith'.[27]

On 22 June Vida watched a very different procession—the Coronation of George V—from an 'exclusive position' along The Mall.[28] The newspaper publishing magnate, Lord Northcliffe, had offered her a seat for the procession. Even though he opposed woman suffrage, he was charmed by Vida and promised he would do anything for her 'at any time or any place on any subject'.[29]

Vida attended the WSPU meeting of 3 July prepared to have a good time listening to the speeches. Suddenly a message came that Christabel Pankhurst wanted to see her. Vida went with the premonition of what was coming—Emmeline Pankhurst had been detained and they wanted Vida to speak in her stead. In all her years of public speaking she had 'never before been called upon to speak at an important public meeting at such short notice'. Her impromptu speech was well received.[30]

About this time Vida wrote a pamphlet, *Woman Suffrage in Australia*, which was published by the WSPU. She outlined how the vote had been won in Australia and gave credit to the broadmindedness of Australian men. The great difficulty had always been the Upper House, the Legislative Council, 'which represented only the propertied classes'. She was convinced that the Australian suffragists' strength had been their policy of concentrating on achieving the suffrage before other social reforms. The first noticeable effect of the vote had been educational, with the women forming all sorts of leagues to ensure they voted wisely. She believed that there had been no noticeable effect on party politics; the 'proportion [of votes] remains the same, but the quality of the vote changes' because women introduced into politics issues of special importance to themselves. Non-party politics, however, was 'visibly affected' because the women who were prominent in the suffrage movement 'hold aloof from the recognised parties, and organise independently'. These women wanted the vote to bring an entirely new element into politics. The reforms they sought, such as equal pay, marriage and divorce bills and protection of children, were not party questions and therefore required non-party solutions. Vida listed the social reform legislation which had been achieved and 'vigorously supported by the women voters'. She concluded, no doubt to reassure her English readers, that 'not one of the prophecies against Woman Suffrage has been fulfilled. Our public men who fought against it have become its warmest advocates'.[31]

During July, Vida continued to address meetings throughout England. She wrote airily that the 'meeting at Brighton last Friday was fine; they all are, so I need not go into details about them'.[32] On a rest day in Liverpool, she visited the Public Gallery and toured the city. Here she saw:

more evidences of animality and poverty than I've seen anywhere else (I have not seen the East End [of London] yet). As it is a seaport city one would likely see the worst types congregating about the docks and ferries. The women especially distressed me; they looked regular viragoes, half-sodden with drink. Little wonder, indeed, when one knows how they live.[33]

That afternoon she was taken to Chester and revelled in the beauty of the historic old town with its Roman ruins and spectacular views—a contrast from the scenes of the morning. The next day she visited a model cotton mill at Bolton, where she was impressed by the skill of the men and women who laboured there, but noted that after twenty years of service they only earned £1 a week.[34]

It was decided that Vida should witness a country by-election, so she was sent to West Somerset. She wrote of one experience with Annie Kenney, the former mill girl who was now one of the WSPU's most prominent speakers:

> Annie Kenney spoke at Bishop Lydiard, and I took the chair—or, rather, the floor of the buggy for her, for we spoke in the open air ... She is a little fair girl, with keen blue eyes, through which a beautiful soul shines out. She is full of life, and true as steel—everyone adores her. Her speech was grave and gay by turns, but always full of political sagacity. The audience hung on every word she said. After the meeting was over the men seized hold of the shafts, others pushed behind, and in this way drove us through the village, amid the wildest enthusiasm and ringing cheers.[35]

The suffragettes were not always so popular. Vida included in her album photographs of the trees planted in memory of two suffragettes whose deaths had been hastened by their suffrage activities. Mary Clarke, the sister of Emmeline Pankhurst, had died on Christmas Day 1910, two days after her release from Holloway. Too ill to join the suffrage deputations, she had taken the 'easier course' of window-breaking and had been imprisoned for a month. The second was Henria H. L. Williams who died on 2 January 1911. She had been badly injured on Black Friday, 10 November 1910, when violence broke out between the suffragettes and the police, following the news that the Conciliation Bill was to be delayed until the next Parliament. Each tree bore a small plaque at its foot; Mary's said, 'I have paid the price of freedom' and Henria's said, 'She Hath Done

What She Could'. The carefully pressed leaves in Vida's album are probably from these trees.[36]

◆ ◆ ◆

For the first week of August, Vida holidayed with Muriel Matters and Violet Tillard in Buckinghamshire. There she saw the 'lovely "Vale of Aylesbury" and the noted ducks! ... The beautiful spot does not suggest poverty, but in some of the very old houses we saw rags and wretchedness that was appalling'. Women were making fine lace for a halfpenny an hour. 'We think sweating in Melbourne is appalling; no words could ever convey the awfulness of conditions here'.[37] In late September she went to Ireland where she traced some relations of her paternal grandmother, but 'finding them very dull and quite unresponsive she made no further attempt to communicate with them'.[38]

Vida was making the most of the opportunities offered her to learn from the suffragettes and the prominent people she met, as well as to travel and enjoy social and artistic events. Nevertheless, Isabella was obviously concerned about her. Emmeline Pethick-Lawrence wrote to reassure the anxious mother that Vida had been very well and 'I think we have followed out your wishes that she should not work too hard'. She credited Isabella with starting the suffrage movement in Victoria, which Vida had carried on 'so splendidly and so successfully'. It was a 'great joy' having Vida and she believed Vida had enjoyed her visit 'as much as we have enjoyed our association with her'. Vida had 'endeared herself greatly to us and her help has been most valuable at a critical time in our agitation'.[39] Vida and the Pethick-Lawrences remained correspondents for the rest of their lives.

Stella Miles Franklin was also in London at this time. She wrote to Isabella in October, saying she had only seen Vida briefly because Vida was so busy, but Stella had

> exhibited her [Vida] with great pride to Miss [Editha] Phelps, who says no wonder we are proud of her in Australia as she never saw such a beautiful, efficient attractive little creature. She was the biggest thing that has happened in the woman movement for some time in England. I heard of her everywhere I went and people asked me what her mother was like and her sisters and so on and I had great joy in telling them as you may believe. Agnes Murphy said she never saw anything like the welcome she got—that a general like Kitchener might well have been proud of it—she

referred to the crowd that came to meet her at the railway, and Agnes Murphy through her Melba experience should be a judge of those sort of affairs.

Stella also told Isabella about Christabel Pankhurst, who, trying to fix someone by description, said, 'You can easily know her as she has her hair flying and is untidy like all the Suffragettes'. Editha Phelps demurred, saying Vida was one of the 'greatest' suffragettes and 'she had never seen any trimmer person'. Christabel concluded that perhaps it was an example of 'how women appeared after they had secured the vote and no longer had to become disarranged struggling for it'.[40]

In November 1911, the Conciliation Bill was again thwarted, when Asquith announced he would introduce a manhood suffrage Bill in the next session. A mass protest meeting at the Albert Hall decided that the following evening Emmeline Pethick-Lawrence would lead a deputation to the House of Commons.

It was a fine frosty night on 21 November 1911. People began to fill the Caxton Hall. There were fears that the police would barricade the demonstrators inside, so the organisers had provided tools to break through the bolts and bars. Suffragettes had been sent out in small groups to support the main demonstration. Emmeline Pethick-Lawrence and Christabel Pankhurst arrived and Vida joined them on the platform. Christabel spoke first, and then Emmeline called on the people to follow her and led the demonstrators out of the hall. When they reached the first cordon of police, a struggle ensued. The police, intent on splitting the march up, let small groups break through. Emmeline and her group pressed on and she was eventually arrested. The groups following her tried to catch up with her, but did not see her again. There is no further record of Vida's role in the night's proceedings. Eventually the groups were absorbed into the crowd that was milling around. All through the night windows were smashed and 223 people were arrested.[41]

The messages in Vida's album reflect the grim and bloody battle of the WSPU's struggle for the vote. While there are flattering comments like 'to know her is to love her, and to be in her company is to be happy',[42] the messages lack the sense of happiness and joyful commitment that shines through the album of her 1902 American visit. Emmeline Pankhurst wrote:

> Come, let us fashion acts that are to be
> When we shall lie in darkness silently.

Emmeline Pethick-Lawrence wrote, 'Thoughts have gone forth whose powers can sleep no more', while Christabel's contribution was, 'Aspirations are proportional to Destinies'. Annie Kenney wrote simply, 'Let us do our duty and all will be well'.

Several male suffragettes also signed her album. Hugh Franklin wrote, 'In memory of a beautiful holiday in Cornwall'. Two years later, when militancy intensified, he set fire to an empty train, was imprisoned and forcibly fed. Victor Duval was arrested at the 21 November demonstration for climbing over the rails of a fence and taking the number of a policeman.[43]

Vida made her farewell speech at the Albert Hall in December. She had been in England nine months and was leaving sooner than expected. She said that she was leaving to carry on the work in Australia, but 1911 had been a year of 'progress, progress all the way'. She listed the advances made and spoke of her conviction that Labour would stay true to the idea of adult suffrage. This was based on her Australian experience, where Labor stayed committed to suffragism, even though they expected women to vote against Labor, but 'because they were faithful to principle they got their reward'. She defined the essential elements of the movement and particularly stressed the sense of sisterhood.

> I have addressed three Albert Hall meetings. Each on[e] has had its own special characteristic, but each has had for centre and circumference an exalted sense of the sisterhood of women, a conception of liberty and justice that the world does not yet understand.
>
> Tonight that sense is still further exalted, for each fresh obstacle, or apparent obstacle rather, will add to and solidify your forces in such a way as to frustrate the knavish tricks and confound the politics of a Government that is making Liberalism in England a sorry and degraded thing...
>
> I go to carry on our work [in Australia]. For it is *our* work. We suffragists are one all the world over. The principles for which we stand, and of which the vote is only a small symbol, have to be woven into the national life everywhere.
>
> ... Dear members of the W.S.P.U., I am proud to have known you; I am proud to have worked with you. I thank your leaders for having invited me to share with them and with you the great privilege of working in your movement — the greatest, the most significant political movement the

world has ever seen. Now, next Tuesday, always, God befriend you, and lead you straight on to Victory'.[44]

◆ ◆ ◆

Vida sailed from England in January 1912. Why she left earlier than planned is unknown. One possible reason was financial difficulties at home. The October edition of the *Woman Voter* was reduced to four pages and the reason given was the cost. In April the *Woman Voter* had reported that it had run at a profit since its inception, but it seems that in Vida's absence the organisation was starting to decline. Vida was painfully aware of her dilemma: that she was a strong leader, with no able deputy to replace her. Vida's support for the suffragettes—and indirectly their militant methods—was also causing a decline in WPA membership.

The *Woman Voter* announced that Vida was due home early in January, but she arrived two months later. Vida was welcomed by the WPA and addressed its members on 'Suffragists, Suffragettes, and Antis'. She spoke at 'electric speed for over two hours, and still the audience wanted more'.[45] Vida realised she must revive the *Woman Voter*. She decided on a bigger format and, no doubt inspired by the fund-raising capacity of the suffragettes, she launched a £1000 Propaganda Fund.

In England, following the demise of the Conciliation Bill, the suffragettes had stepped up their activities, including peaceful processions and militant activities against property. Many arrests were made and the women, denied the status of political prisoners, were sentenced to hard labour. In June 1912, forcible feeding resumed and the suffragettes retaliated with an arson campaign. The barbarities being perpetrated on her newly made friends weighed heavily on Vida. She passionately believed in their cause, even though their militancy was making them increasingly unpopular. Some people asked Vida why she bothered to work for the English suffragettes when Australian women had the vote, but wherever women or children were treated inequitably Vida felt it was her fight, whatever the cost. She devoted more and more of her time to the suffragette cause and this was reflected in the content of the *Woman Voter*. As she got older, Vida became increasingly internationalist in her outlook.

The WPA of South Australia opened a fund for the suffragettes and the Victorian WPA followed suit. Letters were sent to the *Age* and the *Argus*, but only the *Age* published them. There was minimal support for the fund; only £23 was acknowledged. Vida decided that the *Age* and the *Argus*, while courteous, would not help the WPA because of its non-party position. The only way to inform more people was to increase the circulation of the *Woman Voter*. Vida decided on an unprecedented action: she would sell the paper in the streets.

Vida wrote about her first expedition:

> As I pulled up my blind in the morning, and saw the rain coming down in torrents, I must confess to a feeling of relief ... but about three o'clock the sky cleared suddenly, the sun shone out brilliantly, and my heart sank—now, there was no getting out of it ... I despised myself for my cowardice. I thought of the brave W.S.P.U. women, who had overcome all thought of self ...
>
> We got our papers. Off we went, but again, as we took up our allotted posts, I felt profoundly miserable. Only for a few minutes, however. The thought of our W.S.P.U. comrades, the thought that we were doing right, that we stood there for the sake of great principles which are ignored by the party press, these thoughts came to sustain me.
>
> The people streamed by, some amazed, some amused, a few openly contemptuous, but no buyers. Then came a woman, heavily laden with parcels. 'Will you buy our non-party woman's paper, one penny?' I asked. 'Why certainly I will,' and down went all her parcels on the pavement, to enable her to get at her purse. My first buyer! I felt inches taller ...
>
> In the evening we took our stand in Chapel-street, Prahran. Acute misery swept over me once more ... Men stood by watching, wondering. At last one, an elderly man, came forward and bought a paper. I expressed my gratitude. He took off his hat, and, with a bow, said with great respect, 'The debt is all on my side,' showing that he understood what it meant to stand in the gutter for one's convictions.[46]

Vida told a *Herald* reporter she felt numb. 'The first thing that roused me was my own white, scared face looking hard at me from a convenient advertisement mirror'. It also gave her more sympathy for street vendors. 'Only now do I realise how some of these poor people, who stand for hours selling wares, suffer'.[47] She continued to sell papers every week and at length was able to write, 'After the first agonising moments one loses consciousness of one's self in the deep interest aroused by studying those who come and buy and those who come and don't buy, and the work grows more and more interesting'.[48]

The band of female street sellers slowly increased to eight. One of these, a Miss Colley, wrote:

> One of our members has confided to us that the moment of deepest humiliation in her life was when she met our president in the street. She held a bunch of violets in her hand, while Miss Vida Goldstein held up a copy of the *Woman Voter* for sale.[49]

Vida extended her street selling to include *Votes for Women* as another way to help the English suffragettes. Vida and a friend, Catherine Kilkelly, positioned themselves at the corner of Collins and Swanston Streets and started selling the papers at 5.15 p.m. By 6 p.m. they had sold five each. The next day, they sold nineteen on the streets and the rest to friends and members. The following week's papers included information on forcible feeding. Vida pinned a poster to her skirt which read, 'Torture! By Order of the Home Secretary' and the supply was rapidly exhausted.[50] The third week, the papers sold even more quickly and Vida cabled for an increased supply.

May Maxwell, the journalist, remembered seeing Vida selling papers:

> On the kerb at the corner of Swanston and Collins Streets in the homeward rush hour stood a young, attractive woman selling newspapers.
> For fifteen minutes I watched this amazing spectacle. It was 1912—and only boys sold newspapers in Melbourne streets in this era ...
> On this wintry day she had a bundle of papers tucked under one arm and a poster pinned to the front of her skirt, reading: 'Votes for Women' ...
> Most passersby did not even see her. Groups of girls looked sideways and tittered. Occasionally a man would stop and give a disapproving grunt.
> I did not see one person buy a paper.
> Business may have been dull, but once again this Australian leader revealed her moral courage and the strength of her convictions ...
> Each time I met Vida she looked so feminine in every way that I could never understand how she hid her fighting quality. Of medium build with a graceful figure, and brown, intelligent eyes, she was the antithesis of a fighter of any type.[51]

Vida also organised a deputation to Prime Minister Andrew Fisher and a woman suffrage petition[52] to the English House of Commons, which was supported by various women's organisations in Australia. When Emmeline Pankhurst and the Pethick-Lawrences were refused the status of political prisoners, Vida drafted what she considered a 'very polite message, which cannot cause offence' and sent copies to men prominent in politics and the churches, asking them to sign it. The message was, 'Hope Suffrage leaders who break the law from political motives may be treated as political offenders'. Vida realised it might seem she was asking Australians to interfere in English politics, but she argued that England had involved itself in movements for political freedom in other countries, and she appealed for justice 'in the name of our common humanity'. Alfred Deakin was one who refused to sign it, writing that he would not endorse such a 'dangerous and unjust doctrine'.[53]

In August, the *Woman Voter* published Vida's 'Open Letter' to the members of Federal Parliament, calling on Australia to protest against the treatment of the suffragettes on humanitarian grounds and to support votes for women in England. It graphically described forcible feeding.

> The victim is put in a chair, her body tied to it, her arms and legs held down by wardresses, the head is held back, the throat is held, the tube is forced down, and the food poured into the oesophagus. I give the experiences of one of the prisoners, which are typical. Miss Betty Giveen was released from Birmingham because her throat was so swollen that the doctor could not get the tube down. For two days she had severe attacks of functional paralysis in her face, throat, lungs, arms and hands immediately after the feeding. One morning the doctor attempted three times to put the tube down her throat, but it was impossible, as the throat was so sore and swollen.[54]

This letter was discussed in Parliament, but no action was taken. Andrew Fisher summed up the situation saying, 'I think political prisoners should not be treated as criminals, but do not think it necessary to make representations to the Imperial Government on the matter'.[55]

◆ ◆ ◆

It has been argued that Vida became increasingly anti-men after her 1911 visit to England. Norman MacKenzie wrote that Vida's 'bitter sex-hostility... by 1913 had become so irrational that she was attributing all the ills of the world to Man, corrupted by power, sexual excess and venereal disease'.[56] There is certainly a new obduracy dating from this time, but not the blanket sex-hostility or irrationality this passage indicates. Vida maintained good relations with many men as friends and as co-workers for the causes she supported and always gave men credit for their assistance in obtaining the vote in Australia and their work for the peace movement during World War I.

Now in her forties, Vida had achieved international recognition as a suffragist and feminist during her English visit. She had addressed huge meetings with great success and met many people prominent in politics and the arts. This developed her belief in the fundamental rightness and justice of her views and renewed her determination, borne of her increased confidence, not to compromise. With renewed vigour, she supported causes and groups that were not generally popular. The ultimate outcome of this course would be the gradual erosion of her influence in the mainstream of Victorian public life, but undeterred by previous defeats, she once more embarked upon achieving her goal of winning a seat in Parliament.

8

Campaigns for Kooyong
1912–1914

♦

In May 1912, Vida accepted an invitation to stand as the WPA's candidate for the House of Representatives seat of Kooyong. This would enable her to concentrate her campaign within one electorate, which with the WPA's limited resources could prove more effective, but it was also a gamble because she would be calling on electors to give their only vote to her. The campaign planning committee met at once, intent on being fully organised and prepared for the election, which was expected the following May.

When Vida held an election meeting at Camberwell on 28 June, the hall was crowded. She spoke of the necessity of electing a woman to Parliament, gave examples of the 'glaring injustice of the laws affecting women, and showed how men were content to let these laws stand, not through any desire to be unjust to women, but simply because, in the conflict of party interests, the woman's cause must go to the wall'.[1]

In September the WPA moved to a new office and club rooms at Arlington Chambers, 229 Collins Street. In the New Year it opened a shop there, selling home-made jams, haberdashery and various publications on the women's movement and other social and industrial issues. This was later extended to include a Women's Political Library as part of the WPA's educative work. A campaign meeting in January 1913 decided to start canvassing, selling papers and holding street meetings in the electorate. Home meetings had already been organised for some time; this was a clever response to the problem of reaching women who would not attend public meetings. Second-wave feminists took a similar approach with their consciousness-raising groups. A Shakespeare recital was held to raise campaign funds, but while it was an 'artistic triumph' the attendance was poor.[2]

The WPA believed its efforts were being hampered because its activities were not adequately publicised. The *Age* and the *Argus* only gave 'fragmentary reports' of WPA meetings and on occasion the *Argus* would burst into 'hysterical abuse' of both the WPA and Vida. In March the WPA passed a resolution against this 'press boycott of the Woman Movement'.[3] The catalyst was a letter in the *Argus* by an ex-principal of the Presbyterian Ladies' College, the Reverend S. G. McLaren.

> There is one clear principle which condemns [the suffragettes' methods], and that is—we are not to do evil that good may come. Once let this principle go, and there is no extreme in wickedness which may not follow. Miss Goldstein does not condemn these methods. Indeed she seems ... distinctly to approve of them...
>
> Miss Goldstein says, 'The militants will conquer sooner or later.' She is wrong. The militants, as such, will never conquer. And they ought not to conquer ... They say there will be peace if they get the suffrage. How can they guarantee this? They are teaching their followers lawlessness, and in such things the pupils are usually more logical than their teachers. If such methods were to succeed in gaining for women the suffrage, why should they not succeed in gaining the ends for which the suffrage exists? It is easy to open a channel, not so easy to stop the flood which follows.[4]

Vida made a lengthy reply.

> The Suffragette movement is based on principle. The driving force in it is the principle of love, the love of truth and justice, the love of women for women, and the love of women for humanity. The movement is led, and supported by, women and men who have as profound a knowledge of and reverence for the Scriptures as Mr. McLaren himself. They are no more to be blamed for having, after 80 years of constitutional agitation, to make their appeal to Caesar with the 'sword', the only weapon that can pierce Caesar's intelligence, than were those who fought and died for their principles in all the holy wars that have been fought for religious and civil liberty... There have come times in the history of every people when they had to choose between two evils—the evil of tyranny and oppres-

sion by those in authority, or the evil of revolt against tyranny and oppression ...

Mr. McLaren says the militants are 'losing all along the line.' That has been said ever since the Suffragette movement started, and always the 'loss' has been pure gain. The sword and the spear and the shield of the big battalions that are fighting the Suffragettes appear menacing, but they do not dismay the militant women, who know they are only tin toys, and that the victory is, and will be, to those who fight in the name of Truth, and Love, and Justice.[5]

This letter and others supporting her were not published. The women decided to combat the 'boycott' by making the *Woman Voter* a weekly paper and working to increase circulation.

Vida's support of the suffragettes continued to alienate many people. The WPA's effort to find an anti-suffragette speaker for a debate came to nothing. The AWNL refused, although this was only learned unofficially, as did Ernest Scott, who held the chair of history at the University of Melbourne. His letter of refusal, while perhaps an ill-judged attempt at levity, seemed merely insulting:

Dear Madam, —I am very sorry. Your letter of 27th February got hidden under a pile of papers and I did not discover it till to-day, when looking for something else which I couldn't find.

But, in any case, I couldn't debate with Miss Goldstein. She would be sure to get the best of it, and her case being so infernally bad, I shouldn't like that to occur. Secondly, it seems to me to be useless to debate the pranks of the Pancakes, and their maggot-brained following. They have taken the subject out of the region of argument. The example they set is to throw things. If I debated with Miss Goldstein I should come equipped with a basket of rotten apples, and as I can throw straighter than she can, I should be bound to triumph by the use of suffragette methods, and I shouldn't like that either. Please accept my apologies.—Faithfully yours.

This was published in the *Woman Voter* 'as an example of how a man, presumably a gentleman, well known amongst Melbourne *litterateurs*, is willing to disregard the ordinary rules of courtesy in answering a courteous invitation to discuss political methods' with 'high-minded women'.[6]

◆ ◆ ◆

The election was called for 31 May 1913 and the women swung into action. Vida was standing against Liberal Party incumbent Sir Robert Best, in a two-way contest. Labor did not nominate a candidate; the WPA thought Labor had decided it could not win the seat, so had left Vida a clear run. It was hoped she would attract the non-conservative votes. Vida's policy speech was at Camberwell on 15 April. The hall was so crowded that the organisers realised they would need to arrange overflow meetings in future. A special feature was a women's choir, consisting of a dozen young women dressed in white. They sang the 'Women's March' by Ethel Smyth, whom Vida had met in England, and the 'W.P.A. March', with words by Bella Lavender, the first woman in Australia to gain a Bachelor and Master of Arts. The chorus ran:

> Vote for the woman, place her high,
> Woman to woman standing nigh;
> Vote for the woman, she will ring true,
> Faithful to pledges and loyal to you.[7]

The *Woman Voter* reported enthusiastically that Vida 'excelled herself, and her fluent speech and lucid arguments found favour with the large audience. Many questions were put to the candidate and answered to the complete satisfaction of the audience'.[8]

Vida divided her policies into two sections. Her Women's Programme included a federal equal marriage and divorce law; equal custody and guardianship of children; raising the age of marriage (at that time, twelve for girls with parental consent); equal pay for equal work; equal opportunities in the Commonwealth Public Service; amendment of the Naturalisation Act to enable women to retain their nationality and civil rights if they married non-Australians; protection of deserted wives and children and protection of women and girls from the White Slave Traffic (prostitution). Her General Programme included electoral reform; tax on unimproved land values; protection; referenda; elective ministries (necessary for non-party government) and international peace and arbitration.[9]

In the early part of the campaign Vida spent two or three days each week in the electorate, often attending several functions a day. She spoke at home meetings and public meetings, while Bella Lavender and Lillian Harris spoke at open-air meetings and Lucy Paling and

Kate Flynn spoke at home meetings. Vida also had international helpers; Margaret Hodge and Harriet Newcomb who she had befriended in England were visiting and lent their support as speakers. Maurice Blackburn sometimes spoke at the open-air meetings. This gave him experience for his own campaign the following year when he stood as a Labor candidate and won. A pamphlet entitled *Life and Work of Miss Vida Goldstein* was produced by the campaign committee to further publicise Vida's achievements and suitability as a parliamentarian.

Vida spoke to full houses at Hawthorn and Kew and, to avoid disappointing people who could not get in, she agreed to repeat her address at overflow meetings. The *Woman Voter* reported:

> [Vida's] speeches are, as usual, able, clear, convincing, and her straightforward, ready answers to questions delight her audiences... A truly inspiring sight was presented when Miss Goldstein spoke from the balcony at the Kew Town Hall to the crowds which filled the street from one side to the other. The sea of faces, all interested, and, with few exceptions, sympathetic, augured well for the success which Miss Goldstein's spirited and self-sacrificing devotion to the women's cause so splendidly merits.[10]

On 23 April, the *Age*'s editorial called Vida a 'political nobody'. It opposed minority candidates who could prevent others having a 'free run'.

> It is, in fact, in the power of the veriest political booby in the state to do as much as that. Miss Goldstein and Mr Ronald did it in the Senatorial contests of 1910. Everyone remembers how their candidature gave victory to the minority and defeat to the majority. They claimed their rights and their rights were a gross wrong to everybody else.[11]

Five days later a WPA deputation visited the editor of the *Age*. Harriet Newcomb and Margaret Hodge, representing overseas suffrage bodies, assured him Vida was not a nobody overseas. Lucy Paling reminded him of the more than 50 000 votes Vida had received in both elections she had contested, and reminded him that the *Age* stood for non-party politics between elections. The editor retorted that that might be true, but it was unpractical at election time. He then said Vida was practically a Labor candidate; earlier, he had criticised her non-party stance.[12] Faced with such blatant party bias, the women could only renew their efforts through canvassing and increasing the circulation of the *Woman Voter*. It was frustrating to experience such turnarounds at election time and electorally damaging for Vida.

To counter the AWNL campaign against Vida, the election number of the *Woman Voter* gave fourteen reasons why the AWNL members should support Vida. The press boycott continued. The *Argus* reported only one of Vida's meetings and published only one letter in reply to criticisms of Vida by correspondents. The *Age* printed attacks by the AWNL and the *Woman Voter* reported that Vida was refused the opportunity to refute them.[13] In her previous campaigns she had enjoyed extensive press coverage, primarily because she was a woman candidate. Now, in a two-way contest in which she had a good chance of winning, the papers strongly supported her opponent.

Nevertheless her opponents did not discount her chance of election. The Liberal Party told its adherents not to be complacent about Vida's candidature and called on all supporters to vote. The *Age* told its readers to vote for Best and warned against apathy: 'The very strength of the hold which Sir Robert Best has of Kooyong is practically his only danger of losing it' and reminded electors that 'Kooyong has furnished more surprise to political prophets than any other part of Victoria in recent years'.[14] This probably referred to the fact that in her Senate campaigns Vida's best result for a city electorate had been in Kooyong.

Vida published an open letter to electors:

No stone is being left unturned to induce you to vote against me — because I am a woman, because I am a non-party politician, because I am a progressive politician, because I defend the Suffragettes. It is for these very reasons I urge you to vote for me... do not condemn me unheard. Read what I have to say to you, come to my meetings, write to me... cast a *thinking* vote, a conscientious vote!

She also tried to counter the objections to her becoming a member of Parliament. Electors could not see how a non-party system of government would work. She said that party politics was out of date and that women were bringing a new element into politics: 'the home element; all the qualities of honesty, purity, principle and love, which make our homes centres of happiness, and order and good government'.[15]

As election day drew closer Vida increased her speaking

engagements. Despite minimal press coverage, people came from far and wide to hear her. The final rally was at the Hawthorn Town Hall; it seated 1200 people and was the largest in the electorate. The Hawthorn Hall, seating 600, was used for the overflow. This too proved inadequate and a further overflow had to be accommodated on a vacant allotment. When Vida left the Town Hall to speak at the Hall, the Town Hall filled with a second audience and so Vida had to return and deliver her address for the third time. This was followed by a 'phenomenal demonstration' at the railway station. All this went unreported in the daily papers.[16]

On polling day there was another innovation—women scrutineers in Kooyong. The Labor Party had used a few women scrutineers before, but Vida had a large number of women acting for her in an honorary capacity. In a few booths 'extreme discourtesy' was shown to these women, to demonstrate disapproval of their presence, but overall the women won praise for their efficiency.[17] When counting began, the candidates waited inside the hall. It was pouring rain and a small group of Vida's supporters stood outside, under a verandah, waiting for the results to be posted. The first notice to go up showed Sir Robert Best was 500 votes in front. Slowly the little group melted into the night.[18] Despite the months of planning, organisation and hard work, and the increased involvement of WPA members, Vida had been defeated once more.

◆ ◆ ◆

The final results were Goldstein 11 540 and Best 18 777. The Liberal Party had won government by one seat, but Labor maintained its majority in the Senate. It was unlikely that the Parliament would run a full term and the WPA was determined to continue its efforts. At the declaration of the poll Best thanked Vida for the 'courtesy and good feeling she had displayed in the contest', which he believed he had reciprocated. Vida replied:

> I heartily congratulate Sir Robert Best on his victory; but, while he won, and with a very large majority, we were not defeated. We have simply passed another milestone on the road to justice. There is no retrogression, no defeat in justice; it is progress, progress all the way, and our seeming defeats are a series of victories. I use naturally the collective 'we' and 'our', for I did not contest Kooyong as an individual. I happened to be the representative of all that we mean by the 'woman movement'. It is my

privilege to represent the pioneers who won the vote for the women of Australia. It is my privilege also to represent those who are pioneering the way for the women of the future, the women who will be free in the spirit as well as in the letter. In pioneering the way for the women of the future, we are also pioneering the way for the men of the future, for the men born of women free in mind and spirit will be even greater than the great men of the past.

She favoured a system of proportional representation where each constituency would have several members. Under the present system the 11 540 people who had voted for her were not represented in Parliament.[19]

In assessing the campaign the *Woman Voter* admitted there had been an 'undercurrent of opposition' at the meetings but that the 'new note' struck by Vida—her skilful treatment of subjects ignored in the press and her fair dealing with every questioner—had impressed the constituents.[20]

On 5 June Vida addressed a meeting of 150 campaign workers. She believed their campaign had introduced a new element in politics of 'humanity yet of impersonality'. She had been delighted by the support she had received from young and old. She vowed to continue the fight.

Every day the necessity for sending women into Parliament is more apparent. Strenuous times are ahead of us, not only in our own movement, but in the wider human movement. We are helping to mould a national Australia. There are many who believe that Australia will only find herself as a nation through warfare, through a baptism of blood; but Miss Goldstein inclined to the belief that our national sentiment would emerge from a conflict of social and industrial forces, from a war fought on the fields of economics, politics and law. Women must be the peacemakers in that war, and the recent contest had shown them how they could fight for principles and yet bring peace and healing wherever they fought.[21]

Several men and women took part in the discussion of lessons to be learnt from the campaign and they stressed the need to increase the circulation of the *Woman Voter* to combat the press boycott.

In the *Woman Voter*, Vida assessed her third campaign.

What a glorious campaign it was! Something to remember for all time! Never has there been such a political campaign in Australia—enormous attendances at meetings which were strictly political from start to finish, with not a reference, personal or political, to our opponent by ourselves, nor permitted to good but sometimes overzealous supporters. We struck another blow for Freedom, Justice, Truth, Principle, and wherever we could reach people, either through meetings or through our hard-working, devoted canvassers, we had the majority of men and women with us.

I thought nothing could have been more interesting than my Senate campaigns in 1903 and 1910, but this campaign for the House of Representatives outrivalled the others in every respect. I have always been favoured with crowded meetings, but this time the numbers were phenomenal, and the many overflow meetings added to the general enthusiasm. In a Senate contest, when the whole State is polled as one electorate, a candidate flies from town to town, arrives late in the afternoon, speaks at night, leaves early the next morning, and has no opportunity of following up the good work done at the meeting. A non-party association like ours, boycotted by the press, cannot secure the necessary committees and canvassers in distant country towns, and when I consider the work done in this direction in Kooyong I marvel at my 51,000 votes in 1903 and my 54,000 in 1910, for a non-party candidate against whom were hurled all the forces of sex and party prejudice, misrepresentation and calumny...

At our meetings the audience, in the ultra-Conservative parts of a Conservative electorate, were cold and critical to begin with, but always I could feel the mental atmosphere warming up as I proceeded with my address, and my critics one by one began to see that women were not animated by sex antagonism in their desire to get into Parliament; that they had work to do there that no man nor any number of men could do for them.

When asked why she chose the conservative constituency of Kooyong when the WPA consisted of 'good democrats', Vida said that she had received the highest votes there in 1910, that women outnumbered men in Kooyong and that it provided a two-way contest between a conservative and a democratic candidate, without a Labor candidate to split the democratic vote. She had hoped to win the Labor vote, but her canvassers reported that much educative work was necessary to overcome the prejudice against women entering Parliament. Vida believed she had had more support from women in this campaign; men could not bring themselves to give her their only vote, whereas electors could choose several candidates for the Senate. She acknowledged that her task had been difficult because her opponent had been in public life for thirty years and was supported by the Liberal Party and the daily papers.[22]

Vida remained steadfastly non-party. Unable to attend the Congress of the International Woman Suffrage Alliance at Budapest at this time, she sent a message warning suffrage societies against allying themselves with political parties because she was convinced that when there was a conflict of interest it was inevitable that party, not the cause of women, would come first.[23]

A social evening was held on 2 August to honour Vida for her leadership and her election campaign. Cecilia John was one of the performers. She was a tall, strong woman who was to become Vida's closest friend for the next ten years. She had a magnificent contralto voice and had achieved some artistic success, but when forced to earn a living, she built and then ran a poultry farm. After Cecilia sang, there was a dialogue, written by Doris Kerr and performed by Lucy Paling, Cecilia John and Doris Hordern. Vida believed this witty piece showed that the stereotyped views of woman's sphere were being combated by the new spirit of womanhood in the WPA. Unfortunately it was not preserved. Bella Lavender, presenting a cheque to Vida from the members, gave a warm speech:

> having Miss Goldstein for once at her mercy, she would give free rein to her appreciation of their president and her work, which was an impossibility when Miss Goldstein was in the chair, as she always and persistently squashed personality, and pointed steadily and sternly to the 'cause'.

She spoke at length of Vida's qualities and every point was applauded. Vida responded with a few words and drew attention to the work of the pioneers. She averred that it was the bond of love and justice that united and motivated women from all walks of life in the Women's Political Association.[24]

Three days later, at the WPA club, an address was presented to Vida by the Kooyong electors, with a list of one hundred new subscribers to the *Woman Voter*. The tribute, in exquisite calligraphy, recorded that Vida 'offered to the people the wit and eloquence of an orator, the knowledge and foresight of a statesman, and the devotion and courage of a brave woman'.[25]

◆ ◆ ◆

In England the suffragettes had stepped up their attacks on property, which eventually caused a split between the Pankhursts and the

Pethick-Lawrences over methods. The Liberal Government passed what became known as the Cat and Mouse Act, whereby suffragettes on hunger-and-thirst strike were released from prison on medical grounds, but rearrested to complete their sentences when they had sufficiently recovered. Then in June 1913 came the news of Emily Wilding Davison's suicide. A first-class honours graduate from Oxford, she had been imprisoned many times in the suffrage cause and forcibly fed. When she barricaded herself in her cell she was hosed with icy water. She became convinced that 'now, as in days called uncivilised, the conscience of the people would awaken only to the sacrifice of a human life' and that only a death would achieve victory for the suffragettes. On Derby day she ran on to the course and threw herself at the King's horse. She was knocked to the ground and her skull was fractured. She died two days later without gaining consciousness.[26] The WPA passed a resolution recording 'its sense of reverence for the act of self-immolation' and sent a cable to the *Suffragette* which said, 'Place cross for Women's Political Association on Emily Davison's grave. She died that women may live'. Vida wrote, 'Brave Emily Davison! "How long, O Lord, how long" before the men of Great Britain heed her death petition against the wrongs of women?'.[27]

On 16 September the *Woman Voter*, in a statement bordered in mourning black, strongly championed the suffragettes. Henceforth most of the paper and all political work was to be devoted to the suffrage campaign. A Protest Fund was opened to help support the WSPU and Vida gave public lectures entitled 'The Truth About the Suffragettes'. On 10 October she spoke at Gisborne, outlining the history of the suffrage movement and relating the horrors being endured by the suffragettes. She held the large audience rapt, and 'many who come to scoff remained to pray'.[28] By deciding that an international issue would take precedence over issues at home, Vida opted to become an international feminist first, but her allegiance to the suffragettes placed her in a minority radical position and eventually led to a decline in membership of the WPA. She made this sacrifice for a principle. She could only help the suffragettes through publicising their cause and offering moral support. The money she could raise would be infinitesimal compared with the WSPU's funds.

Rose Scott wrote a letter to the *Woman Voter*, asking how Vida reconciled her opposition to compulsory military training and her defence of militant tactics in England. Vida was sorry to differ from 'our good friend', but 'we do not see any inconsistency... Militancy with the object of taking life, and militancy with the object of saving life, are very different things'.[29] Although Vida was to become one of the foremost peace activists during World War I, she never did see any inconsistency in her support of the suffragettes, even when they committed crimes against property. To her the suffragettes' fight was a holy campaign:

> Those who take the sword in the spirit of revenge against persons will perish by the sword; but those who hurl the sword, in passionate love for those oppressed and helpless, against intolerable conditions of living are hastening the day of human freedom.[30]

These eloquent words show her deep compassion and passionate defence of fundamental human rights, in particular the right to self-determination.

◆ ◆ ◆

Vida's friendship with the Pankhursts was also responsible for her adopting a higher public profile in relation to sexual issues. At a WPA meeting in September 1913, Vida read an article by Christabel Pankhurst on venereal disease. Christabel wrote that between 75 and 85 per cent of men were affected; they passed the disease on to their wives, who either became sterile, miscarried, or bore deformed or mentally defective children. As well, the women often had to undergo horrendous operations. Women's weakness was one argument used against giving women the vote: this was not natural weakness, but the result of gonorrhoea passed on by husbands. The suffrage would make women the equals of men and make the relationship between the sexes pure, because men would no longer treat women as slaves to be 'bought and soiled and degraded and then cast away'. Vida had considered whether the WPA should tackle the 'Red Plague', as VD was known. She realised it would open the WPA to 'abuse, misrepresentation, and calumny', but knew that would never deter the WPA members. The conspiracy of silence about VD was 'a hideous wrong to women and children'. Women must band together to fight for women and children, but not in bitter antagonism to men; the best men supported their crusade and the 'most abandoned men were the victims of wrong education, of low ideals, of no ideals; they would be glad to be free from their slavery'.[31]

In the same issue of the *Woman Voter*, it was reported that the

Bishop of Riverina had blamed 'race suicide' (the declining birthrate) on the New Woman, who displayed 'an inordinate love of pleasure, rivalry in display, and wilful shirking of responsibilities'. This was the same argument Dr James Barrett had used in 1901 and which Vida had addressed in the *Woman's Sphere*. Vida now asserted that venereal disease was largely responsible for the declining birthrate. She also believed that 'with self-respecting men and women, quality rather than quantity is the determining factor in deciding on the number of their family'.[32]

The WPA monitored the progress of the Age of Consent Bill which would raise the age from sixteen to eighteen. The WPA wanted the age to be twenty-one, the same as property rights, but was prepared to support the Bill as an interim measure. Vida wanted to debate the issue with Walter Manifold, MLC, but he declined, saying that he could not discuss it with her or any other young lady. Vida was now forty-four and had been competently discussing sexual issues for a quarter of a century.

An *Argus* editorial supported Manifold's refusal, arguing that civilisation had (rightly) erected a set of barriers around all questions affecting sex to protect the moral life of the community and prevent the worship of 'the great goddess Lubricity'. The women who criticised Mr Manifold did not represent the community and 'though their constituency is so small, their wisdom might have been larger... They call themselves "advanced", but they are not really advanced, they are merely unmarried'. They were too young to have learned that 'perfect frankness is quite impossible in a civilisation that has learned to use clothes'. The suffragette may thoughtlessly break down the barriers that protect juveniles and 'introduce a frankness that is an open door to lubricity'. The pressing sex problems of the day should be discussed in private and only with the same sex.

> The unmarried women whose minds are obsessed with this morbid 'sex antagonism' must get their minds cleansed from this perilous stuff before they can help at all ... They are steadily souring their own natures... The 'emancipated' girl has been heard attempting to discuss the 'white slave traffic' with a male acquaintance whom she meets in the train. That will not stop the 'traffic', but it is an unspeakably dangerous thing both for the 'emancipated' girl and her friends ... their minds are quite unhealthy — one might almost say diseased ... If one of the consequences of broadening the suffrage is to be that some women are to be given the right

to indulge a taste for discussing with men in public questions which healthy-minded women would shrink from talking about even among themselves, then we will be confronted with one of the most sinister developments in public and social affairs that it is possible to conceive.[33]

This contemptible piece shows the entrenched patriarchal attitudes Vida had to contend with: that a virtuous woman could not be interested in sexual matters and that an unmarried woman was an affront to society, either to be pitied for not having a partner or condemned as unnatural for threatening the status quo by rejecting the institution of marriage. Vida courageously challenged these prejudices.

The *Woman Voter* retorted that the result of such ideas and the advocacy of reticence was that 80 per cent of men had venereal disease.

> Therefore, we say the day for the removal of the barrier has arrived, and no longer will woman be relegated to the boudoir as the plaything of the wealthy man, or to the kitchen as the slave of the poor man; but will stand by his side ready to face these sex questions as belonging not to half, but to the whole race.
>
> We conceive true manliness to be a quality that in its fundamentals is equal to that of true womanliness, and the true man or true woman must have a wider horizon than that bounded by sex, and seek the good of the whole race if either is to lay claim to manliness or womanliness.[34]

Ignoring the *Argus* and its aspersions about their minds and natures, the WPA convened a conference of delegates from various reform societies to consider the Age of Consent Bill, which 'had been seriously mutilated in its passage through both Houses'.[35] Vida presided and Mary Fullerton read the main paper.

◆ ◆ ◆

The work to recruit members continued and the WPA decided to attract publicity by entering a boat and setting up a barrow at the Henley Regatta. Doris Hordern, who had worked as Vida's campaign secretary and was still working for the WPA, wrote to her future husband Maurice Blackburn that the clubrooms were full of 'enthusiastic folk' preparing for it. She was glad to have an excuse to 'keep me off that barrow; but I do feel a mingy sneak you know—for none of them like it anymore than I do and only do it from a sense of duty'.[36] For many of the members such a public profile was something they were not used to or necessarily comfortable with, but their loyalty to Vida and their commitment to the goals of the WPA helped them overcome their reluctance. The WPA created a sensation, but not in the way it had intended. The barrow was decorated with lattice work in the WPA colours and draped with bunting and posters of the *Woman Voter* and the WPA. There were many remarks from bystanders about the boat being 'manned' by women and when the cry of 'Suffragettes!' was raised, the crew bowed and smiled acknowledgements. Suddenly a lantern caught fire and in no time the WPA decorations were blazing. The women managed to extinguish the fire before the police boat arrived.[37]

Early in November, Vida and Cecilia John went to Gippsland and addressed several meetings arranged by the Bairnsdale branch of the WPA. A new branch was formed at Paynesville and copies of the *Woman Voter* were at a premium—some sold for a shilling each instead of the usual penny. In Bairnsdale when Vida gave her 'The Truth About the Suffragettes' talk, it was reported that one man refused to attend because 'Miss Goldstein was one of those dangerous, persuasive women'. They then motored to Orbost, taking twelve hours to cover the sixty miles of rough bush track. Vida spoke to a full house and managed to convince many of the need for the suffragettes' militancy.[38]

Vida then worked in Adelaide for three weeks for the Women's Non-Party Political Association of South Australia. It was her first visit in five years. She was the guest of the president, Lucy Morice, the niece of Catherine Spence. Vida had successful meetings, many new members joined and the papers vied with each other to write leaders on non-party politics, the woman's movement and issues such as the divorce laws. This was especially pleasing after the Victorian newspapers' lack of coverage of her campaign.[39]

Vida continued to campaign for equal pay. In July 1913 she presided at a monster meeting of women's societies on equal pay. An example of the inequities faced by women was the plight of female teachers. In 1883 they had four-fifths of a man's salary, but they were now reduced to half. After forty-two years' service, with an unblemished record, a female teacher received £250 a year—a salary which a man received after only eight years service. This woman would have responsibility for more than 300 infants, plus the supervision of needlework throughout the school, and have to train one assistant and five juniors. A man on the same level earned £320, taught eighth grade with less than forty pupils and had no junior teacher to train.[40]

Now, when the Sixth Class Lady Teachers' Association started campaigning for restoration of their four-fifths of a man's pay, Vida condemned it as a 'tactical mistake'.[41] She found it particularly galling that they were campaigning on anything less than equality when the suffragettes were suffering so much for equality. She also called for the employment of married female teachers and an end to the regulation in the 1889 Public Service Act that forced women to resign when they married.

Maurice Blackburn suggested that instead of campaigning for equal pay Vida should work for a legal minimum wage for women not covered by the wages board. When Vida refused to consider the idea, he told Doris that Vida's motivation was 'sex antagonism [because] capital can be made out of the refusal to give equal pay and equal work. It can't out of the other'. Doris agreed there was a 'growth of sex antagonism' in the WPA, but the leaders were 'in deadly earnest ... even if they do not always act wisely or see clearly.[42] Doris was twenty years younger than Vida and sometimes chafed at the Goldsteins' protectiveness. On one occasion Doris made inquiries about another job. They found out and Aileen Goldstein made remarks to Doris which she called 'cheek'. Doris wrote to Maurice, 'Funny is'nt [sic] it, how these folks make our business theirs and are so deeply interested in us. I suppose it amuses them, and we ought not to mind'.[43]

Cecilia John was employed as Vida's secretary and then she became the WPA's business manager. Her friendship with Vida and her rapid rise in the WPA caused jealousy among some of the other members. Doris told Maurice how one member grumbled, 'When Miss John wants a thing there does not seem to be anything to do but to cave in'.[44] In the early days of the association, Vida had been astutely aware of keeping everyone working in harmony, but now she was more inclined to follow her own path. Doris privately voiced the concerns of some members.

> As to finances: The Club and Association are above water but the *Voter* is now in Miss John's entire charge; she undertook to manage it alone and if it is not paying she alone is to be held responsible. I don't think it was wise

to give such a large responsibility into the hands of one so new to the game as Miss John, do you? But it was by the vote of the executive that it was done, so nothing much can be said on the subject.[45]

Soon after the Christmas holidays the WPA resumed the Kooyong campaign. At Hawthorn, on 29 January, the women found that their 'pitch had been taken by swinging boats, ocean waves, and various other amusements, including a brass band, so that we felt we had a very small chance of being heard', but Bella Lavender and Jenny Baines, an early WSPU member who had emigrated to Australia on medical advice, were equal to the task and an excellent meeting was held.[46] Open-air meetings were resumed and new branches were formed, three in one week. In February, with Cecilia at the helm, the *Woman Voter* was enlarged, 'urged forward by the rapid increase of advertisements', and a direct cable service with the WSPU was introduced, as well as a column on gardening and a monthly column for girls. The WPA tea-rooms were refurbished and at-homes were held there every second Sunday.

This was probably the zenith of the WPA's fortunes, but the forces that would divide and fragment it were already surfacing. WPA members, including Lucy Paling, had misgivings about the direction Vida was taking. Doris Kerr and other members were 'annoyed' by the space devoted to the suffragettes in the *Woman Voter*. Maurice Blackburn commented that Vida had been 'so loyally helped by men [she] ought to be the last to lead a holy war of the sexes'.[47] The *Woman Voter* began to lose subscribers because of the suffragette campaign. One disgruntled subscriber called the campaign 'hysterical propaganda of a matter which is no business of yours', adding that there was enough work to be done in Australia and that the suffragette campaign was being conducted at the expense of the other seventeen items on the WPA platform.[48]

Undeterred, Vida pursued her chosen course and continued to make speeches on behalf of the suffragettes. The 17 March edition of the *Woman Voter* carried a horrendous account by Mary Richardson of forcible feeding. A poet and novelist, she had served several imprisonments, including one for arson of a deserted mansion and one for defacing the Rokeby *Venus*. She called on believers to pray at 9.30 a.m. and 4.30 p.m., the times of forcible feeding, that the women should be delivered from it speedily and that the nation should be forgiven for its torture of women. Describing her own experience, she told how she was forced down by as many as nine wardresses. Then the doctor entered:

> He introduces the tube cautiously into the nose, but then thrusts it with violence through the small nasal opening into the throat. This is where the laceration occurs and swelling—and the greater the swelling the more acute the agony.
>
> Then the tube, a yard long, is run through this nasal passage, down the throat into the stomach. Medicine or tonic is then administered from an opaque glass, so that you see nothing. Food is run through the tube, and, being rich and thick, it runs slowly. Struggling at this point is impossible, choking and coughing begin, and last spasmodically through the feeding. Tears stream from the corners of the eyes, though one is not crying voluntarily, and this pain and injury to the eyes alone is a fine torture apart from all other things.
>
> After the feeding the doctor removes the tube by two vigorous jerks, that seem as if they were splitting the face in half.

This hideous torture was being inflicted on Vida's friends. It is no wonder she remained true to their militancy and supported their efforts, even if it adversely affected WPA membership and her electoral chances.

The WPA did gain a new member at this time: Adela Pankhurst, the youngest daughter of Emmeline Pankhurst. Adela had begun militant campaigning for the suffrage while still a teenager and had been jailed many times. Now aged twenty-six, Adela had been banished from England by her mother. The reasons are unclear, but she said her sister Christabel became jealous of her successes as a speaker. Adela was sent to Australia with £20 and no plans. She later wrote that she often wondered what her mother had thought she would do, once the money was spent. 'I knew nothing of the country and neither did she. My problem was solved by Miss Goldstein who persuaded me that my banishment from the movement did not extend to Australia.'[49] She was greeted in Melbourne by cheering suffragists and was soon involved with the WPA. She was probably paid by the WPA. She lectured in Adelaide on the 'Woman Movement' and was well received.

Adela was short and lithe, with fine long hair which would work loose when she spoke at meetings.[50] A new element had entered feminist politics in Australia in the guise of the 'untidy' English suffragette. When interviewed by Freda Sternberg for the magazine *Lone Hand*, she was asked 'Why do you bite policemen?'. Adela replied that militancy was the result of the treatment of the suffragettes. 'If we had been men we would have killed them long ago.' Readers were assured that 'there was no trace of the ogre' about Adela, that she looked 'essentially feminine' and managed to 'retain an old-world charm and aloofness that was part of the days when women were but women—the wives and mothers of the world, but still, only women'. Adela said that Australian women did not value the vote because they got it so easily and could not understand what it was like in England. The article, entitled 'The Militant Suffragettes', included photos of the Pankhursts, Emmeline Pethick-Lawrence, Annie Kenney—and Vida.[51]

◆ ◆ ◆

On 5 June 1914 a double dissolution of Parliament was announced; the election was called for 5 September. The WPA immediately rallied to support Vida in her fourth election campaign—the second for Kooyong. There were many open-air meetings, usually with Lucy Paling, Jenny Baines and Kate Flynn as speakers. Bella Lavender and Mabel Singleton spoke at and sometimes chaired meetings, while Vida concentrated on women-only meetings, public meetings and at-homes. Adela Pankhurst was also a prominent speaker. By July Vida was speaking almost every day except Sunday. Usually her afternoon meetings were for women only and the topic often was 'The White Slave Traffic and Assaults on Children'. Sir Robert Best renominated and an Independent Liberal, E. W. Terry, also nominated. The *Age* predicted that Vida 'should have a reasonable chance of success' because there were three candidates.[52] The *Argus* accused her of trying to split the Liberal vote.[53]

Vida opened her campaign on 23 July in the Hawthorn Town Hall. It was full, with almost equal numbers of men and women. Introduced by Mabel Singleton, Vida was greeted with loud applause.

> Quietly, but in words so warm as to touch the heart, the women's candidate declared for a political policy which would ensure national purity. All true women were mothers at heart, and [she] proved it by her tender pleading for little boys and girls whom the law allows to enter the holy bonds of matrimony when they should be at play.

She spoke of the duty enfranchised women owed to the native women and children. Candidates are not apt to talk much about those who cannot repay them by votes, so that Miss Goldstein's plea for these most helpless of all victims of a cruel oppression, with her championship of children, the Suffragettes, and the voteless boys under military rule, has awakened the mirth of her opponents. She has not got a programme at all, they say! No politician, in their sense of the word, puts justice and the rights of the helpless in the forefront of their campaign.

The audience appreciated Vida's unique programme. One man shouted out, 'You'll get my vote' and this was met with applause. Nobody wanted to leave and even after the meeting closed people lingered on.[54]

Vida's policies were basically those of her 1913 campaign, with the addition of preference to unionists for employment[55] and the abolition of compulsory military training. It was decided that Vida would ask women to vote at her meetings on compulsory military training of boys under twenty-one. The members of the WPA were free to decide for themselves as it was not a WPA platform, but there was an 'increasing feeling of uneasiness' among members about it.[56] At one meeting, when the vote went in favour of it, Vida said her objection to it was 'mainly the moral danger of camp life to boys'.[57]

On 4 August 1914 Britain declared war on Germany. The previous day, the Australian Government had promised troops and warships to support the British in the event of war. The election campaign continued against a background of war fervour. In this atmosphere, Vida's opposition to compulsory military training would lose her votes, but the WPA continued to campaign vigorously, full of hope that this time Vida would be elected.

The AWNL was again supporting Sir Robert Best. Vida published replies to their assertions that a Labor Government would take children away from their parents and that Labor would nationlise everything and dispossess everybody. For the first time in a campaign, however, Vida won the support of some individual party women. Members of the AWNL and the Labor Party openly supported her. A letter from Ella Gavan Duffy enclosing a donation said:

> As you know, I am not in sympathy with you in your advocacy of certain planks—preference to unionists, abolition of military training etc—but for many reasons I have come to think I have strained at a gnat while cheerfully swallowing a camel. As far as I can see, women and children

have nothing to hope for from manmade legislation, and there are evils which shriek to high heaven for redress, and it is increasingly clear that only women will deal with them.[58]

The *Socialist* also supported her. In the pre-election issue the editorial called Vida a 'brave and gifted lady', who spoke on issues 'with clarity, wisdom and vision'. Vida had proven herself a 'priestess and prophet in the big and best sense of the terms as symbolising fundamental knowledge, living enthusiasm and flaming sincerity'. The socialists would like to see her in Parliament 'as an assertion of the right of womanhood to be there; and we also know that she would be a prominent and useful figure in a gathering of chiefly male mugwumps'.[59]

The canvassers reported the main objections to voting for Vida: though the reforms she advocated were needed, one woman alone could not do anything to secure them; women could do more for morality by staying at home and training their children properly; and women should concentrate on State politics (where they could not stand for election) and leave the Federal Parliament. Vida did her best to counter the prejudice, but failed to acknowledge the difficulties of being an independent in a party system, because she optimistically thought that the party system would fade away.

The *Woman Voter* called on voters to support Vida 'for the sake of womanhood'.[60] Twelve years after her first campaign, it was still necessary to prove that she was a fitting representative of women. It published a glowing report from the *St Arnaud Mercury* which noted that even though Vida had been in the public arena for nearly twenty years 'you would not think it to look at her. She is still as bright, vivacious, and full of practical ideas, as she was when she was making her way to the front'. One only had to listen to her speak to note that 'public speaking and general public activities do not necessarily rob womanhood of its bloom and charm'.[61] The pre-election edition of the *Woman Voter* called on women to support Vida and to give a woman a chance.

> It is hard to put wrong things right, all women know, but if this [war] is the best men can do, women cannot make more fatal mistakes ...
>
> At this moment, when greed and brutality seems to be the strongest force in the world, women can stand firm for peace and love by sending into the House of Representatives their own representative to voice those great principles there.[62]

Vida's campaign committee had organised more and better canvassing and covered a wider area than the previous campaign. The campaign committee called for 150 honorary scrutineers for election day and for motor cars to convey electors to booths. Despite their best efforts, Best's cars outnumbered theirs twelve to one.

Vida polled less than the previous year, even with a slightly larger number of voters in the electorate. She had lost votes to the Independent Liberal. The figures were: Goldstein 10 264; Best 18 545 and Terry 2420. The Labor Party had won government with substantial majorities in both Houses. One Independent had been elected. The *Woman Voter* concluded, 'More courage, more devotion, more sacrifice is needed'. It believed Best's increased majority could be attributed to the 'wave of militarism which is passing over the civilised world', whereas Vida had been the only candidate to make a stand for the principles of international peace.[63] A meeting of supporters was organised to discuss the next campaign.

Adela Pankhurst's assessment of the election was that the issues were 'utterly trivial', the AWNL ladies merely adorned the platforms or read from well-thumbed speeches 'only too obviously written in the *Argus* office' and the Labor Party's campaign was uninspiring. Best's meetings were usually empty, 'for his speeches were too dull for endurance', yet the electorate voted for him. Adela concluded Kooyong was hard for a progressive to win, because most of the electors were owners of small property, caught between high wages and the high cost of living. Women in Kooyong saw politics as a 'bread and butter question' and they voted for Best out of self-interest.[64]

In her analysis of her defeat Vida commented on several factors which had cost her votes: the entry of another Independent, which allowed 'sex prejudice' to triumph in the non-Liberal vote; the disenfranchisement of about 2000 working men and women who were removed from the rolls because they had moved, although they were still living within the electorate; her campaign against compulsory military training and war; her campaign for the suffragettes and her policy of preference to unionists. She believed the majority of her votes were from women and that the WPA was succeeding in reaching women through its meetings and the *Woman Voter*. She vowed to resume work at once and to reach every woman in the constituency. She declared, 'In spite of defeat, the victory is already ours'.[65]

At the declaration of the poll, watched by 'half a dozen adults ... six or seven small and curious boys and two dogs',[66] Best was angry about the allegation that the Liberals had set out to remove the names of working men and women from the rolls. The WPA had resolved to ask the government to inquire into the matter.[67] Vida replied that the WPA was not complaining about individuals but about the law which allowed this disenfranchisement, and added that she did not want any ill feeling over the campaign, which she thought had been a 'great moral victory' for her.

The election campaign over, Vida now faced a new battle—the fight for peace, in a war-mad country intent on achieving nationhood through bloodletting, and the fight to retain individual freedoms of speech and assembly when wartime measures promoted their suppression.

9

Casualties of war
1914–1915

◆

The outbreak of World War I was greeted with fervent patriotism by most Australians, accompanied by a corresponding vilification of all Germans and everything German in war propaganda, recruiting rallies and pro-conscription meetings. People with German-sounding names or connections were persecuted and towns were renamed. People playing German music were assaulted and pianos with German trade names were smashed. Even dachshunds, or their owners, were attacked. Volunteers flocked to recruitment centres. Such was the enthusiasm that young men lied about their ages or forged their parents' signatures on permission forms to enable them to enlist. In this atmosphere, pacifists were considered unpatriotic, even traitorous. Vida was passionately committed to international peace, a position which would bring her into conflict with many of her friends and colleagues.

Vida's response to the declaration of war was reported in the *Herald*.

> I think that it is a fearful reflection on 2000 years of Christianity that men have rushed into war before using every combined effort to prevent this appalling conflict. It is my earnest hope that women in all parts of the world will stand together, demanding a more reasonable and civilised way of dealing with international disputes.
>
> The time has come for women to show that they, as givers of life, refuse to give their sons as material for slaughter, and that they recognise that human life must be the first consideration of nations.[1]

The Federal Government quickly enacted the War Precautions Act. Ostensibly to ensure national security in wartime, it also allowed the abuse of individual liberties. Vida was determined to ensure that these were not eroded; the first that came to her attention was the freedom of the press. Under the War Precautions Act, all copy had to be submitted to the censor before publication. The authorities told Vida that the *Woman Voter*'s issues of 25 August and 2 September contained prohibited material and that she must promise not to offend again. Vida asked the censor whether it was permissible to plead for love and peace. A man from the censor's office was sent to see her. He reiterated that it was forbidden to print anything which might deter military enthusiasm, but Vida insisted on her right, in a Christian country, to publish the ten commandments, including 'Thou shalt not kill'. She agreed to abide by the guidelines about not reporting shipping and cargo movements, but refused to stop talking of love and peace.[2]

The next week, when Vida and Cecilia went to the printers to make up the *Woman Voter*, they were 'greeted by an armed guard, with fixed bayonets, a commanding officer, an officer in mufti, and a detective!'. The men threatened to seize the paper and the printers' plant. When Vida told them she would report this incident in the next issue, more police were called for. The men tried to make Vida promise not to publish anything about their actions. Vida ordered the printers to make up the paper 'in the cause of civil liberty and the freedom of the press'. As soon as the proofs were prepared, Cecilia, accompanied by an armed guard, took them to the censor's office. The censor ruled out a report on the attempts to prohibit Vida publishing, a brief appeal to mothers and a quote from Ruskin. The metal containing the censored material had to be destroyed and the proofs were torn into tiny pieces.

Vida was forbidden to indicate that the paper had been censored, so she published the *Woman Voter* with blank spaces where the material had been censored. The censor could not prohibit a blank space. In the next issue, she attempted to publish another account of events, but this was also censored. The newly elected Fisher Government took office at this time, so Vida arranged a deputation to protest about this censorship. The deputation was assured that it was not the intention of a Labor Government to interfere with peace propaganda. Vida had won the first round in the fight for freedom of speech and freedom of the press.[3]

There was, however, nothing she could do about the invasion of privacy condoned by the War Precautions Act in the name of national security. In a vigilant search for spies, patriots were called on to report suspicious people and events to the military police. Great dossiers were compiled on all the prominent pacifists, like Vida and her friends, as well as on many ordinary citizens. The censor read and withheld mail and the military police sent shorthand writers to meetings which might pose a threat to the war effort and recruiting, but as they only had two reliable people available, they were unable to attend every meeting and soon became well known.[4] Despite the paranoia, not one spy was discovered in Australia during the war.

Lucy Paling, a prominent WPA member, and her family were investigated by the authorities. In December 1914 an unsigned note was sent to the military police saying that the Palings' landlady was being paid extra rent to ensure they were not disturbed. It said the flat was not furnished and no one was allowed to go near it. The back of the flat commanded a full view of Port Phillip Bay and was a good place for a wireless. It was assumed the Palings were Prussians and 'their actions have aroused suspicions'.[5] The report was followed up; the police discovered the Palings were in fact Belgian (an allied country) and that the house was run by an ex-constable. It was, however, noted that Lucy had been expelled from the Australian Women's National League for 'pro-German utterances'.[6]

In October 1916, at the height of the first conscription campaign, a scrap of paper was sent to the military police by Captain Anderson, who lived below the Palings. He said he had found it in their backyard. It measured 1 × 3 inches and read:

> If you should use the code given in the little...
> And they will send you, it is American...
> a copy of my code barstop.

Captain Anderson said he could 'always tell when there has been a German victory a few days before it appears in the papers, because they have a great jollification (they play the piano and consume a quantity of liquor)'. No action was taken, but the surveillance continued.[7]

Vida, Cecilia and Adela were all under surveillance, as was the *Woman Voter*, which was under 'strict supervision'.[8] Their mail was read and some of their letters were withheld.[9]

◆ ◆ ◆

War fervour was now so intense that it took great courage to sell the *Woman Voter* in the streets. May Brodney, wrote of one experience early in the war when she and Rachel Helsy were selling the paper. An angry crowd gathered around them, incensed by their poster, which said 'Germany Wants Peace'. The poster was torn down and people tried to snatch their papers. May's companion, a seasoned suffragette although only nineteen, told her to drop her papers and run, but May refused to do that and the women were attacked by the crowd, which 'behaved more like wild animals than human beings'. The police arrived but seemed annoyed at the women for disrupting peak-hour traffic. May managed to save her papers.[10]

In October the *Woman Voter* announced that the WPA's wartime contribution would not be an appeal for funds to relieve distress because others could do that work better. Rather, the WPA would offer its 'priceless gift of knowledge'. The *Woman Voter* dared tell the truth and this would convert the public to the side of peace.[11] At Vida's instigation, the WPA pledged to begin an educative campaign to promote international peace and arbitration. Vida still made time for her other commitments, but she was convinced that working for peace had to come first because this was the linchpin: war destroyed families and took life; what use then was equal pay, custody rights or increasing the age of consent?

Some of her readers implored Vida to desist from her peace stance and criticism of warmongers, but she firmly asserted that even if the WPA lost every member and the *Woman Voter* every reader, she could do nothing differently.[12] Some WPA members did resign and so, on 26 October, a meeting was held to decide whether the WPA should become anti-militarist and anti-conscriptionist. After heated debate the meeting was adjourned. Hilda Moody and Doris Kerr resigned as secretary and treasurer because they were opposed to the anti-war campaign.[13] Doris Hordern wrote that they resigned 'because when the question of a peace campaign was voted on and negatived by 3 to 2 the opinion of the majority was put aside'.[14] They were the first casualties in Vida's fight for peace.

At the subsequent meeting, several amendments, aimed at postponing the decision until the annual general meeting, were ruled out of order by Vida in the chair. The meeting finally voted 22 : 8 to add 'Opposition to Compulsory Military Training and Militarism' to the WPA's platform. Readers and members were invited to send in a vote on the issue, but this proved inconclusive (41 voted Yes to anti-militarism and 33 No; another 6 Noes were disallowed for being late).[15] The voting shows the divisiveness of the issue, but the peremptory way in which Vida dealt with it indicates her commitment to it. The WPA had managed to survive as a non-party association, but it could not accommodate Vida's pacifism and those who supported the war.

At the general business meeting held to fill the vacancies on the committee, Cecilia John was elected financial secretary and Adela Pankhurst organising secretary. Meetings held in December instituted a new method of governing the WPA. All members were to be involved in organisation and finance, working as a committee 'taking the full responsibility upon themselves of providing the sinews of war, and running the activities of the Association on sound business lines'.[16]

The second casualties were the WSPU and Emmeline and Christabel Pankhurst. When the WSPU announced it would suspend its activities for the duration of the war and support the war effort, Vida immediately dissociated herself from it.

> From the first we have stood by the Suffragettes because they have put justice and the sacredness of human life before everything else, because they were fighting the cause of emancipated womanhood throughout the world.
>
> It is extremely painful to us, after nine years of the closest sympathy with Miss [Christabel] Pankhurst, to find ourselves ranged in opposition to her over the war ... Miss Pankhurst blames Germany alone. We blame the war parties, the secret diplomacy, the armament firms, the newspapers of all nations ... [We] maintain that the women of all nations should unite in demanding arbitration here and now.[17]

Pacifists realised it was vital to organise in order to counter the increasing militarism pervading the country. Many new peace organisations were formed and Vida was prominent in this process. She formed her own pacifist association and later chaired the first meeting of the Australian Peace Alliance, which was established to affiliate all the peace groups.

Vida knew that some pacifists would not join the WPA because of its non-party politics, so she decided to form the Women's Peace Army which would be closely connected with the WPA, but devoted solely to peace propaganda. The new association was to be 'a fighting body, and would fight for the destruction of militarism with the same spirit of self-sacrifice as soldiers showed on the battlefield'. Eighty 'peace soldiers' enlisted at the first meeting on 8 July 1915.[18] At the next meeting it passed resolutions which opposed the use of women to support war. It protested against the War Census as a forerunner of conscription, proposed co-operation with the 'Stop the War' committee in England, and supported the principle that governments which used women to replace men in the workforce should pay them equal wages.[19]

The objects of the Women's Peace Army were similar to those of the Sisterhood of Peace which had been formed in March 1915 by the Reverend Charles Strong at the Australian Church. Some people were members of both groups, including Lucy Paling, who was the first president of the Sisterhood of Peace. Eleanor Moore, one of the Sisterhood's corresponding secretaries, later wrote that where the two groups differed was in 'tone'.

> In wartime... when the public is excited and revengeful and Government censorship is severe, the way a thing is said matters as much as the contents of the saying. Sometimes it matters more. When public opinion is inflamed, there are two ways of seeking to influence it. One is to be provocative, taking the risk of reprisals, in the hope of making converts on the recoil. The other is called educational. It studies to avoid the particular phrase which will irritate listeners, and tries rather to draw them into discussion based on propositions with which, at the outset, all will agree. Inevitably, followers of the first method will incline to think of the second as timid, and 'playing safe, while the second type may think of the first as apt to mistake truculent assertion for convincing argument. There is a place for both, but they are better to work apart, especially at a time when a severe penalty may follow an unwise word. If one is to go to gaol for hindering recruiting... or to be ducked in the river by indignant men in uniform, it is something to know that the trouble springs from the assertion of one's own principle and not from the indiscretion of a colleague.[20]

The two groups did work together to celebrate the first conference of the International Committee of Women for Permanent Peace at the Hague in April 1915. The Hague conference resolved to meet again when the war ended, in the same place as the peace treaty negotiations would take place, and both groups decided they would send representatives to this conference. The International Committee later suggested the two groups merge, but the Sisterhood declined because of the groups' different methods; the Sisterhood had resolved not to actively oppose the current war, accepting that the nation was geared up to fight it, but was working quietly to gather support for action for peace after the war ended. This was not Vida's way; she would never accept that the status quo could not be changed once she saw a wrong that could be righted.

◆ ◆ ◆

Vida's main goal was to 'War on War', but she could never turn away from suffering and, within a month of writing in the *Woman Voter* that the Women's Political Association would leave charity work for others, she decided to investigate conditions of distress caused by the war. The war had caused a rise in unemployment and food prices, yet wages were frozen. On 4 December 1914 the WPA held a large open-air meeting to protest the 'unnecessary' rise in the price of bread. The *Woman Voter*'s message was 'Hands off the people's bread'.[21] This action attracted praise from unlikely quarters. Broken Hill's *Barrier Daily Truth* called Vida, Cecilia and Adela 'a brave and brilliant trio, fair, fearless and free' because they were not afraid to hold bread meetings on street corners and further praised them by saying that 'in their militancy they leave Labour women speakers far in the rear'. It added that years ago Barrier Labor would not have Miss Goldstein to visit because she was 'outside the fold'.[22]

The WPA also monitored the growing unemployment, especially among women. Vida wrote that when unemployment was mentioned, invariably it referred to male unemployment. For women, however, unemployment was 'a much more dangerous question' because it was assumed they were not breadwinners,[23] so there was minimal government, union or charitable support for them. Vida, maintaining the philosophy of the Charity Organisation Society that 'Charity is useless and harmful', decided to organise female workers into cooperatives from which they would draw all the profits.

There was no response to the *Woman Voter*'s appeal for work orders for the women, so in January WPA members approached the Lord Mayor's Unemployment Committee to ask how many women were registered. They were told there were none and that there were no facilities for women to enrol. The WPA then opened a register for employers and employees at its club rooms. Within a few weeks there were 200 names on the register and small donations were being sent in. At first this money was spent on food for starving families, but Vida believed that the money should be used to provide work. A workroom was set up in the club rooms and calls were made for work for the women. The *Woman Voter* remarked on the irony of society ladies being taught to knit socks and make shirts for soldiers at the Lady Mayoresses' League room, while across the street, in the WPA rooms, starving women were begging for work to feed and house their children.[24]

The *Herald* contributed £50 and arranged for baskets to be placed at the entrances of railway stations so that clothing could be left for those in need. This was collected by the Women's Political Association, the Crusade Clothing Club and the Australian Church Social Improvement Society. The *Woman Voter* reported: 'Some have been given the opportunity of re-clothing themselves almost entirely, Miss John giving them the finishing touch by knotting their new ties for them, and they have left our rooms with renewed hope in their hearts and increased self-respect as they surveyed their new attire'.[25] The collections were most successful, but without warning the *Herald* stopped them; the last collection was the largest with 1040 items.

The WPA was spending £4 to £6 a day on wages and relief. Adela wrote that the situation was worsening daily and that the only possible solution was for the people to take over certain industries and run them for the profit of the people.[26] These were radical—and unwelcome—ideas for many WPA members. Meetings were held with the director of the Government Labour Bureau and Margaret Cuthbertson, now the Chief Inspectress of Factories. The WPA put forward a detailed proposal to train unskilled women and provide work and relief for unemployed women. The aim was to employ 300 women for two days a week. The landlord at Arlington Chambers objected to his premises being used as a factory, so in March 1915 the WPA and the Women's Bureau moved into new rooms at 213–215 La Trobe Street, with offices on the ground floor and a factory on the first floor. The government had agreed to pay rent of £20 for one month but, after three weeks' fruitless searching, they were forced to take the building on a six-month lease (that being the minimum available) at £5 a week.[27]

The Women's Bureau provided work and a hot midday meal for

Vida persuaded some eminent women to join the foreign contingent of the WSPU's demonstration march of June 1911, including Margaret Fisher, the wife of the Australian Prime Minister and Emily McGowan, the wife of the Premier of New South Wales.

Vida, passionately concerned about the forcible feeding of the suffragettes, took the unprecedented step for a woman of standing in the streets selling *Votes For Women* to publicise their plight.

The great suffragette procession in London on 17 June 1911, led by suffragettes who had been imprisoned, was, with 40 000 people marching, the largest to that time.

The 'robust and ladylike girls at work' at the Women's Farm at Mordialloc are Rica Kirby (left) and Connie Gardiner.

Vida, campaigning in her 1913 bid for the House of Representatives seat of Kooyong, is accompanied by the Hordern sisters: Doris, Marjorie and Mollie. Lucy Paling is on Vida's left.

Vida spent the war years working for international peace and striving to alleviate the suffering at home. She and Cecilia John collected donated clothes for the *Herald* clothing fund for distribution from the Women's Political Association's rooms.

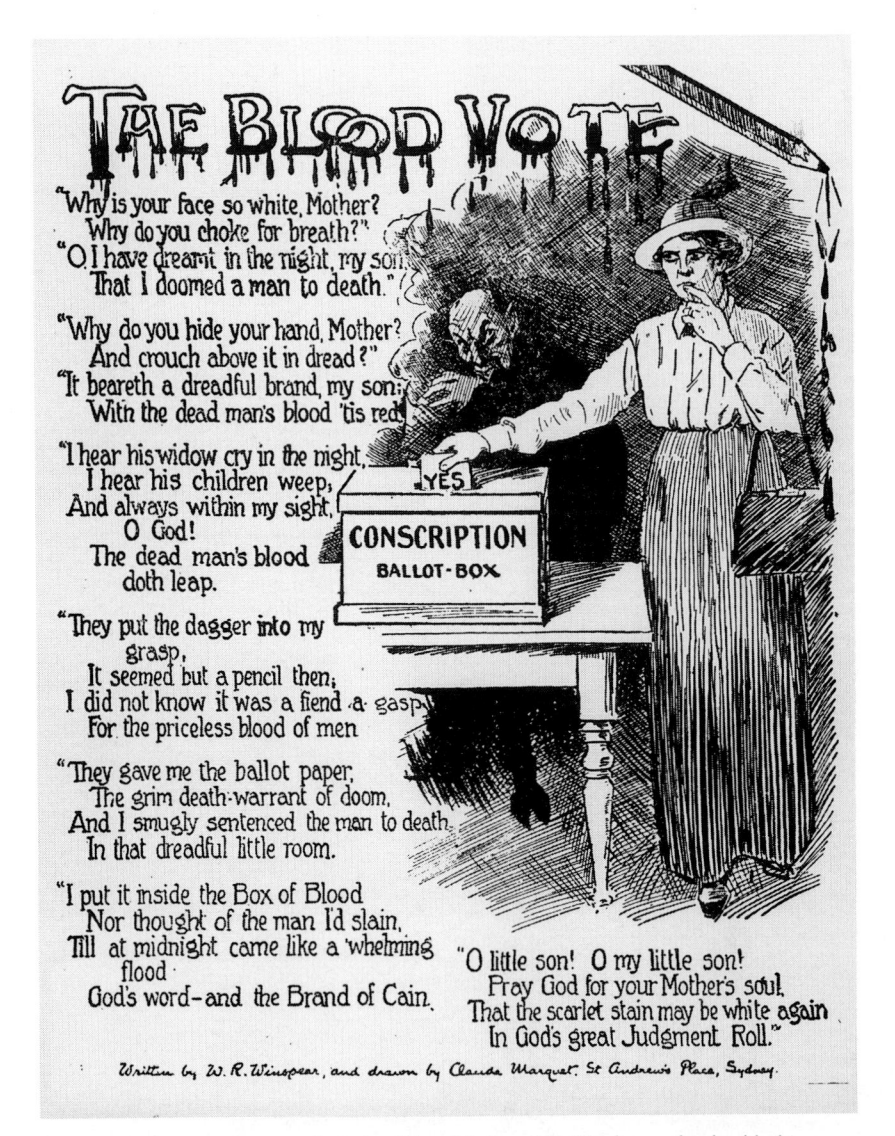

An anti-conscriptionist poster depicting Prime Minister Billy Hughes as the devil lurking behind the wavering voter

Vida in 1930—although disillusioned with the lack of progress in the social and political reforms she advocated, she continued to urge young people to become involved in politics and the women's movement.

Madeleine, the youngest child of Edith Gardiner, the Women's Political Association's vice-president, was given the role of leading the United Women's No-Conscription procession of 1916 in a deliberate choice to appeal to people's finer instincts.

The banned peace song 'I Didn't Raise My Son To Be a Soldier' was parodied by supporters of the war and adopted for this enlistment poster.

unemployed women and also organised lectures on domestic economy and the care of children. By May it was threatened with a withdrawal of government support. Vida appealed to the Central Unemployment Fund (mainly funded by unions) but was told that it was for men only and that the government should be responsible for the women. Despite this, she managed to obtain a further £50 from the fund.

The WPA held a sale of gifts and raised about £31, but on the three tables displaying the work of the unemployed women, only £8 was taken, with goods worth £40 unsold. The *Woman Voter* praised 'Our glorious band, the chosen few' who made goods and then bought them back themselves. It said the WPA managed to achieve so much because of such devotion. It also reported that large sums of money were being donated to the National Belgian Fund and that the distress of Belgium had so fascinated Australians that they were blind to suffering at home.[28]

The *Woman Voter* emphasised that the Women's Bureau money was kept separate from the WPA's funds; the government would not support a political organisation, and also the WPA wanted to show that its work was not duplicating the work of the Ladies' Benevolent Society. There was a growing antagonism between the two agencies, based on ideological and personal differences. True to COS philosophy, the WPA opposed handouts and only gave them when the LBS had refused the person relief. Vida and Cecilia investigated one case where the husband was unemployed and there were seven children. One child earned thirteen shillings a week and the family paid ten shillings rent. They interviewed the secretary of the LBS, who admitted she knew nothing of the case, adding there were so many needy cases. Vida said the name of the society was degrading (men did not have to apply to a Gentlemen's Benevolent Society) and many of its members were less than benevolent; one widow and her 9-year-old son were told by LBS members that one loaf of bread ought to last a week.[29] The WPA vice-president, Edith Gardiner, later recalled how unemployed women vowed to starve rather than apply to the LBS again. They were 'humiliated and shamed when the "ladies" opened drawers and cupboards to find some little not needed article, then said they weren't "deserving poor" '.[30]

The women at the Labour Bureau were 'greatly disturbed' when it was announced in the press that the government grant would be discontinued. They decided to form a deputation to Frederick

Hagelthorn, the Minister for Public Works, and invited the officers of the WPA to accompany them. Almost a hundred women assembled at the Bureau. Bearing a banner which read 'Unemployed Women Demand Work—Not Charity', they marched to the Public Works Department. The procession caused quite a sensation—it was a novelty to see women demonstrating in the streets.

Vida introduced the deputation to the Minister and then called on the speakers. In turn, the women told of their plight: they had sick or unemployed husbands, or were deserted or widowed; they had large families, were behind in the rent and their children were starving. For some, their sole income was the eight shillings a week they received at the Bureau. One woman paid 3s 6d rent, which left her 4s 6d for 'epicurean living'. The Minister replied that the government decision to put funds for the unemployed into public works at the Yarra Bank would provide work for married men and therefore help the women and children, as well as providing the State with a permanent legacy. Vida countered that the money the WPA was spending was going to produce healthy mothers and children, the 'best assets the country could have'. Hagelthorn retorted that Vida was helping 'a lot of old women who cannot do any good in learning a trade at their age' but Adela said only about 10 per cent of the women were older than fifty-five. The Minister was not convinced, but said he would consult the Premier. Eventually the Bureau received another £50. This was only a stopgap measure and the following week most of the women had to be dismissed.[31]

Vida was working feverishly and in one week joined five deputations, which reflect her wide range of concerns. The first was a deputation to the Central Unemployment Committee on 29 June 1915, asking for £50 a week to keep 150 families 'from destitution'. The case was also presented to the Lord Mayor's Unemployment Committee. The submissions were successful and the Bureau re-opened on 1 July with work for fifty women.

The next deputation was to the Chief Secretary, John Murray, asking for female police, jurors and magistrates, and a special department for the protection of women and children, as well as inquiries into the age of consent and the white slave trade. Murray replied that if women were to be police, they should take all the responsibilities of men, like fighting at Gallipoli. When the women asked why he was not at the front and added that women risked their lives in childbirth, he beat a hasty retreat from that line of argument.

Two days later, there was a deputation to the Victorian Parliament on the cost of living. The members, told of the impending deputation, had adjourned an hour and a half earlier than usual, but the deputation managed to 'catch' a few and presented to their 'astonished gaze' exhibits of groceries to illustrate the difference in purchasing power since the war. The price increases ranged from 80 to 150 per cent compared with the 17.8 per cent the government claimed. The deputation asked that women be on the Price of Goods Board and said that families earning less than £3 a week should be able to buy food at pre-war prices, with the difference subsidised by the government.

The final deputation was to the Minister of Defence requesting the appointment of women as military police. There was an increasing incidence of attacks on women by soldiers and the deputation argued that it would be easier for the victims if there were female military police to investigate these cases.[32]

The WPA had also bought land in Mordialloc to establish a women's farm. The philosophy was similar to the Leongatha Labour Colony which Vida's father had helped establish, but this venture was to be run as a company on co-operative lines. Registered as the Women's Rural Industries Co. Ltd, it was always known as the women's farm. Cecilia John and Ina Higgins were the WPA members most involved; Cecilia provided expertise in raising poultry and Ina in growing flowers and fruit. Fourteen acres were bought, a well was sunk and a windmill erected. The venture employed and trained girls and women, about six at a time, throughout the war.[33]

The farm progressed well and within a year had 24 acres under crop, in addition to rearing cattle and hundreds of white leghorns. The produce was sold at the WPA rooms and the farm was open to the public on Saturday afternoons. A reporter from the *Socialist* visited the farm and wrote that what caught the eye was 'the robust and ladylike girls at work ... who looked as intelligent and as healthful as it was possible to imagine'.[34] Two of these young women were Connie Gardiner (daughter of Edith Gardiner) and Rica Kirby. Connie's younger sister Madeleine recalled how she and Rica's young brother were allowed to stay for a few days at the farm. After the children had finished their chores, Cecilia told them to keep 'out of the way till tea-time'. The children played by the Mordialloc creek where a child had drowned the week before. Madeleine wrote that some time later at the WPA rooms

I was with Miss [Mollie] Hordern in the office, when we overheard a 'ding dong row' between my 5' 0" mother and the large tall Celie about this. At its height Vida passed us, and went into the other room, where she said firmly and chidingly, 'Children! Children!' Sudden silence, then my mother laughed and said 'Peace!' Then Celie laughed too. That was Vida.[35]

◆ ◆ ◆

In July 1915 Adela was appointed WPA delegate to the National Council of Women. She had been attracting unfavourable press, mainly for speaking against the war, but also for her WPA work. It was WPA policy to monitor court cases involving offences against women and to be available as friends and advisers for them. When Adela attended a case relating to offences against young girls, the *Argus* condemned her for being 'prurient'.[36] The *Argus* wrote editorials against her[37] and a reader suggested a ducking stool would be a good thing for her.[38] There was also antagonism between the WPA and some NCW members who were also members of the LBS. Some NCW members objected to Adela's appointment as a delegate, but under the constitution an affiliate could appoint delegates. A by-law was proposed that no one could become a delegate unless approved by the NCW. When Lucy Paling (a WPA delegate) tried to move an amendment against this she was told she could not speak or vote because the WPA was unfinancial. Lucy said the fees had been paid, but was told that, as the NCW treasurer was in Sydney, this could not be verified. Other organisations were permitted to pay and vote at the meeting.

Vida was present as an associate and claimed the right of the WPA's delegate to speak and vote. This was disallowed. According to the *Woman Voter* Lucy Paling 'put up a spirited fight against the Prussian methods of the Council, but there was no intention of showing justice or fairplay'.[39] The by-law was pushed through and Vida immediately challenged its legality, but the meeting was closed. Janet Strong resigned from the NCW in protest at the 'autocratic and unconstitutional way business was transacted by the Executive'.[40]

When the new by-law was used, to vote on whether to accept Adela as a delegate, Lucy Paling tried to move a motion against its propriety, but the chairman steamrolled the vote through. The vote went against accepting Adela as a delegate and forty delegates and associates walked out of the meeting in protest.[41]

At the next meeting, Lucy tried once more to move a motion on the issue, but was again ruled out of order. The *Argus* reported the exchange that followed:

> The President [Mrs McInerny] called for order and said, 'I will be forced to ask the constable to remove you'. (Uproar)
> Miss Vida Goldstein (angrily), 'The veriest criminal is heard in self-defence'.
> The President (sweetly), 'But Mrs Paling is not a criminal, is she?' (Laughter)
> Miss Goldstein (with more anger), 'Well you seem to think she is'. (Dissent)
> The President, 'It is very degrading to the council that an affiliated society can give such trouble'.

Vida, Lucy and their supporters then left 'among the hoots and hisses of the crowded meeting'. It was reported that Vida 'expressed her opinion of the National Council while cranking up her motor-car in Flinders Lane'.[42] Vida objected to the press coverage of the meeting, claiming it made the WPA women seem like 'hooligans of the most wicked type'.[43] The depiction of Vida being angry is unusual. Usually, in public at least, she was calm; people who knew her often mentioned her even temper and serenity. In the Palings' home, there was stress too; Lucy's husband was reportedly 'off his head with rage' when Lucy's name appeared in the papers associated with 'that woman', Adela Pankhurst.[44] This glimpse of domestic strain is a reminder that every woman fighting for the causes Vida espoused was bravely stepping beyond her sphere and confronting the issues in her personal life which this process created.

At the next NCW meeting Adela once more attempted to take her place as a delegate. When she signed the delegates' book, her name was crossed out by the person in charge, who also refused to conduct the meeting in Adela's presence. After a vote demanding that she leave, Adela rose and left. Vida had been the NCW delegate to America in 1902 and had been impressed even then by the NCW's platform of international peace, but the local NCW was patriotically pro-war and would not tolerate the pacifism of the WPA. Vida's peace stance, compounded by her differences with the LBS over the Women's Bureau, had led to another parting of the ways.

A few months later the breach was apparent in a *Woman Voter* article which scornfully reported a NCW recruiting rally where only men spoke.

> Two deplorable recitations were given, the first to the effect that mothers bring up their sons 'for the Empire', and not as members of the human family, and the second hysterically gloating over the broken life of a poor fellow cut off in the flower of his youth.

The article concluded that the 'only Australian women who understand the war sufficiently to speak about it in public are against it'.[45]

◆ ◆ ◆

In September 1915, citizens were required to complete a Wealth Card as part of the war effort. Vida used the occasion to explain her convictions:

> I furnish this information under protest, because it is asked for in the interests of war, which, I believe, is contrary to God's law of love and universal brotherhood, and is fought to retain or acquire territory and markets, which are wrung by the strong from the helpless peoples of the earth ... I believe that war should be fought and paid for by those who, believing in war, have incomes of and over £300 per annum. Those who have less are engaged in one long war against unjust social conditions, and I believe they should be exempt from any other compulsory national service than that of trying to obtain for themselves and their children the bare necessaries of life: good housing, good food, good clothing, good education, choice of occupation, recreation, amusement, books, holidays, and a competency for old age—so that they may not become a burden on the State.[46]

In fact lack of money for her work was once again causing Vida concern. The *Woman Voter* was in financial trouble and Vida appealed for support to prevent it becoming a fortnightly paper. It was losing readers and advertisers and Vida was being accused of being pro-German. Another constant problem was finding sufficient funds to keep the Women's Labour Bureau operating. The Central Unemployment Committee's provision of £35 a week was inadequate. A massed band concert raised £218. The *Woman Voter* reported there were 16 000 people present, but the well-to-do were absent.[47] The WPA started to document the living expenses of the poor, to prove they were living frugally, but in November the Unemployment Committee lowered its contribution to £15 a week. The committee was then disbanded because male unemployment had decreased; the State Government agreed to support the Women's Bureau.[48]

In March 1916 the government raised the grant to £45 a week, to offset the decline in donations being raised by the WPA. Vida said this was because when male unemployment fell the papers stopped reporting the problem, even though the women were still suffering, and consequently the donations had decreased. In May and June there was more debate in the papers about the Bureau. The main criticism was that the WPA was a political body and was using the Bureau premises for its meetings and to publish the *Woman Voter*. The *Argus* dubbed the WPA's work 'political charity'.[49] The WPA replied that it had paid all the rent until March, then used government money to pay for half of it, even though the Bureau occupied two-thirds of the site. The WPA believed that the unemployed women were the government's responsibility and it was therefore reluctant to do the work, but it could not stand by and watch women and children starve. It also stated that it had raised 45 per cent of its funds, compared with the LBS which had raised only 4 per cent.[50]

In July the government stopped the grant and promised to establish a similar bureau. In fact it provided a central office for the less controversial LBS, which offered charity doles to women who wanted work. In deference to Vida's arguments, special provision was to be made for 'ladies of refinement'; they were to be dealt with in such a way as to minimise any objection they might have to taking charity.[51] The acrimony between the WPA and the LBS was aired in the papers. LBS vice-president Mrs McInerny wrote to the *Argus* saying Vida had phoned her about a case in Collingwood which she had 'ferreted out', but it was an old LBS case. Mrs McInerny alleged that what the WPA called 'sewing employment' was in fact giving women material and eight shillings a day to sew it into garments for themselves. She considered this charity.[52] Vida replied that she had not ferreted out the case; the woman had appeared on the doorstep at six o'clock, as she was leaving for the night. She said the women were paid four shillings a day for two days' work a week and that they wanted work, not charity.[53] The WPA continued to do what it could for a few women, but it was now totally dependent on donations. It continued to help women obtain legal advice and pensions if they were eligible and Vida continued to appeal for relief work for the women in the *Age* and the *Woman Voter*. In the WPA's annual report for 1916, Vida wrote:

> We greatly regret that the strenuous work of the W.P.A. in its anti-militarist campaign prevents us from keeping the Government up to its duty to women who want work ... we demonstrated the most reasonable and advantageous methods of dealing with a pressing social problem, but it was, of course, only a palliative, and we could not give our lives to a palliative, since we wish to deal with the causes rather than with the effects of unemployment.[54]

Vida blamed the war for the increased unemployment and reduced living standards of the working class. Militarism had to be resisted at all costs.

As the number of war casualties rose, recruitment began to falter and attitudes hardened on both sides. With every death, the pro-war lobbyists called for vengeance and reinforcements, while the pacifists pleaded for an end to the carnage. At times the tensions between these groups resulted in violence. Vida and her WPA women now risked their personal safety as they continued their fight for peace.

10

Battles for peace

1915–1916

◆

The WPA members continued to campaign energetically against the war, despite the best efforts of their opponents to silence them. When the WPA women were refused the use of the Mechanics' Hall in Sunbury, Cecilia used their car as a platform. The listeners assured the women they would get the hall next time, but the women were pleased to be 'quite independent of hall accommodation'.[1] On occasion the *Age* and the *Argus* refused to insert advertisements for their meetings.[2]

When Adela spoke at meetings she was often heckled by soldiers and supporters of the war. The *Age* reported that Adela was heckled at a WPA meeting at Northcote on 30 September 1915, although the *Woman Voter* disputed this, saying there was only one man, who interjected three times.[3] At this meeting the police alleged that the crowding of aisles constituted a danger in the case of fire and Cecilia was charged with neglecting to keep the aisles free. She pleaded that she had done her best to ask people to move forward and sit in the vacant chairs at the front and that the main crowding was caused by the councillors who stood in the doorway near the end of the meeting. The case was adjourned because the bench disagreed on a verdict. When it was reheard, Cecilia was found guilty and fined £1 with ten shillings costs. She refused to pay the fine and asked for the case to be reviewed in chambers. It was, and the conviction was quashed. While the conviction had been featured in all the papers, only the *Argus* reported that it had been quashed.[4]

In November 1915 Cecilia and Adela set out on a peace mission to Brisbane and Sydney. This was partly funded by donations sent to the *Woman Voter*. In Brisbane they were met by the reception committee of the Old Franchise League. They were surprised by Adela's appearance. 'Instead of a big militant person looking unutterable strength', they saw 'a small modish lady with an English complexion'.[5]

The next evening Adela was to speak at the Centennial Hall.[6] Fourteen hundred people were waiting in a packed hall on a hot night for her arrival. Margaret Thorpe and the chairman, Cuthbert Butler, extemporised and kept the audience amused. Adela had been delayed by a car accident, but when she did arrive, her 'eloquent advocacy for the peace movement roused hundreds of citizens to remarkable enthusiasm. Her plea for the suffering womanhood of the nations moved many to tears'.[7] Before the meeting, the chairman had been notified by the army authorities that anyone singing the banned peace song 'I Didn't Raise My Son To Be a Soldier' would be arrested. Copies were distributed to all those present and, as Cecilia started to sing, everyone joined in the chorus:

> I didn't raise my son to be a soldier,
>   I brought him up to be my pride and joy.
> Who dares to put a musket on his shoulder,
>   To kill some other mother's darling boy?
> The nations ought to arbitrate their quarrels—
> It's time to put the sword and gun away:
> There'd be no war today,
> If mothers all would say:
>   'I didn't raise my son to be a soldier'.[8]

The authorities decided it was not politic to arrest an entire audience. Copies of the *Woman Voter* sold out in five minutes and Adela's pamphlet *Put Up the Sword* also sold well. Published by the Women's Peace Army in July 1915, this set out to show the causes of war. It 'does not take the extreme view that all Wars are caused by Capitalism, but shows how a mixture of motives slowly but surely combines, to bring about armed conflicts'.[9] It was popular enough to go into three editions. Further successful meetings were held in Brisbane and Cecilia continued to sing the banned peace song. Copies of it were sold at the meetings for one penny and it 'caught on splendidly'.[10]

The women enjoyed a river trip on board the Q.G.S *Otter* lent by the government. This seems strange, when the women were flouting the War Precautions Act and spies were being sent to all their meetings to record what was said. Newspaper reports of the meetings were also filed and annotated by the authorities. The Brisbane publisher of the song sheet was 'noted'. One secret report by G. A. King (a private in the Main Guard) gives an insight into what was considered detrimental to the nation's ability to maintain the war effort. He found 'only two outstanding statements' in Cecilia's speech: 'This pernicious form of boy conscription is the vilest on the face of the earth' and 'So long as one man is killed this is a dishonourable war'. He found more in Adela's speech, including 'The Germans are a better nation than ours and their leading men are wiser' and 'We do not want a big army. The war is dragging us lower than the beasts and mothers send their boy sons to destruction without regret. If all would stand together all war would cease'. The authorities took no action at this stage.[11]

The women left Brisbane pleased with their well-attended meetings and the formation of branches of the Australian Peace Alliance and the Women's Peace Army. They held a successful meeting in Toowoomba, which Cecilia considered was 'a wonderful achievement for an ultraconservative country town'. After the meeting:

> We were told by one gentleman, who does most of the recruiting there, that he would see that we did not continue our work any longer in Australia. We told him we thought he could not possibly stop us, and we left him with mixed feelings. At two o'clock next morning the house in which we were staying was attacked with stones and other missiles. As the roof was iron the noise was deafening, but no one stirred, and the attackers, after two valiant attempts to draw us, left us in 'peace'.[12]

They were unable to prearrange their engagements in Sydney because the 'NSW peace propagandists had been terrorised into silence' by various prosecutions under the War Precautions Act, and ten organisations had turned them down. Despite this, their meetings were successful and Cecilia wrote, 'It is wonderful how the people everywhere just drink in every word of peace'.[13]

◆ ◆ ◆

Vida always maintained the Women's Peace Army was fighting the system of war, not the soldiers, who she considered were the victims of capitalism and militarism. In fact she helped individual soldiers, lending her car to bring wounded soldiers from their ships to hospital.[14] Vida blamed the daily papers for promoting dissension between the soldiers and the peace movement. Most of the soldiers respected her and this, combined with her courage, enabled her to quell a riot at the Bijou Theatre on 19 December 1915. Adela had been billed to speak on 'Shall Men Enlist?—The Women's Answer' at the Socialist Party's meeting. The theatre was overflowing an hour before the meeting was due to start, and there were many soldiers present who were determined to 'take it out' on a male socialist who had spoken slightingly of soldiers. The soldiers began singing and caterwauling, drowning out the speakers. The rest of the audience responded by singing 'The Red Flag'. When Cecilia rose to sing 'I Didn't Raise My Son To Be a Soldier', the soldiers counted her out, but she managed to finish, despite loud 'boo-hoos' and much stamping of feet.

Pandemonium reigned as Adela rose to speak and she could not be heard even on the platform. A returned soldier clambered on to the stage and made a deal that the soldiers would desist if he could speak for five minutes after Adela had finished. The truce lasted a few minutes, but then some soldiers rushed the platform and one started to play the piano. Men in the audience rushed to protect the speakers. The audience responded by attacking the soldiers. One old man seized a chair and brandished it at the soldiers. Mabel Singleton courageously jumped on to the platform. She and Cecilia stood each side of Adela. Some of the soldiers 'were brutal in the extreme' and used the 'filthiest language' to the women. The military police refused to control the crowd, saying it was the Socialist Party's meeting and so they should control it, and the civil police were 'helpless'.

Vida walked into this scene and quickly assessed the situation. She climbed on to a chair, helped by two soldiers who supported her with their arms around her waist. She called for order and a fair hearing for the soldier who wanted to speak. When the soldiers realised she was present, they cleared a way for her to mount the platform. She pleaded for fair play and the audience allowed the soldier his five minutes. Adela finished what she had wanted to say and the meeting was closed.

Almost everyone had left when Major McInerney entered the hall and ordered the civilians out. They refused, resenting the militaristic order, and the situation began to look ugly again. McInerney, puffing on a cigarette, repeated his order. Vida approached him. The *Woman Voter* reported their exchange:

> Miss Goldstein: Major McInerney, if you ask the audience quietly to go they will do so.
> Major McInerney: I couldn't ask them more quietly than I have done.
> Miss Goldstein: You have not asked them, you have ordered them.
> Major McInerney (in his bullying manner): I won't only order them to go, I'll make them go.
> Miss Goldstein: You are making a mistake in ordering the audience to go; it is likely to cause trouble. If you ask them quietly and courteously to leave they will go.
> Major McInerney: If you say I have spoken discourteously, I beg to join issue with you, madam.
> Miss Goldstein: You have done so, and you are making a mistake.

The speakers then left the theatre and Major McInerney joked with his men as he marched them out. Later it was discovered that the soldiers had thought it was an anti-recruiting meeting.[15]

A few days later, a Corporal Hewitt gained considerable publicity when he boasted to an approving crowd outside the *Age* office that he was one of the men who had stopped the Pankhurst meeting in the Bijou. He finished by singing the peace song in a revised version for returned soldiers:

> I didn't raise my son to be a soldier,
>   But as a soldier he's my pride and joy;
> I'd have him bear a musket on his shoulder,
>   Like every patriot mother's darling boy.
> God grant Australia never will have mothers
> Like Pankhurst, Goldstein, John and all their crew;
>   Our boys must fight to-day,
>   And never will I say
> I didn't raise my son to be a soldier.[16]

The increasing tensions between the pacifists and militarists resulted in acts of brutality. Just before Christmas 1915, Fred Katz, the secretary of the Federated Clerks' Union, was held down in his office by at least fifty returned soldiers and members of the Expeditionary Force, while hot tar was poured over his head and feathers were spattered over him. He was then kicked down the stairway. When a female journalist who had heard about the attack arrived, she was also rolled in the tar on the floor, 'presumably because she remonstrated with them for their cowardly attack'.[17] The reasons given in the papers for this treatment of Katz were that he had spoken against the government's recruitment cards, and also of course his German-sounding name. Vida and Cecilia reported the affair to the State Commandant. Vida's involvement in this case (especially with her surname) took great courage. The soldiers had shown they were not loath to mete out similar treatment to a woman. The *Argus* said that the woman had not been attacked, but had slipped. It called Vida's action 'premature and unnecessary, not to say theatrical',[18] but Vida assured readers that 'the facts are as we have related them'.[19]

In its Christmas Day editorial, the *Argus* argued that while Christmas was the time of goodwill to men, this could not be extended to Germans or those who worked against the war. It said women who fought against the war were unnatural and dangerous:

> The physiological problem presented by the craving for notoriety by certain women is not new. An unbalanced mind, a glib tongue, an absolute lack of self-restraint, and a wanton delight in giving offence are characteristic of this type of woman. But the few women who are so constituted as we have described would be comparatively harmless were it not for the use made of them by crafty men who arrange the meetings and carry on pernicious propaganda ... In normal times the vapourings of socialists, feminists, and pacifists can be tolerated without much risk of harm resulting. But in a period of national crisis no one should be permitted to outrage the sensibilities of a loyal community.

Having witnessed the 'organised ruffianism of certain soldiers' at the Bijou riot and then the treatment of Fred Katz, Vida was convinced that the civil and military authorities were not prepared to maintain law and order. The WPA had organised a Christmas Women's Peace Service, with the Children's Peace Army leading the singing, but it was decided to cancel it because without police protection the WPA 'could not accept the responsibility for saving the little ones from attack by a mob of hooligans'.[20]

Instead, a Great Peace and Free Speech Demonstration was organised at the Yarra Bank on Sunday 30 January 1916, with more than twenty organisations co-operating. Unfortunately it rained and only seven to eight hundred people turned up. About a hundred soldiers were present but the only disturbance was when the Reverend Lynch tried to address the crowd in favour of recruiting. Losing his temper with an interjector, he leapt from the platform and struck him in the face. The crowd was so incensed by the Reverend's behaviour that they refused to let him continue and forced him to leave.[21]

◆ ◆ ◆

A few weeks before this, on 12 January 1916, Vida's mother died after a short illness. The *Woman Voter*'s tribute to Isabella credited her with preparing the way for Vida's work, at a time when the fight was much harder and the pioneers were 'ridiculed and abused'. It said Isabella's influence had helped to make Vida a 'leader amongst women'. Vida had had the benefit of her mother's experience and the 'example of her worthy life to assist her in making use of her own great gifts'.[22] Vida had lost a true companion and supporter of all her work, but sustained by her faith that those who pass through the experience called death 'waken to a fuller and truer sense of life', she continued her public work.[23]

The WPA still befriended women and children appearing in court. Adela attended court proceedings related to the white slave trade and the WPA continued its campaigns relating to venereal disease and the age of consent. In March 1916 Vida, Cecilia and Adela were at court to hear the case of Joseph Skurrie, a member of the Victorian Socialist Party, who was charged under the War Precautions Act on the evidence of a newspaper report of a speech he had made at the Yarra Bank. He was jailed for three months, even though the reporter could not produce his notes and admitted the words could have been changed by the editor. As the women were leaving they heard the next case being called and realised it involved a 14-year-old mother they knew. They had helped her get a maintenance order from the baby's father, but now he was requesting the order be struck out. Neither the girl nor her solicitor had been notified of this case and when Cecilia explained the situation to the judge the case was thrown out. The *Woman Voter* wrote that while the girl had received some financial compensation, nothing could compensate for the suffering she had undergone and concluded, 'Everytime it is the women who really pay'.[24]

In similar vein, Vida responded indignantly to the Catholic Archbishop of Melbourne, Dr Daniel Mannix, who had criticised women for the declining birthrate. Although she had been addressing this issue since 1901, the war heightened her passionate defence of women's right to choose not to have children.

> Women are not going to be made breeding machines for the god of war ... for women will ever increasingly refuse to give life that men may take it. The prostitution of the brain of man in making all science but a means of dealing death in more horrible forms will not be followed by the prostitution of women in giving life to a child that it may grow to manhood but to murder his fellow man.[25]

In May 1916 the WPA held a women's convention on venereal disease, the 'Social Evil'. The convention attracted delegates from twenty-four organisations including various suburban Political Labor Councils and municipal councils and from unions as diverse as the Pastrycook's Union and the Federated Seamen's Union. The Victorian Lady Teachers' Association and the Society of Friends were also represented. Interstate delegates, Emma Miller from Queensland and Kathleen Hotson from South Australia, were enthusiastically welcomed.

Vida gave the main address. She paid tribute to Annette Bear-Crawford, who had established the Vigilant Society in Victoria in 1891 to raise the age of consent from fourteen. Before Bear-Crawford's work, no respectable woman would talk about sexual matters. Vida had continued the campaign and now Victoria had the highest age of consent, eighteen. Vida said the convention heralded a pleasing new development: men and women of differing political opinions coming together to help women. She said this new spirit of co-operation could be continued on other issues, so that men and women could be emancipated, 'For men cannot be free while women are in chains'.

In speaking to the first resolution, 'That education, showing the physical, moral and spiritual value of purity of thought, word, and deed, should be the chief agent in combating venereal disease', Vida stressed that this resolution embodied her

> own deep personal conviction [that] only a spiritual conception of life will give us the strength and understanding to work out the problem of the sex relationship between men and women. The problem is as old as human existence, and the perversion of the relationship from the function of

procreation to that of physical gratification has caused the great social evil we are discussing.

Other resolutions submitted opposed the compulsory examination, treatment and detention of prostitutes, because this legislation gave police a 'dangerous power' over the poor wage-earning girls who were forced by poverty into prostitution. The legislation would legitimise 'the trade in human bodies' and acknowledge that 'Women must be sacrificed to the worst passions of men'. The convention also recommended that a seduced girl under the age of twenty-one should be given the rights of a legitimate wife, and if the man was already married, he should be prosecuted for bigamy.[26]

◆ ◆ ◆

After the Bijou riot the authorities banned the use of licensed halls on Sundays. A deputation, representing twelve organisations, asked the Chief Secretary to withdraw the prohibition. Vida said the press reports were a travesty of the Bijou incident and that the suppression of free institutions meant the triumph of the Prussian spirit.[27]

When there were disturbances at the Women's Peace Army meeting at the Yarra Bank on 26 March, there was a move to ban meetings there too. About 4000 people were present. It had been reported in the papers that a woman at the previous meeting had called the soldiers murderers, so about a hundred soldiers had come to 'take it out of' the women in revenge. Many speakers now untied their shoelaces before beginning their speeches, so they could kick off their shoes if they were thrown into the Yarra.[28]

Vida stood on the improvised platform, with the soldiers milling around in an angry mood. She said she would let the soldiers speak if they did not agree with her. She began to submit her resolution, calling on the 'mother-half of humanity to prepare the way for a constructive peace'. The soldiers shouted that they would not let her speak because she had called them murderers and assassins. Vida denied this, calling on them for fair play. The grim response was, 'We don't want fair play; we want a fight'. She repeated that she would let them speak, but Clemence (an instigator of the Bijou riot) mounted a barrel and said, 'I'll speak now'. Hogg, an English Corporal, jumped on to the platform waving a Union Jack. He stood in front of Vida and Adela, using vile language. Clemence said, 'If anyone here would do to these women what the Germans did to the women of Belgium, I'd stand by and watch them do it with pleasure'. The soldiers cheered. They tried to push Vida off the platform and pull away the planks on which she stood. Each time they surged forward Vida faced them calmly and fearlessly.

Fred Riley, the secretary of the Australian Peace Alliance, was beside Vida trying to protect her. A soldier snarled, 'Let's get this— mongrel out of the way, then we'll get her'. One of the soldiers tore up a placard and used it to light a fire at his feet saying, 'That will shift him'. Riley was struck violently on the head and about thirty men responded to the call to throw him in the river. He hit out vigorously in self-defence and was then arrested for riotous behaviour.

Vida put her resolutions to the meeting and they were passed. The crowd was incensed by the behaviour of the soldiers, but fearful of being involved, and the meeting was closed. Then Vida, Cecilia and Adela went to the police station to bail out Riley. His face was badly bruised and clawed.[29]

Riley went before the City Court on 27 March. Hogg was a prosecution witness. He denied that he called the women 'lice, crawlers, things dressed up as women, not fit to be alive', saying that would be introducing some words he used after the women had left. He admitted he called the women parasites. Riley was fined £2 or fourteen days' jail.[30] On principle he refused to pay the fine, but the officers of the Women's Peace Army, who were in court to testify for him, paid the fine because he had so 'chivalrously defended' them and they could not allow him to suffer further on their account.[31]

◆ ◆ ◆

At Easter 1916 the first Interstate Conference of the Australian Peace Alliance was held in Melbourne. The peace organisations agreed it was vital to become as strong as possible because a new threat was looming which would need their greatest endeavours to combat: the possible introduction of conscription.

11

Conscription, strikes and spies

1916–1918

◆

Throughout the war years peace advocates were in the minority, and the *Age* described the peace societies as 'factious and freakish bodies'.[1] Most Australians supported the war to 'the last man and the last shilling',[2] yet there were many who opposed conscription. Even before the war, compulsory military service had been fiercely debated. The threat of conscription in Australia increased with its introduction in Britain in late 1915.

Prime Minister William Morris Hughes, 'the little digger', landed in Britain on 6 March 1916, just four days after conscription began to be enforced. He attended the War Conference in London and was fêted by the British military leaders, who were seeking increased support from the colonies to compensate for their casualties, which now approached one million. Hughes's war fervour grew and he addressed patriotic meetings around the country, extolling war because it 'prevents us slipping into the abyss of degeneracy and from becoming flabby'.[3]

Hughes returned to Australia in September 1916, determined to introduce conscription, but in his absence a majority of the Labor Party had pledged not to introduce it. A compromise was reached: the matter would be decided by a referendum to be held on 28 October 1916. The battle lines were drawn. The issue of militarism and conscription had split the WPA; now conscription would divide the country and split the Labor Party. Even church leaders differed on the issue. The Anglican Synod in Melbourne announced that God was on the side of the Allies and conscription was morally necessary. Dr Mannix opposed conscription, but his counterparts in Sydney, Perth and Hobart supported it.

The major newspapers supported a 'Yes' vote. Those papers which opposed conscription were subjected to severe and often grossly unfair censorship restrictions. The promise to Vida that a Labor government would not interfere with peace propaganda had held until March 1916, and then the *Woman Voter* and the *Socialist* were subjected to increased censorship. Once the referendum was announced censorship became more severe. The *Woman Voter* of 21 September was heavily censored, but forbidden to write this fact, Vida announced in the empty spaces, 'MR HUGHES SAYS WE MAY HAVE A FREE PRESS'. There were attempts to prohibit the publication of the blank spaces, but Vida continued to publish them. Vida wrote an 'Open Letter to Members of Parliament', outlining the earlier censorship and the promises the Labor Government had made about freedom of the press. She feared that if this freedom were withheld and conscription was forced upon the country by deliberately trying to manufacture support for it, while denying those opposed to it basic rights of speech and assembly, then 'there will be such serious trouble that Civil War is a certainty'.[4]

She printed the letter in the *Woman Voter*, although parts of it were censored. Reference to the armed raid in September 1914 was censored. The words 'The daily papers are permitted to lie freely about anti-militarists' were allowed, but the next part, 'we are not permitted to give the truth about ourselves and our work, and thus refute the false statements made by the daily papers with the object of inflaming the soldiers and public opinion against us', was censored. In another article, which said 'Labour will come into its own again ... and will make for peace, justice and humanity the wide world over', the word 'peace' was censored.[5] After these protests, the censorship was modified to a certain extent, 'but not enough to permit the anti-Conscription, anti-Militarist standpoint to be put fairly', according to the *Woman Voter*.[6]

The Women's Political Association had just moved into new premises at the Guild Hall in Swanston Street. The office gave the WPA 'what we have long desired in the way of light, air and roominess'.[7] It also had two halls with seating for 700 and 1700 people. These were hired out for use by other organisations, and unions often held meetings there. There was little time to settle in because the anti-conscription campaign began almost immediately the referendum was announced. During the WPA's tenancy the Guild Hall would become a rallying point for the anti-conscriptionists and, later, the site of a strikers' commune.

Vida and the Women's Peace Army campaigned for a 'No' vote in the referendum, with debates and meetings. At a Yarra Bank meeting on 17 September, Vida addressed a crowd of about 30 000 people. The *Woman Voter* published points for speakers against conscription and the Women's Peace Army printed leaflets opposing conscription. The Women's Peace Army was involved in the People's Proclamation Day on 4 October. It was organised by the trade unions to protest against Hughes's proclamation, to call up single men and draft them into camps, in anticipation of a 'Yes' vote. This action incensed many people and, despite the rain, 40 000 people assembled. Hilda Moody (who had resigned as secretary of the WPA because of its pacifist policies, but who was opposed to conscription) was there and said that even though it was impossible for many to hear the speakers, 'It was the wettest, dirtiest, happiest day I ever spent. The spirit of the crowd was wonderful'. The Women's Peace Army provided seven speakers; four women and three men, including a returned soldier. In the afternoon it held a meeting at the Guild Hall. There was tremendous enthusiasm when Vida announced that when four young girls present had walked out of a shirt factory to support the men, 130 girls at the factory had followed their lead.[8]

As the day of the referendum drew closer, antagonisms on both sides increased, no doubt inflamed by lurid advertising campaigns. Disturbances at the Yarra Bank were frequent and even schoolchildren became involved. When Adela Pankhurst spoke at Box Hill on 19 October, schoolchildren sang patriotic songs to drown out her words. Adela was forced to take shelter in a house to escape the children.[9] Adela's anti-conscription campaigning exacerbated the rift between her and her mother. Emmeline Pankhurst sent a telegram to Hughes which read, 'I am ashamed of Adela, and repudiate her. Wish you all success. Make any use of this'.[10]

A Women's No-Conscription Demonstration and Procession was organised for Saturday 21 October by the United Women's No-Conscription Committee. It was the first time Australian women had walked together in a peace procession. The march began at the Guild Hall.[11] The four to six thousand women were led by eight-year-old Madeleine Gardiner. She was dressed all in white and carried a satin-bound wand topped with a feathered dove of peace. Behind her there were two young girls carrying a banner which said 'A Little Child Shall Lead Them'.

Cecilia John followed on horseback. She was dressed in white and carried a staff decorated in the purple, white and green colours of the WPA. She was followed by the committee members of the Women's No-Conscription Committee led by Vida and Lizzie Wallace as presidents. The women wore white frocks with purple, white and green sashes.[12] Then there were eight lorries with tableaux representing 'Free Australia', 'Happy Childhood', 'War and Peace', 'Peace', 'Food Exploiters', 'International', 'No' and 'White Australia'. Many women carried banners or wore sandwich boards proclaiming 'Thou Shalt Not Kill', 'Our Sons Are Our Own' and so on. Motor cars were provided for 'hoary-headed but free-souled women who were unable to walk'. The children on lorries won the hearts of many. One old man said, 'I was going to vote "Yes", but when I look at those children I see I must vote "No"'. At a signal, several dozen doves were liberated from the children's lorries.

As the procession reached Bourke Street an attempt was made by about thirty soldiers to disrupt it, and a few soldiers attempted to unharness the horses drawing the lorries. Fortunately Fred Riley had gathered a group of supporters and the soldiers were quickly pushed back. One of Riley's men picked up Madeleine, 'our little herald of peace to protect her from the soldiers, and she remained mounted on his shoulder, with her white dove held aloft'.[13] Madeleine recalled she felt very proud leading the procession but was

> disgusted when about six big men joined me. More so when one smiled, and lifted me on his shoulder. When he said it was because people at the back of the crowd could not see me, I looked to Celie, but she smiled and nodded. I saw a distant struggle. Later I heard that a group of drunken men had been urged to 'throw the kid in the Yarra', so wharf laborers came to protect us.[14]

Knots of soldiers attempted to disrupt the procession, but other soldiers linked arms to prevent them and many returned soldiers along the route cheered the women. Individual soldiers attacked the women and children, snatching their 'No' banners from them and smashing them in their faces. One soldier 'bit off a piece of a finger of a woman who resisted his savagery'.[15] Muriel Heagney was marching with her mother. A soldier grabbed her mother's umbrella and struck the old lady with it on the forehead. Even though blood was streaming from the wound, she insisted on continuing the march.[16]

At the Yarra Bank, despite minor scuffles, the twelve women speakers delivered their speeches to about 80 000 people. Madeleine sat next to Vida, and Cecilia led the singing.

A week later the people went to the polls and a majority voted 'No'. Many WPA members spent the referendum evening in the *Argus* offices watching the results being posted up.[17] The anti-conscriptionists held jubilant celebrations. Vida, writing of the victory, called on Australians to demand that differences be settled by negotiation, not war, and said that 'a true nationalism can only be rooted in Internationalism'. She believed the 'No' vote had been secured by women and soldiers.[18] (When the soldiers' votes were eventually released, a majority of them had rejected conscription.) Vida said that many women who had differed with the WPA were now coming to agree with it. Conscription had roused women politically as nothing else had since their enfranchisement and she hoped that the unity obtained during the fight would remain. The battle was only half won, however, and the unity did not last long.[19]

The Labor Party was the first to suffer in the aftermath. Hughes had lost many supporters within it and when Caucus moved a no-confidence motion against him he angrily walked out. Four ministers and twenty-six others joined him to form the Federal Nationalists Party, which then governed with the support of the former Opposition. It won government when elections were held on 5 May 1917. Labor did not achieve federal re-election until 1929.

◆ ◆ ◆

Vida and Adela had always differed over the question of party politics and in January 1917 Adela resigned from the WPA and joined the Victorian Socialist Party. It was stated in the *Woman Voter* that Adela and the WPA differed 'fundamentally' about policies and that Adela's resignation was by 'mutual agreement'.[20] Adela did not make the decision lightly. She wrote to Bob Ross of the Victorian Socialist

Party: 'You must not judge me as you don't know what I have to go through. I am determined that I will not work for the Women's Political Association anymore—Socialism is the only thing—but I may have to give up work altogether'.[21] Vida continued to publish Adela's writing in the *Woman Voter* and maintained a kindly interest in her. When Adela was imprisoned later in the year, Vida campaigned for her release and became her guarantor.

In March 1917 Vida announced her candidature for the Senate. This time her stalwart supporters included Cecilia John and Mabel Singleton, who were the honorary secretaries of the campaign committee, and Kathleen Hotson who wrote for the *Woman Voter*, spoke at factory meetings and organised women's meetings in the industrial suburbs. This campaign was to be Vida's hardest yet, with the war and conscription clouding the issue of a non-party woman in Parliament.

The Labor Women's Campaign Committee and the Socialist Women's League asked Vida to reconsider her nomination because she would weaken the anti-conscription vote. They acknowledged her right to stand and the good work she had done. 'Forgetting our differences, you stood with us in our fight to defeat the Referendum on the 28th October last. Will you not stand with us again?' they pleaded. Vida replied that while she understood their point of view, she did not agree with it, because it was 'based on fear, and not on fidelity to the principle of international goodwill and brotherhood'. She said only the Australian Woman Movement, 'of which I am privileged to be the leader', had not forsaken this principle.

She also reminded them that the Labor Party had not come out against conscription until late 1916, whereas she had always opposed it and the Women's Peace Army had condemned it in a resolution of 15 July 1915. She said the labour movement had not come into the anti-conscription fight until the other societies had 'made it safe for them'. Her main opposition to Labor was that they had placed the Defence Act on the statute-book, which compelled men to fight and was just as reprehensible as overseas service. She regretted that they did not support her in these principles, but she knew they would 'continue to respect each other's convictions'.[22] Relations remained strained, although after the war, in an article for the *Christian Science Monitor*, Vida wrote, 'It must not be thought that there is strife between Australian party and non-party women; they agree to differ, they respect each other's viewpoint and the utmost good feeling exists between them'.[23]

Even some of Vida's supporters were not convinced her candidature was wise.

> It should be apparent to her [Vida] that the majority of Victorians are crazy over the war, and that her high principles of justice and honour and her humane love of peace are not in the least likely to find any understanding or appreciation from a host of war-mad reactionaries. The only votes that in my opinion Miss Goldstein is likely to receive will be votes which in the ordinary way would be cast for the Labour candidates. Therefore I regard her candidature as a serious danger, which will almost certainly lead to three conscriptionists being returned instead of the three anti-conscriptionists ... I hope, therefore, that Miss Goldstein will decide not to stand, as her doing so will surely benefit the cause of militarism. I know of no one in Australia who would make such an ideal Senator as Miss Goldstein, no one who would so surely and so nobly inspire the people to lofty action, and, if my vote and influence could secure her return, she would have them before all-comers. But she will be appealing to people who are blood-mad, and cannot at present be converted, so I hope she will wait for another occasion.[24]

In reply, Cecilia John wrote that the WPA would 'fall in and help' Labor if it stood for the people instead of the 'greatest institution the capitalist class possess—the military machine'. She also wrote that the Labor Party had almost ignored women in its manifesto.

Women in the Labor Party were also disillusioned with the way they were being treated. Bella Lavender, who had left the WPA and joined the Labor Party, gave a controversial lecture entitled 'Poodle or Packhorse'. She praised the WPA, saying no organisation had reason to be prouder of its work for women and children and that it had kept the flag flying for women's political equality, whereas the Labor executive had 'tactfully exerted a repressing influence on any talent for even loyal independent action that we Labor women possess'. Vida agreed that the Labor women had allowed themselves to be poorly treated and perceptively stated this would continue to happen until women had faith in their own understanding and aims.[25]

Vida's previous campaigns had forced people to choose between their loyalty to a political party and loyalty to feminist principles; now, in wartime, her nomination forced people to choose between party loyalties and the principle of international peace. Even members of the Australian Peace Alliance chose Labor before Vida, the peace candidate. Former colleagues had to choose publicly. At the interstate peace conference of the Australian Peace Alliance, Fred Katz (who Vida had supported when he was tarred and feathered) moved that precedence be given to the proposal that Vida be asked to withdraw her nomination because her candidature might harm Labor and lead to the election of pro-conscriptionists. The motion was ruled out of order.[26] On 12 April Vida's friend Fred Riley resigned as secretary of the Australian Peace Alliance, saying he had been forced to choose between the Labor Party and Vida. He could not remain secretary and opposed to a candidate who claimed she stood for peace. He opposed any action that might split the anti-conscription movement and, while he had the greatest respect for Vida, he felt she was making a mistake standing at that time.[27]

Vida called herself the 'People's Candidate' and campaigned on anti-militarism and anti-conscription, in addition to her regular policies. She told her audiences that the war was caused by Britain's fear of losing commercial supremacy and that she hoped for 'a revolution—a bloodless revolution—to remove the capitalistic system', which would occur through the ballot-box.[28]

She opened her campaign in Bendigo, which Hughes was to win, on 29 March 1917 and addressed an audience of 1500 people. According to the *Woman Voter*, her message was listened to with 'rapt attention'.[29] The *Bendigo Advertiser* reported the meeting at length. She seems to have received a reasonable hearing, although no one volunteered when asked to help take up a collection to defray her expenses. Vida then said her friends would collect at the door and because they had no plates they would use the helmets of the two policemen standing there.

She wanted all returning soldiers repatriated with a guaranteed £200 salary a year. She tried to defend her pacifism against questions like 'How can you have peace if the other fellow won't have peace?'. When she said Empire was the curse of the world and the 'vastness of the British Empire makes it the most abominated nation in the world', many people started to walk out, presumably without availing themselves of the helmets. Mabel Singleton had to shout above the din to declare the meeting closed.[30]

Vida concentrated her campaign in the country and spoke in about twenty-five towns. She reasoned that city people had opportunities to hear the WPA and the Women's Peace Army speakers and only held five meetings in the city and suburbs of Melbourne. At the Yarra Bank meeting, Vida and a group of WPA women used a table for a platform from which to speak. At the conclusion there were three cheers for the peace candidate. Vida responded by calling for three cheers for peace and humanity.[31]

Political candidates were asked to use their meetings to try to enlist recruits. When Vida received this request from the Recruiting Committee, she replied that she recruited for peace. Much later she learnt that her manifesto was not included in candidates' policies sent to soldiers overseas.[32]

Once more there were rumours spread against her and these were addressed in the *Woman Voter*. A letter asked if Vida was against marriage and an advocate of free love. The *Woman Voter* replied that Vida was

> a strong opponent of Free Love, which she regards as a euphemism for Free Lust. Miss Goldstein's marriage philosophy is summed up in the words of Olive Schreiner: 'Marriage for love is the beautifullest external symbol of the union of souls; without it, it is the uncleanest traffic that defiles the world'.[33]

For the fifth time Vida failed to win a seat in Parliament, but this time she lost disastrously. She suffered the ignominy of receiving only 7000 votes and forfeited her deposit (the other candidates polled over a quarter of a million votes each). However, of all her campaigns, she said she was proudest of this one, because she had stood for the principle of international peace. She wrote in the *Woman Voter*:

> It is not the fact that your [sic] licked that counts,
> It's *how* did you fight, and *why*.[34]

◆ ◆ ◆

Undaunted by the defeat, Vida went to the Yarra Bank as usual on the Sunday after the election, to continue her campaign for peace. The Women's Peace Army now held regular weekly meetings at the Yarra Bank if fine and at the Guild Hall if wet. The main speakers were Cecilia John, Jennie Baines, Mary Fullerton and Eileen McMahon. Factory meetings resumed and a ceremony was held to launch the WPA flag. Members climbed to the roof of the Guild Hall to see Vida and Cecilia unfurl the purple, white and green flag.

By the winter of 1917 Australians were war-weary and plagued by high food prices and strikes. Prices had risen 29 per cent and many people were suffering terribly, yet grain was rotting in storehouses and frozen meat was accumulating in storage, because there were not enough ships to export the food. The wharf labourers went on strike and women took to the streets to protest against the high food prices. Adela Pankhurst and other women interrupted proceedings in Parliament and sent two unsuccessful deputations of women to Parliament House to demand a reduction in the cost of living. They were refused admittance. Adela called on the women to reassemble the next day, 15 August, and the government hastily framed a regulation under the War Precautions Act, forbidding more than twenty people to assemble within a prohibited area.

Two to three thousand men and women assembled in defiance of the Act and Adela addressed them. She was arrested and charged with obstruction and escorted to the watchhouse followed by a 'hooting, hysterical crowd of women'.[35] The *Age* erroneously reported that the Women's Peace Army had organised the demonstration and a raid on the One Woman One Recruit League where a woman had been attacked and kicked.[36] Adela was released on bail and fined £2 in court the next day. The *Woman Voter* wrote that it supported the aims of the deputation, but was concerned about the methods employed (militant methods were undesirable for a peace organisation) and the name of the group, the Women's Peace League, which could be confused with the Women's Peace Army. The WPA's letter to the *Age* dissociating itself from the deputations was not published until 24 August, but even a month later, the *Age* continued the misapprehension when it referred to 'that curiously named body the Women's "Peace" Army'.[37]

At another demonstration on 22 August, Adela, Lizzie Wallace and Jennie Baines addressed the crowd of seven to eight thousand assembled in the Treasury Gardens. Adela stood on a chair under a tree. She denounced profiteers and the government who let food rot in storehouses while people starved. The police moved in, the women used umbrellas and fists against them, and Adela and Lizzie were arrested. Adela was sentenced to a month's gaol but was soon released on appeal. Lizzie was fined £1. Again the *Age* said the Women's Peace Army was responsible and pointed out the presence of 'several lavishly dressed women whose adornment certainly betrayed no pretensions to impoverishment'. The police warned that they 'did not want to see a repetition of the suffragette episodes in England, when Churches and other buildings were destroyed', and said they had been instructed to 'take prompt action and stern measures to repress any future disturbance of the kind'. Throughout the last week of August there were daily demonstrations.[38]

In early September Adela was again arrested, this time under the War Precautions Act, along with Jennie Baines and other women. Jennie was fined £10. Cecilia stood in for her at a meeting of the North Fitzroy Political Labor Council and the money for the fine was raised at the meeting. The *Argus* leader of 4 September called Adela a 'notoriety hunter' and a 'public nuisance'. The women organised a monster torchlight demonstration for 19 September. Adela addressed the meeting and then led the crowd from the Yarra Bank to Parliament House. The people in the procession got bolder as the numbers swelled to 10 000. Mêlées broke out near Parliament House and the crowds flowed through the city. The streets were unlit because of coal shortages and demonstrators started smashing windows. About £6000 damage was done. Adela and Jennie were held responsible for introducing suffragette tactics into Australia. An *Age* editorial accused the government of weakness because it permitted 'a comparatively few degenerates and weak-minded people to riot through the city'.[39] Suggestions were made in the press and in Parliament that they should be deported. Prime Minister Hughes privately wrote, 'Adela Pankhurst is making herself a damned nuisance and I really don't know what to do with the little devil. I hate punishing women but I fear I shall have to deport her'.[40]

The government reacted by releasing some staples like rabbits and butter from storage. They prohibited meetings at the Yarra Bank and enacted provisions to use the Riot Act and to give police the power to move people on if they did not leave voluntarily within fifteen minutes. Extra volunteer constables were sworn in. These measures, combined with the loss of support due to the violent tactics and events in Adela's private life, led to the end of the riots.

On 30 September Adela married Tom Walsh, an Irish-born seaman who had been in Australia since the 1890s. He was a militant socialist and probably one reason why she left the WPA. He was a widower with three children. Shortly after the wedding Adela appeared in court to face the charge of encouraging injury to property on the night of the torchlight procession. She was released on a bond and said she would retire from public life and devote herself to training her three stepdaughters. There were other charges, however, and appeals pending. She failed to win her appeal for an offensive behaviour charge and was sentenced to one month's imprisonment. When she refused to sign a bond she was sentenced to four months under the War Precautions Act. She was taken to Pentridge on 1 December. From there she wrote to her new husband:

> I'm very, very tired of it all, Tom ... I get frightened, sometimes wondering whether I shall ever get out and find things all right when I do —whether we are ever to have our happy life together. Oh darling, I was so happy for those few weeks. It was a lovely dream. Can it ever be again—I dar'nt hope it ... Dear Husband I am afraid I am going to give way and ask you to let me come home. Please let me—I am afraid I can't stand any more of it. I've done my best.[41]

A deputation of women, including Vida, waited on Prime Minister Hughes to request Adela's release before Christmas. He promised to bring the matter before the Cabinet at the earliest opportunity. The second conscription referendum campaign was in progress, so there was no incentive for him to have her released. The women started a petition calling for Adela's release. They collected 5000 signatures in less than a week and said the signatures would keep coming 'until we get this brave woman released'.[42] The *Argus* editorial of 24 December 1917 argued against clemency for Adela, but she was finally released on 17 January, two days after Cabinet had dealt with the petition. Hughes set conditions for the release with Vida. A large meeting was held at the Socialist Hall to celebrate.

◆ ◆ ◆

While Adela and the women were protesting on the streets, the unions were also calling for a reduction in food prices. On 29 July 1917, a meeting of 500 members of the Wharf Labourers' Union agreed to refuse to load any food for overseas shipment, until the cost of essentials was brought down to pre-war rates. Throughout the war, the WPA had been campaigning against the high food prices and so Vida and the WPA immediately decided to help the striking families. The *Woman Voter* of 30 August 1917 called on families to take in one or two children of the strikers for the duration of the strike. The Hampton branch of the ALP offered to accommodate 1000 children and by early September 'a number' of children were 'happily located' in WPA and Labor Party homes. All strikers and families were given free admittance to the WPA picture shows held on Wednesdays and Saturdays at the Guild Hall.[43] Supporters of the war thought it was disloyal to strike during wartime, but Vida defended the strikers and denied they were disloyal, pro-German or tools of the Industrial Workers of the World.

During the strike the number of WPA meetings was increased and the WPA speakers were joined by members of Parliament and union leaders. At the Yarra Bank on 26 August Vida, Cecilia John and Mary Fullerton spoke on 'The Strike and After' to crowds larger than those drawn for the anti-conscription meetings. Throughout the meetings a well-to-do couple interjected that men should not strike during the war. They were invited on to the platform, but failed to convince the crowd. The WPA speakers said the government had struck against the workers by raising prices and introducing the card system, even though it had promised that working conditions would not be changed during the war. The *Woman Voter*'s report of the meeting concluded:

> If the Commonwealth Government persists in its determination to ignore the strikers, it will lose even should it seem to win. The present strike is the first rumble of the thunder of the conflict that is coming if our 'rulers' are not wise enough to see that the capitalistic system is doomed, are not wise enough to unite with the workers in adjusting the old to the new conditions.[44]

The idea that capitalism was doomed was very real with the Russian Revolution only four months old and the war causing political, social and economic upheaval throughout Europe. Vida wrote in her 'Open Letter to Workers, Unarmed Australia' that the Russian Revolution was '*the* Sign of the Times, of the approaching social and industrial revolution, which it is our aim to accomplish through education and negotiation instead of bloodshed'.[45]

In the first week of September, the fifth week of the strike, the Guild Hall was formed into a Registration Bureau to register all families in need of help. WPA members and friends liberally provided donations of cash and food. Some members paid a weekly amount to board the children with their own mothers.

Nursing and expectant mothers were especially cared for. Vida admired these wives 'who show heroic devotion to the principles for which their husbands are fighting' and wrote:

> And yet it is inspiring to see the spirit they manifest—no anger, no bitterness, no resentment—just quiet, earnest, dignified realisation of the issues at stake, and a resolution to suffer any personal privation themselves, if only they are helped to provide for their children.[46]

Meals were available for all strikers and their families who came to the Guild Hall. Soup was supplied every day. A Mr Nicholls gave many vegetables and promised a ton of turnips. Volunteers made mountains of sandwiches. Suburban Political Labor Councils donated groceries and supplied volunteers. Rabbits were trapped 'to take the place of meat' and a bootmaker called Mr Peddie fitted up a bench for the repair of boots. Eventually men from the union were taught bootmaking. A barber's saloon gave the men free haircuts and shaves. Vida believed that by providing for the welfare of the people involved the WPA was demonstrating how a strike should be fought.[47]

By the middle of September the Guild Hall, 'the home of true democracy', was operating as a commune, with kitchens, dining rooms, grocer's shop, baker's shop, smoking rooms, barber's saloon and boot factory all being established in a few days by a handful of women for thousands of men whom they were 'proud to stand by'. Vida saw it as a 'miracle' and promised even greater things. Donations continued to come in strongly and gift nights with dancing and games were organised. Collections were taken at the Yarra Bank meetings, although this source ceased when meetings at the Yarra Bank were temporarily prohibited after the food riots.[48]

In New South Wales the General Strike had ended in total defeat of the unions by early October, but the striking Victorian wharf labourers remained steadfast. The eleventh week of the strike was one of the most momentous for the commune. When a Mr Stapleton suggested they ask the workers at Newport for supplies, Vida and Cecilia jumped at his suggestion and said they would take a cab. Mr Stapleton said that was no good, a van was needed. So some of the wharf labourers borrowed the Carlton Brewery's lorry. Vida and Kathleen Hotson addressed the men on the Wednesday and Thursday, and then on the Friday Cecilia and a Mr Smith brought back six tons of provisions. The arrival of the lorry was greeted with cheers by the wharf labourers; a 'moving picture of the animated scene' was taken and shown the next Saturday. The workers at Newport became one of their major sources of supplies.[49]

By November provisions for 5000 people were being distributed from the grocer's shop every week. Twelve to fifteen hundred meals were being provided weekly, including hot evening meals for the men helping the WPA volunteers. Twenty tons of food were being donated weekly, with half coming from the workers at the Newport workshops and the Sunshine Harvester Works, but 100 tons was needed and the remainder was bought from donations. There were now two boot shops. Vida gave the credit for all this to the 'phenomenal business ability' of Cecilia. She hoped it would become a permanent institution for unionists. Vida said non-unionists, who were not prepared to sacrifice individually for the collective good, could go to the Ladies' Benevolent Society for handouts when they were unemployed, but unionists working to change the social system deserved help lovingly given by their fellow workers and other friends; this was not charity. Vida also helped organise a Women's Union, the condition of membership being union membership if eligible, being a relative of a trade unionist or a supporter of trade unionism.[50]

Vida also gave public speeches to raise money for the commune. She was still under surveillance by the military police and although 'so far no gross breach of the Regulations has been brought to notice', two shorthand writers were sent to a meeting she held at Bacchus Marsh on 1 November 1917. Her topic was 'The War and Industrial Democracy'. Mabel Singleton chaired the meeting and told the audience that Vida's only brother had been killed in the war and that 'it is very hard for those who have lost one so near and dear to them to take up the attitude we are taking'. Selwyn Goldstein had voluntarily enlisted in England and was commissioned into the Royal Engineers in October 1915. He died fighting in the war that his sister opposed and was buried in Poperinghe, near Ieper, in Belgium.

Mabel Singleton said the WPA was always misrepresented in the press and that when she first came to Melbourne twelve or so years ago 'I should have formed the conclusion, from the reports, that Miss Goldstein was the most silly and senseless person that had ever spoken on a platform'. The WPA had been blamed for the recent food riots but the members 'very strongly condemn' them. In her speech Vida said that 'all wars are more or less trade wars' and that she hoped the people would learn from this war and have a press of their own.

She opposed conscription because 'no man is free if he has to go away against his will'. She wanted peace with democratic principles, 'true industrial democracy', where the control of industry was in the interests of the people. Then she spoke about the strike and the WPA's efforts for the strikers' families and called for donations. All this was dutifully recorded by the shorthand writers and put on file in Intelligence Records in the interests of the war effort.[51]

The commune closed after the strike ended in February 1918. By then it had supplied 60 000 food parcels, prepared 30 000 meals, provided 6500 haircuts, distributed 30 000 items of clothing and repaired 2000 pairs of boots. Children had been boarded to their mothers and they had assisted 200 cases of confinements and sickness. The WPA had collected £1500 in donations and almost 700 tons of food. It was a magnificent achievement.

On Eight-Hour Day the wharf labourers marched to the Guild Hall and saluted the Women's Peace Army and the Women's Political Association in recognition of the work they had done during the strike. Vida deeply appreciated the 'graceful action'.[52]

◆ ◆ ◆

Nine weeks into the strike, on 4 October 1917, meetings of the Women's Political Association and the Women's Peace Army had passed resolutions unanimously inaugurating a second Women's No-Conscription Campaign. This illustrates the merging of the two organisations by this time. Later in the month the two groups joined anti-conscriptionists in celebrating the 'glorious 28th', the first anniversary of the conscription referendum. The Women's Peace Army called on members to be vigilant and prepared to resist another conscription campaign. As feared and predicted, on 8 November Hughes announced a second conscription referendum, to be held on 20 December 1917. This campaign was even more intense and bitter than the first. Rocks were thrown at Hughes at a huge rally at the Melbourne Cricket Ground.

While continuing to fulfil its commitments to the commune, the WPA once again campaigned vigorously against conscription. It provided speakers for Yarra Bank meetings and held factory and open-air meetings. Cecilia and Vida travelled more extensively than in the previous campaign. Vida travelled to Sydney and was well received on the Women's Peace Army's platform at the Domain. Then she attended meetings in the Western District, accompanied by a returned soldier, Mr Heather. Vida also had what she considered successful meetings in Tasmania. According to local reports, however, the crowds were noisy and boisterous and there were frequent interjections. One fellow shouted out how many sons did Vida have at the front, which outraged her supporters and led to further commotion. At an open-air meeting in Hobart a truckload of people collecting for On Active Service Funds arrived. They sang and rattled their collection boxes so loudly that Vida could not be heard. A policeman persuaded them to move on before the audience set upon them. The Hobart *Mercury* condemned Vida as 'a mixture of Karl Marx and Lenin' and said that her name suggested 'German-Jewish ancestry'.[53]

The WPA also printed leaflets against conscription. Cecilia was charged with 'having procured the commission of an offence under the War Precautions Act' for having a leaflet printed. The case broke down because the leaflet had been printed before the regulation was drawn up. Small costs were granted, but they were insufficient to cover the cost of the counsel the WPA had engaged.[54] Cecilia travelled to Brisbane and her letter to Vida saying she had obtained a film which she thought would be 'great propaganda value' was recorded by the authorities. Four days later, on 14 December 1917, a warrant to search was issued against Cecilia. This entitled the bearer to 'enter, if need by force... any time of the day or night... [and to] examine, search and inspect' any part of the premises and any person and to seize anything prejudicial to public safety or constituting an offence under the War Precautions Act. It is not certain if it was in fact used.[55]

On 15 December a peace rally was organised as part of the anti-conscription campaign. About 2000 people, mostly women, set out from the Trades Hall in forty or fifty covered wagons. The sides of the vehicles were covered with streamers and posters. The *Argus* report said the women were singing 'revolutionary songs, and shouting defiance'. The wagons drove along Russell Street and turned into Swanston Street, where some of them stopped outside the returned soldiers' rooms in the Alexandra Buildings. 'Boo-hoos' and counter-cheers were exchanged, then a returned soldier rushed across the road and tore a sign off one of the wagons. 'This precipitated a general mêlée. With hoarse threats of vengeance the "antis" dashed upon the returned men, whom they outnumbered by ten to one, and a furious battle ensued, from which several men emerged with bruised and bleeding faces'.

When the procession arrived at the Yarra Bank there were about 5000 people assembled to hear the fourteen women speakers. The women's speeches were described as 'inflammatory' by the *Argus*. Vendors of 'No' buttons did a good trade, as did the thirty or so ice-cream carts flaunting 'No' placards. Two blind musicians twanged their instruments and sang the 'anti' songs in tremulous voices and were well rewarded for their efforts.[56] At some point in this campaign Cecilia defended the WPA flag by turning a fire hose on to the soldiers who tried to wrest it from her.[57]

Once more the people rejected conscription. Hughes had said he could not continue to govern if the 'Antis' won. After many calls for his resignation, including one from the *Woman Voter*, he resigned on 10 January 1918. The Governor-General, unable to find anyone else who could command a majority, recommissioned Hughes the same day. Hughes re-formed his ministry without alteration. Eleanor Moore summed it up well when she wrote that 'the work and money which pacifists had put into the struggle, and the special opprobrium which they had drawn upon themselves in doing so might be considered a bad debt'.[58] Vida fought passionately against conscription and the majority of Australians had voted against it, but there was no mass popularity to be gained from the stand she had taken. It was as if in a secret ballot Australians could say 'No', but publicly they would mouth the opposite.

◆ ◆ ◆

The WPA's annual report for 1917 noted successes in reform of the intestacy laws and the appointment of female police. The women's parliament had had several sessions, but the successful picture-shows had had to be stopped because it was impossible to find films suitable for children. In January 1918 Cecilia resigned as secretary, although she remained on the committee. Then in February Mary Fullerton resigned as vice-president because of ill health, but continued as a speaker and a writer for the *Woman Voter*.

In February 1918 Vida went to Brisbane to take part in a great peace demonstration. She gave support to the Labor Party's peace proposals but maintained that the Women's Peace Army had more definite and far-reaching international and anti-capitalistic proposals. She also stayed in Sydney to confer with the Women's Peace Army there.

In March Vida became the honorary secretary of the committee formed to celebrate the first anniversary of the Russian Revolution. Vida had followed the events in Russia with interest and although 'we may not write as we would wish', she believed it was a good movement because it helped the masses. The Australian Socialist Party, the Women's Peace Army and the Victorian Socialist Party were the organisers. The evening began with a balalaika orchestra and there were numerous speakers.[59]

At Easter Cecilia was the Women's Peace Army's delegate at the Peace Conference in Sydney. Fifty-four organisations were represented. In May Cecilia and Annie Macky launched a new venture, the People's Conservatorium. The prospectus said that education was a right, not a privilege, and that no education was complete without the arts. The aim was 'to hold up before the students the high ideals of Unionism and to point out that an educated Revolutionary movement will be a far greater force for good than an uneducated Revolutionary movement'. This venture was dear to Cecilia, who knew what it was to be talented but poor.[60]

Vida's mail was still being read by the censor, whose annotations were becoming increasingly peevish. A letter to Vida from Edith Abbott about WPA work in Portland told how the propaganda work was slow because 'the war atmosphere is so thick' and added, 'Were I a Loyalist and wanted to punish the Kaiser ... I would advise that he should endeavour to do a fortnight in Portland'. The censor wrote:

> Is there no end to the latitude which the Pacifists are allowed? ... [The letter] tell[s] the whole story of a loyal District, with keen war workers, obviously standing for the Empire who are to be disturbed, mis-guided, and probably led astray by the disgruntled Pacifists.[61]

Circulars sent to Vida from the Committee of Women for Permanent Peace were withheld and Vida's letter to Clara Tybjerg, a Danish member of this group, was also withheld. In it Vida said the WPA was finding it harder than ever to carry on its anti-militarist work. The censor noted this was 'good to learn', although he felt the evidence 'would seem to indicate quite the reverse'. Vida said Australians seemed 'prostrated' by 'having their liberties interfered with' but that the WPA kept 'sowing the seeds' and there were indications that the people were stirring. The censor agreed that 'they have every reason to flatter themselves that their dangerous propaganda is making its influence felt in many quarters'.[62]

When Bob Ross invited Vida to speak at a send-off to Peter Simonoff, the Russian Consul-General, the censor noted that Simonoff 'may be more appreciated in his own country than he is here'. He added with unaccustomed humour, 'What a truly representative gathering of M. F. [Military File] members there should be on that night'.[63]

Later in the year when W. J. Miles from Sydney wrote to Vida suggesting links with the Sydney and Melbourne pacifist groups, the censor was not at all happy about this development and referred to them as the 'rebels of Sydney and Melbourne'.[64] When a Mr Hills wrote to Vida regretting she had had the expense of setting up an article only to 'have had the Beast draw his paw over it', the censor noted that it was a 'rather complimentary simile between the Censor and one of the latest recruiting posters'.[65]

From Vida's letters the censor also learned that throughout 1918 the *Woman Voter* was in financial trouble. It went fortnightly in the middle of the year and in August doubled the price to twopence. Near the end of the year Vida wrote to her printers that her financial condition was poor and the *Woman Voter* might have to close.[66]

◆ ◆ ◆

Within the constraints of declining membership and the general weariness of members exacerbated by the demands of the war campaigns, the WPA continued to monitor and work for issues related to women and children. One of these was the problems resulting from the high number of war dead. The general belief was that with nearly 60 000 Australian men killed in the war, fewer women would have the opportunity to marry and have children. (This has since been disproved. The balance of the sexes remained almost unchanged, offset by heavy immigration of men before and after the war.[67]) Also, because the soldiers were considered the best of the nation's manhood, it was feared that the quality of the prospective fathers would be diminished.

In August 1918 the WPA held a conference on Scientific Motherhood, which was a scheme to address this problem. It was advocated by Marion Piddington to help the 'war heroines' (married or unmarried) who had lost men in the war and so were doomed to childlessness. Older couples (of the highest moral and physical type) with grown-up children would have intercourse using a 'shield' and send the 'life' to a Eugenics Institute staffed by doctors of exalted character where the heroines would be artificially inseminated. Vida said they should all be big-minded enough to examine any social issue, but added that she personally found the scheme 'essentially animal and materialistic'. She believed that only 'hearts and minds united to spiritual ends... could justify and sanctify the creation of another human being'. She opposed the idea because it removed a woman's responsibility to choose the father of her child and the man's responsibilities as a husband and father.

Mary Fullerton developed this further in her speech:

> In the activity of a noble sex love there is a spiritual mingling as well as an atomic bodily mingling—an embracing of spiritual atoms. Human passion at its sublimest in action is a condition of soul as well as a physical emotion; it is a state of being—something far beyond the mere activity of bodily cells. The etherialization and sublimation of the human nervous system causes—makes possible—such a spiritualisation of passion that it is no longer a mere animal function.[68]

Kate Flynn admitted she expected to be shocked by the scheme but,

> before I had read a page, I had forgotten it in horror at the way it was presented. For the shameless materialism of the thing was overlaid with biblical quotations with an ingenuity that would have been satanic had it not so obviously been just sheer innocence...
>
> One thing offends me particularly in this suggestion we are considering: the insistence of its supporters that the woman in the experiment is 'fulfilling her destiny' in becoming a mother.
>
> That motherhood is necessary to the fulfilment of our destiny I deny absolutely... Motherhood is an experience... a great and holy experience it should be—but only an experience... As things are, as they have been made by the acceptance of an unequal standard of morality for the sexes, the enlightened woman must often put away the hope of

motherhood, because she has no hope of contracting a marriage wherein the conditions demanded by her ideal of true conception can be fulfilled creating a perfect mental, physical, and spiritual atmosphere to which to invite a human soul.[69]

In 1945 Vida wrote to Mabel Singleton and Mary Fullerton, who were living in England. She enclosed a cutting about test-tube babies and recalled this WPA conference 'and Mary's outraged feelings — summed up in the words "Imagine a child having a syringe for a father!" I have frequently quoted that comment!'.[70] Although this letter was written many years later, Vida's and her friends' failure to move with the times in attitudes to sexuality was already apparent at this conference and in Vida's earlier response to the question of free love. The conference generated many letters to the *Woman Voter* opposing the scheme and then it disappeared from its pages, overshadowed by the 'Dawn of Peace'.[71]

The war ended on 11 November 1918. The Women's Peace Army rejoiced at the cessation of hostilities, but feared internal warfare in many countries unless free speech, free assembly and a free press were guaranteed to all peoples.[72] In Australia the War Precautions Act was not repealed. Vida joined the Socialist Party, Trades Hall Council and the Labor Party in signing a memorial calling for its repeal. Arrests were still being made under the Act; Jennie Baines and Bob Ross were imprisoned for displaying the red flag. (When Jennie was rearrested in 1919 she went on hunger strike, the first person in Australia to do so, and was released after four days.)[73]

◆ ◆ ◆

The cost of Vida's pacifism was enormous. The war had forced women to choose between party and sex loyalties, between patriotism and pacifism, and to decide on the methods they would adopt to achieve their aims. It had highlighted their differences. It had divided the WPA and isolated it from other women's groups which commanded wider support, while bringing it closer to the minority radical left. It left the WPA mortally wounded and the *Woman Voter* in financial straits. Vida's electoral support had dissipated. Principle had exacted a high price.

12

The world moves

1919–1922

◆

Vida and Cecilia had been nominated in 1917 to represent the Women's Political Association and the Women's Peace Army at the Women's Peace Conference to be held in Europe after the war. As soon as the war ended, they began their preparations for the trip. They realised that travelling would be difficult, but the WPA considered it vital to send them: women had not been included in the Peace Conference of the Powers, yet women and children were the greatest sufferers from war, and post-war decisions would affect the children of the future. WPA members were asked to give donations, hold fund-raising events or advance £10 'until the conclusion of lecture tours by our delegates on their return'. It was estimated that £350 would be needed for each delegate.[1] The censor, who was still reading Vida's mail three months after the war ended, noted that the effort to raise the money 'seems doomed to failure'.[2]

The news came through in March that the conference would be in Paris and begin on 5 May 1919. The women would have to leave immediately, and hope that there would not be any delays during the journey, if they were to reach Paris in time. The influenza epidemic sweeping Melbourne had made it impossible to hold fund-raising activities, so it was decided that only Vida would go. She was departing with very little money, but a 'great heart of faith in us [the WPA members], and in the eternal "coming right of right things"'. At the eleventh hour this decision was reversed and Cecilia joined Vida. They sailed on the *Orsova* on 24 March.[3]

Vida and Cecilia had a rough crossing of the Bight and while Vida realised it was unfair to compare shipboard conditions with those before the war, she was nevertheless unimpressed. The ship was so crowded that meals were served in relays—and more troops were to be taken on in Bombay. She expected some comfort for her £3 a day, but had to 'turn the ship upside down to get anything for those who are ill'. Vida noted that the stewards were 'so fearfully overworked' that she hesitated to ask them to do anything more, so she tended the sick herself and reported that she had become quite adept as a stewardess. With characteristic perception, she observed that the shipping company and the stewards were not on good terms and that the stewards' most essential needs (such as air and bathing facilities) were being ignored; ninety stewards slept together, twelve feet below the waterline. She wrote, 'It is these constant pin pricks that lead to the more serious trouble at what is considered the favourable moment'. She also remarked with wry irony that, 'Judging by the swarms of children with us, there is no evidence of race suicide in Australia; they are all over the place'. The children placed a great strain on the stewardesses and also on their mothers, many of whom were unwell and looked 'the essence of misery'.[4]

The ship docked at Fremantle but overseas passengers were not allowed to disembark. Vida was most disappointed at missing the chance to meet her West Australian friends and supporters and admitted feeling 'a grudge against the medical profession for the absurd laws it has laid down in its fear of influenza'.[5]

They arrived in Colombo early on 9 April and were pleased not to have a medical inspection, which Vida opposed on religious grounds. Walking through the market and native quarters they acquired a 'self appointed' thirteen-year-old guide. Vida wrote, 'He was such an attractive youngster ... the heat making us feel inclined to yield to anything but the enormous prices asked for every commodity'. Men, women and children were 'greatly struck with Miss John's size as she moved amongst them, a Trition [Titan?] amongst minnows'.

In the afternoon, friends drove them to Mount Lavinia eight miles away, passing the native quarters which Vida described as 'another mass of life and colour, and of poverty and wealth'. At the hotel at Mount Lavinia they sat on the terrace feasting their eyes on the Indian Ocean, the palms, the golden sands and the people dressed in colourful sarongs. Driving back at sunset, the tall coconuts were silhouetted against a backdrop of 'green, blue, flame, amethyst and burnished gold. No pen could begin to do justice to the magic of the scene'. Dinner at the Galle Face, followed by a rickshaw ride and a motor launch to the ship, completed a perfect day.

> Most people seem to find that one day at Colombo is enough for all time, but I have now been there three times, and my enjoyment was as keen the third time as the first. The natural beauty of the place, the picturesqueness of the street scenes, the glorious colouring, could never pall upon me. Of course, in the background is the social question, which brings to one's mind many perplexing problems. The motor car is already beginning to triumph over the rickshaw, and that marks the beginning of the end—the awakening of the teeming millions of India. I found the idea of the rickshaw driving as repugnant as on my first visit. There was the same feeling of degradation for myself and for my runner, in the fact of his being made to play the part of a human horse ... the pant, pant, pant of the runners was almost more than I could stand.[6]

At Bombay the Indians unloaded the ship's cargo of wool so the ship could be converted for the 1700 troops due to come aboard. Then the military authorities changed their minds and decided the troops would stay in India. Gandhi's Passive Resistance movement was only a few weeks old and trouble was expected. This meant the wool had to be reloaded: the Indians were inexpert at this, and the ship had to be converted for civilians. All this was wasting precious time—the opening date of the conference was now less than a month away.

Although advised not to, Vida and Cecilia visited the native quarters several times and encountered no trouble. Vida remarked on the increased anglicisation of Bombay, 'in its most inartistic aspect', since her 1911 visit. Beautiful stone and wood had been painted over and 'hideous' enamel had supplanted brass utensils. Leaving Bombay after ten days, Vida wrote, 'We have enjoyed this glimpse of India immensely, but the call of the West silences almost completely that of the East'.[7]

On 25 April the ship was in the Gulf of Aden. An Anzac service was held and the sermon was preached by an army chaplain. Vida was probably thinking of her brother Selwyn and speaking for herself when she wrote that the service was

> a glorification of the Australians, with some humorous sidelights; it had none of the dignity and impressiveness that one would have thought the

occasion demanded, and offered no comfort to those present who had lost relatives at Gallipoli and on other battlefields.[8]

As the ship passed through the Suez Canal, Vida rose at 4.45 a.m. so she would not miss 'the effect of a sunbeam on the barren but beautiful hills'. She was overjoyed by the beauty of it all and described Suez itself as a 'city set with opals'. Their ship had to wait while two ships and six submarines came through the canal. Vida called it a 'hideously impressive sight'; the submarines were 'like long snakes typifying exactly their venomous nature'. The soldiers on board these vessels answered their cooees and called out, 'Have you got Billy Hughes there? Pitch him overboard'. (Hughes was travelling from London to Paris for the Peace Conference.) They passed Kantara, which was transformed by the war, with prisoners behind barbed wire and burial grounds full of crosses. Passing the troopship *Sardinia*, Vida called out, 'Are you glad to be going home?'. She was answered by roars of delight from hundreds of throats. Passengers on both ships waved everything that could serve the purpose, from puttees to china plates. When the cheering could no longer be heard Vida experienced a 'very homesick feeling'.[9]

When they reached Port Said, Vida and Cecilia spoke to Australian soldiers who had not spoken to Australian women for four years. The women spent their time trying to establish if the ship was going to Naples as originally stated. Eventually they discovered it was going directly to London. They had planned to travel overland from Naples. Time was running out.

◆ ◆ ◆

In 1911 it had taken Vida thirty-three days to travel to London. This voyage took fifty days. The ship docked at Tilbury at 8 a.m. on 12 May, a week after the conference had been scheduled to start.[10] After seven weeks' travel to get to the conference, they had missed it. Vida and Cecilia arrived in London at 3.20 p.m. and while Cecilia waited for the luggage, Vida went to Cook's head office. A telegram waiting for her announced that the conference had been postponed a week and the venue had been changed from Paris to Zurich in neutral Switzerland to enable women from all countries to attend. This meant a longer journey, but so far they had only missed the first day. Vida turned to the clerk and said she wanted tickets and visas for Zurich, leaving immediately. He looked at her with a pitying smile and said, 'Impossible!'. He did not know to whom he spoke.

Visas usually took two to three weeks to obtain. Vida took a taxi to the Agent-General's office to ask his help and arranged to see him the next day. Then she went to the office of the Women's International League and met a woman who was just leaving for the conference. Vida told her to pass on their greetings and to hold up the proceedings till they arrived. The League had arranged their Swiss entry permits, but had been unable to get their French visas. They would have to get them the next day. Vida rejoined Cecilia and they tried to find a hotel. They rang several but they were all full. Eventually they found accommodation with a friend of Vida's. After dinner they had their passport photos taken, arriving two minutes before closing time.

The next day they started operations at 9.20 a.m. They collected their photos. (Vida thought they made them look like 'habitual criminals'.) The Agent-General's office sent them to Australia House, where they were given personal letters to the Chief Passport Officer and the French Consulate. These 'acted like magic' and they got the visas in six hours.

> When one is waiting amongst hundreds of weary, anxious people, and rushing from one office to another, at opposite ends of a great city, six hours seem like six days; but wherever we went we received the utmost consideration and courtesy.

Clutching their documents jubilantly, they went to Cook's to buy their tickets to Zurich. One hopes the same Cook's clerk was in attendance. They collected their baggage, had dinner and then set off on the two-hour train journey to Southampton. Vida tried to write about the day's events but she was distracted by the sight of the sun setting over the English countryside, resplendent in the first flush of spring.

At Southampton passports had to be cleared. Row after row of passengers sat waiting, as first one official and then another checked and rechecked the passengers and their luggage. They had a comfortable cabin to themselves and got six and a half hours' sleep.

They arrived at Havre at 7 a.m. on what was the third day of the conference. Vida, spoiled by Lizzie's cooking, described their breakfast in detail:

> [It was] the most awful meal I have ever had; a roll of brown bread, hard as a bullet—to suit the times—no butter, no margarine; something that looked like tea, but tasted like anything else; and two little pellets of saccharine, about a fifth of an inch round and nothing of an inch in thickness.

They arrived in Paris at 11 a.m. and from then on considered they were travelling *de luxe*—not in terms of comfort, but because of the cost. They were travelling through war-torn Europe only six months after the cessation of hostilities and racketeers were flourishing.

They travelled all through the night and all the next day, arriving at Zurich at 11 p.m. on 15 May.[11] The next morning, when Vida and Cecilia walked into the conference with Blanche Reverchon, the first French woman to arrive, they received a great ovation. Cecilia, in response to their welcome, told the assembled women that 'as she was leaving, a soldier had said to her that only women could prevent war in the future. It was to be hoped that women might succeed in this mission'.[12] Eleanor Moore, the Sisterhood of Peace's delegate, had left three weeks before them. She had arrived after the opening session, but had shorthand notes of the proceedings to show them.

The president, Jane Addams, had travelled via Paris where the Powers Peace Conference was being held and had obtained a copy of the Peace Terms, so this Women's Conference was the first group to pass 'impartial judgement' on this document. The women passed a resolution that the peace terms were unacceptable. There was considerable debate, especially about the proposed League of Nations. All the delegates agreed that the proposals were disappointing, but some argued that they were better than anarchy, while others deemed them totally unacceptable.[13]

Addressing the conference, Vida said Australia was as enslaved as Europe by militarism and had the iniquity of boy conscription under the guise of compulsory military training. She appealed for help to fight this and militarism worldwide. Conferences such as this were important to 'develop the international conscience, instead of the selfish spirit of nationalism'. She called on women in 'troublous times' to 'take as our watchword that wonderful word "Love". It is the only thing that keeps the world moving, it is the only weapon that counts, it is the sword of the spirit that alone will bring an enduring peace'. Vida also moved a motion that the League of Nations should abolish censorship of the press; it was carried, but her motion to prohibit compulsory medical examinations in all countries was unsuccessful.[14]

In her summing up, Emily Blach (who Vida had met in America in 1902) noted the absence of 'incidents' at the congress and remarked on the growing sense of coming power among the women. Acutely aware that they had been members of small minorities in their own countries, the women were hopeful that in the world of the future, women would have more power and would use it to work against militarism and to improve the quality of life.

The final meeting was a banquet at the Tonhalle. The tables were bright with flowers and the delegates engaged in animated conversations in many languages. Students in national costumes sang songs, including a peace song specially written for the occasion. Jane Addams, in the closing address, said they had shown that women could come together in genuine friendship and understanding and that if it could be done on a small scale it could be done on a larger scale. Eleanor Moore later wrote that the saddest part was farewelling the German women. One woman said to Eleanor, 'Think of us; we are going back into the night'. She could see all too clearly the future for post-war Germany, which would ultimately lead to another war.[15]

The moment that remained etched in Vida's mind was the arrival of Madame Melin from war-devastated northern France. She was presented with a bunch of pink roses, symbolising the beauty of universal love, by Fraulein Heymann in the name of German women. Madame Melin replied with a moving speech in French. 'It is not my country, it is not your country that is guilty of the crimes against humanity—c'est La Guerre, c'est La Guerre.' She called on all present to fight war.[16] (In contrast, the men at the official conference in Paris humiliated the defeated Germans and set punitive conditions that laid the foundations of World War II.)

There was scarcely a dry eye in the hall, but

> they were not tears of emotionalism, they sprang from deep wells of grief that hate, and jealousy, and ambition, and brutal malice should seem to have power to crush the love and trust that are the common attributes of

all mankind; they came also as tears of gratitude that there were some women in every country who had remained true to the universal sense of love.[17]

Vida looked about her, her eyes moist. Beside her were German women who had been imprisoned for their pacifism, French women who had suffered terribly in war zones, German women who had worked to help French women interned in Germany. She was part of an international movement of women who had suffered for their pacifist beliefs. Surely together they could build a future of world peace.

◆ ◆ ◆

In contrast to their dash across the continent, Vida and Cecilia returned to England in short stages to avoid spending the nights in trains. They would arrive in a town, book a hotel and then hurry off to explore the sights. They arrived in Paris in the middle of a public transport strike. The taxi drivers were 'coining' money. They visited Reims, where only seven houses remained intact at the end of the war. Vida wrote how flimsy things like lampshades had survived undamaged inside the ruined houses. The magnificent Gothic cathedral had been reduced to a shell and had been left as a reminder of the war. She wrote that the visit 'bring[s] home to one the ghastly wickedness of war and its absolute futility'.[18]

They crossed the Channel at Bologne and stayed at Folkestone, before going on to London, where they parted. Vida remained in London and Cecilia returned to Australia via America. They probably kept in contact, but there is no further documentary record of their friendship. Cecilia arrived in Melbourne in October and was greeted by her friends. She spoke of her experiences and said she was more determined than ever to continue her work, particularly to bring music to the people, to set up a Save the Children fund in Australia and to promote Dalcroze Eurhythmic dancing which she had studied while overseas.[19]

Vida felt some disillusionment with the way the peace plans were being handled and with the proposed League of Nations. There was still terrible suffering in Europe; babies were starving, strikes were crippling the poor and many countries were still at war or under the domination of a foreign army. In July Vida wrote, 'Peace has been signed and proclaimed, but no-one believes that peace reigns'. She maintained her 'simple faith in moral force' and her conviction that 'Righteousness exalteth a Nation'.[20]

Vida was now fifty and took this time, alone in England, to reassess her life and work. She decided to remain in England for some time rather than return immediately to Australia as she had originally intended. The *Woman Voter* explained, 'In the heart of the upheaval of things, and after earnest reflection, she has made her change of plans'.[21] Vida later wrote that 'in 1919 I felt I could no longer work in the political field because the people did not seem willing to tread this path'. In her notes she added that the people 'preferred party politics and questions of principle were sacrificed', but she crossed this out.[22] She told the WPA she would not be returning to Australia for some time and waived any further claim for monies from the delegates' fund. She had only received £238 4s 6d. Cecilia had had to pay her own costs and had carried out business connected with the People's Conservatorium to defray expenses.

Vida argued that the post-war world called for new methods and new endeavours. This was accepted, and both the WPA and the *Woman Voter* were disbanded. In the last issue of the *Woman Voter* the acting editor wrote of the demise of the WPA:

> The step has been well considered on the part of Miss Goldstein, and is endorsed by the Association, whose individuals, by the passage of events, feel with her that the changing of the old order calls for a more comprehensive outlook upon the world's affairs than ever before ... The aftermath of the war, even more than the war itself, has shown us the utter futility of the tinkering processes of reform that each and all of the methods adopt that do not aim at a complete upheaval and reconstruction ... The world is sick unto death, and the sources of Government—if we may put it so—polluted ...
>
> The present intention of the Association is to go into recess (not to vegetate, but to possess our souls); into what we shall then emerge, it doth not yet appear. But we MUST not, DARE not be idle.[23]

When the news of the disbandment reached Vida, she was not surprised, 'although she greatly regretted it'. She had come to realise that 'no organisation could have a proper life or an assured future, when it leant so entirely on one person'.[24] In Vida's final letter to the

WPA, her first word was 'international' and the last was 'spiritual'. More than ever she was convinced of the importance of both, and that without the latter the former could not become a reality.[25] She intended to work in a new way—through her Christian Science faith.

Privately her staunch supporters were dismayed. Mabel Singleton recalled after Vida's death:

> Someone remarked that 'when Vida retired into the Christian Science world it was almost the same as entering a Convent' and people soon forget. I shall always retain my love and deep admiration for her, as a friend and leader, but this does not prevent my feeling of disappointment through the years that she should have taken such a step. I believe she would have become one of the foremost women leaders of her day. Probably if I knew her reasons I should think differently.[26]

Little is known of Vida's personal life during this time in England. She did visit Selwyn's widow and their four children in Buckinghamshire. She was still in contact with friends she had made on her 1911 visit. She wrote affectionately to Adela Pankhurst and told 'My dearest Adela' about visits to her sister, Sylvia Pankhurst, and the latest news about Emmeline and Christabel Pankhurst. Vida also gave Adela advice about an insurance policy and told her she must inform the company of her marriage, which had taken place three years before. She finished with greetings to Adela's husband and family and 'plenty of love to yourself'.[27]

Vida watched the procession for Peace Day in July. She joined the South Londoners and stood by the roadway, surrounded by Australian soldiers, as the countries marched by in alphabetical order. She followed the crowds into a park and heard a choir sing the 'Hallelujah Chorus'. She joined the rush to see the Queen as she drove past. Even though it was raining, the Queen ordered that the cover be put down so the people could see her. Vida decided she 'could visualize the fireworks' so went home, soaked through, but feeling very satisfied.[28]

In September Vida attended the National Council of Women Conference on the proposed League of Nations and spoke at the British Dominions' Women's Citizens' Union about women being represented on the League of Nations. She attended the final convention of the No-Conscription Fellowship. It was held at the Society of Friends' headquarters, the first time another group had been allowed to use it on a Sunday. Vida thought the conference was 'wonderful' and was delighted when the Quakers joined in singing 'The Red Flag'. She remarked, 'Certainly the world moves'.[29]

Vida wrote to Hyde Champion, hoping he could arrange to have her writing published. She was writing fortnightly letters, under the title Sidelights on Peace: A Warning and an Appeal, in which she dealt with the political situation in England and a wide range of issues; Italian socialists, Russia (the 'eighth wonder of the world'), Constantinople, Lady Astor's maiden speech, the Miners' Campaign and the third International.[30]

As a new decade dawned, Vida wrote more hopefully of the League of Nations, saying it

> might be a stepping stone to higher things ... In all the medley one thing stands out sharply, clearly—the insistent demand on the part of thinkers to get back to fundamental 'truths', fundamental 'principles' of life ... the conviction that life is essentially a unity.[31]

Vida watched the March of Labour on May Day 1920, in Piccadilly near Hyde Park corner. Although some of the marchers looked tired as they neared the end of the march, they remained in good spirits. The National Union of Returned Servicemen turned out in force. As one marched past Vida, he said, 'We're walkin' for what we were fightin' for and ain't got'. Vida thought the 'most pathetic' group was the Blind Men's Union demanding State Aid. The Communist Party struck the 'most artistic note'. She was disappointed at first that none of the others had decorated their transport, but realised that 'the feeble, methodical machine like efforts at decoration on the carts and cars were the only striving after beauty and joy of expression that life and education had hitherto offered them'. Vida thought this 'mighty march was the first hint that a new world really has made its appearance ... It was a great and vital procession, aglow with the hope of the future and lighted also with the best of England's past—her traditions and liberty'. She wondered whether Australian authorities would permit 'Bolshevism, the I.W.W., Sinn Fein, to hurl their propaganda against all comers, to fly triumphantly the Orange and Green, and Red flags'.[32] Vida admired this liberalism of the English and was impressed when she attended the World Woman's Christian Temperance Union Convention to see people there selling literature of all creeds. The only objection came from an American woman. Vida told her she admired such tolerance.[33]

Vida went to Geneva for the Women's International Suffrage Congress in June 1920 and wrote an article for it entitled 'A Bird's Eye View, 1902–1920'. There were delegates from thirty-one countries. Nineteen countries had enfranchised women since 1913, including Britain in 1918 and the United States of America in 1920. Vida saw this as the 'spirit of the new world that is rising from the ashes of the old'. She wrote one of her most charming descriptions:

> The enfranchised women sat in a large half circle at one end of the platform, wearing their national colours, their chests puffed out like pouter pigeons, their faces beaming; the unenfranchised women, a small group, sat at the other end, their drooping shoulders, and dejected countenances being a delightful piece of play acting belying altogether the joy which animated them at the recital of the victories won by their enfranchised sisters by means of the vote and the hope of swift-approaching victory in their own land.

Carrie Chapman Catt, the president, dressed in black and flanked by the women of India, China and Japan in their 'gorgeous saris and silvery kimonos', said, 'I never thought that I should live to see the day when I should have to ask enfranchised women to hurry up with what they had to say because there were so many of them!'. Delegates were urged to take home with them 'a new spirit of international unity based upon that new conception of love which, in spite of wars and rumours of wars, is beginning to fill the hearts of all peoples'.[34]

In August Vida wrote about the League of Nations, dubbing it the 'League of Some Nations'. She said governments were trying to reconstruct it on pre-war ideas; they did not realise that the pre-war world had gone forever. There was also a mellowing in her thinking and a certain fatalism when she wrote:

> In public affairs there are such wheels within wheels, such violent clashing of interests, that it becomes more and more difficult to see where right lies, and so I am not going to judge anyone or anything ... Those who want to oppress will always endeavour to find a way to make war ... will always argue that the end justifies the means ... There is no difference in principle between a capitalist war and a class war.

As if writing her farewell speech, she said:

> The easiest thing in the world is to criticise, and it is a relief to turn from the overheated political atmosphere and breathe the pure air of the things

that endure — the commemoration of the sailing of the *Mayflower*, the unveiling of the statue of Abraham Lincoln in Canning Square opposite Westminster Abbey. The cargo of conviction and conscience that the *Mayflower* carried to America, the greatness, the simplicity, the invincible integrity of Lincoln, remain for all time, and League of Nations or no League of Nations, are gradually drawing the Anglo-Saxon peoples together encircling them with invisible cords that are stronger than all the armies of all the world.[35]

She continued to write the fortnightly letters throughout 1921. She reported the Coal Strike of 1921 and wrote that she had witnessed three great industrial crises in England: the Railway Strike of 1911 and the Coal Strikes of 1919 and 1921. She believed that the outstanding feature of each had been the lack of cohesion among the workers.

During her time in England the course of Vida's life changed. 'There came to her a great distaste for public life and political campaigning' and she 'shrank from all the old accustomed limelight'.[36] The letters stop at the end of 1921 and some time after this, she left England and returned to Australia, where her arrival went unheralded.

During her absence the world truly had moved. At fifty-three, Vida quietly retired from public life. She did not intend to be inactive: a new career awaited her, as a Christian Science practitioner.

13

A spiritual woman

1923–1949

◆

When Vida returned to Australia she lived quietly with Aileen Goldstein and Elsie and Hyde Champion in a flat at 462 Punt Road, South Yarra. Vida and Aileen maintained an office in the city where they counselled people on religion, psychology and health according to Christian Science principles. Elsie continued to operate the Book Lovers' Library. Their niece Leslie Henderson worked there and was shocked when Elsie refused to employ Roman Catholics. Vida shared Elsie's prejudice and when Leslie challenged her, Vida admitted that this was against Christian principles, but that it was justified because Catholicism was a false religion, contrary to the teachings of Christ. She told Leslie that the 'coming struggle in the world' would be between Christian Science and Catholicism.[1]

After Hyde Champion died in April 1928 the sisters decided Elsie should travel abroad before she got too old and that Vida would accompany her. They left in early 1929 and Leslie, now a partner, remained in charge of the bookshop while they were away. The sisters travelled to London and Keith Murdoch was one of their fellow travellers. At Colombo the group was keen to visit the native bazaars and dine there but Murdoch, fearful of contagion, invited them to be his guests at dinner in the leading English hotel.[2]

In England, Vida and Elsie had lunch with George Bernard Shaw. Vida had met Shaw on her first visit to England in 1911. Champion had published him in the early days of his career, when others had rejected him, and Shaw never forgot this. Shaw made Champion his dramatic agent in Australia and after Champion's death transferred the agency to Elsie. In London Elsie sold some of Shaw's first-edition books inscribed to Champion. They raised £250, which helped to finance the trip.[3]

Meanwhile at home the shop was in financial difficulty, exacerbated by the recession and imminent depression. Leslie wrote anxiously to Elsie, but the 'only result was that she and Vida went off to America to visit the Christian Science Church (the Mother Church) in Boston'. The sisters returned to Australia late in the year and the partnership between Leslie and Elsie was dissolved. With the Book Lovers' verging on bankruptcy, Vida and Aileen tried to help Elsie, 'sacrificing practically all their savings to keep the business afloat', but it was to no avail and Elsie was forced to close the shop, much to the sadness of her many loyal customers and subscribers.[4] Stella Miles Franklin, in a letter to Vida, also admitted to feeling a certain disappointment. While agreeing there was 'no sense in working to pay rent', she confessed the closure ended a small ambition of hers: to have a window display full of her novels.[5] She believed Elsie's shop would have been her best hope. In actuality, Stella never did achieve much literary recognition or financial success in her lifetime. She died in 1954 and her bequest established the Miles Franklin award for literature. Elsie was undeterred by the closing of the Book Lovers', and at the age of sixty-six she set out to find a new position. She worked briefly at Collins Book Depot, then at Robertson & Mullens until she was retrenched in 1953. She died that year at the age of eighty-three.[6]

On her return from overseas Vida wrote an article, based on her observations in England, which was published in the *Herald* in 1930. Entitled 'Women Can Help Australia More' it is characteristic of Vida's writings in later life. It presents many of her major convictions and a certain disappointment she felt in the failure of the women's movement to capitalise on the gains that had been so hard won by her generation. Vida had been impressed by the young women in England who were working to help solve the problems England faced. She believed women had unique abilities and could provide a spiritual side to life and 'provide a brake on mere materialism'. In Australia, however, the women who were doing 'unselfish, exacting public work' were the women who were involved years ago; young women had not 'shown themselves alive to their responsibilities' as their English counterparts had.

She believed that 'Youth instinctively looks upwards and onwards; it is unnatural for us to stagnate, to be satisfied without achievement', so it was vital to establish organisations for young women to involve them politically and to keep them abreast of world events. Australians still felt isolated because of their geographic position and they did not realise that what happened in the rest of the world affected them. She now opposed tariffs and protection because they were a form of war, and believed people must think globally not nationally. What was needed was 'idealism, service, a conscious turning from the material to the spiritual, for "where there is no vision the people perish"'. The article was published with a photo of Vida, now aged sixty-one. Her greying hair had been cut short, but her mouth was still resolute and her dark eyes still stared challengingly at the world.[7]

Vida channelled her energies into Christian Science work and refused most invitations to attend or speak at various women's associations. She did not seek personal honours or the public limelight, but occasionally she could not resist the opportunity to publicise her views. She declined the invitation to the fourth triennial Conference of the Australian Women Federation of Women Voters, even though the organiser, Bessie Rischbieth, assured her she would be welcomed 'with open arms'.[8] Vida did send a telegram of greetings and apologised to Bessie for not having helped her more in her 'unselfed service for women, for humanity'.[9] Vida's time had been fully occupied, being 'lost to the world for some months preparing the affair which exceeds our wildest hopes'. This was the Christian Science Monitor Exhibition of 27–9 April 1933.[10]

Vida continued to write some articles, using them as a means of education and dissemination of her ideas. She must have felt a certain sense of achievement when she compiled a list of Women's Progress in Victoria for Victoria's Centennial in 1934:

> Political freedom, the right to enter the professions; to act as Inspectors, Police Matrons, and Justices of the Peace; Widows' Maintenance, a share in the Custody and Guardianship of their children, and every measure of freedom the women of the State enjoy today they owe to the women suffragists, who faced obloquy and the cruellest ridicule in carrying on the educational work in order to rouse the public from its opposition to women's complete social, political, and economic emancipation.[11]

Vida was acknowledged for her assistance in the foreword to the *Centenary Gift Book*. The profits were to fund a memorial to pioneer women and the articles focused on women's achievements. Vida was featured in an article by the journalist and suffragist Alice Henry, outlining the struggle for the suffrage.[12]

Vida wrote 'Towards a New Social Order' for the twenty-fifth anniversary of the Women's Non Party Political Association of South Australia in 1934. She recalled the 'eager vision' of her youth that women would achieve equality and the young would be protected, but wrote ruefully that this still seemed far off. The country was in the grip of the Great Depression and there was no social, industrial or political question of greater importance to women than high unemployment. She wanted the association to consider if it were time to work differently and suggested the solution was to build on spiritual foundations. The year before, she had written to the Women's Conference in Sydney proposing that women organise a Campaign of Education for a New Social Order. She called on the South Australian women to consider this idea.[13] Privately she hoped 'for something inspiring and practical' from the meeting.[14]

Vida acknowledged the multiplicity of organisations already in existence, but believed it was vital to establish one that concentrated on the 'supreme necessity', education. She argued that the 'inspiration, art and beauty that characterised the Suffragette Movement need to be re-born, without the militancy of the Movement'. She advocated the revival of the suffragist colours.[15] The movement would be based on the fatherhood of God and the brotherhood of man and work for security of employment, adequate purchasing power instead of artificial restriction of production, and would 'Build Friendships not Battleships'. It was her 'absolute conviction that the only remedy for the existing conditions is the establishment of a Just Social Order based on the Ten C[ommandments] and the S[ermon] on the M[oun]t'.[16]

◆ ◆ ◆

Vida now spent her days in her 'loved and familiar environment'; her office in the city, her flat at 74 Leopold Street, South Yarra, and, within walking distance, her beloved church, the First Church of Christ, Scientist, in St Kilda Road.[17] In June 1935, members of the church elected Vida second reader, for a term of three years. In Christian Science services the sermon is made up of scriptural texts, read from the Bible by the second reader, and their correlative passages from the textbook *Science and Health with Key to the Scriptures* by Mary Baker Eddy, read by the first reader. Vida found it 'a great joy reading the Bible'.[18] Vida also served as president twice, chairing business meetings of church members.[19]

Her friend Julia Rapke, describing Vida at this time, wrote how one was 'conscious of the depth of that great inner force that is her driving power'. Her 'passionate love of freedom and justice' was still evident although she had withdrawn from the 'hurly burly of life'. She still read widely and studied deeply and did the occasional crossword puzzle. She was 'a contented woman happy in the society of her sisters and her friends'.[20]

The friendship and correspondence with Stella Miles Franklin continued. When Stella's mother died in 1935, Vida's letter of condolence touched on what her faith meant in her own life:

> With all my heart dear Stella, I wish one could feel that you feel life has still much to offer you; that you could find comfort and joy in what, to me, are the very fundamentals of being. In these days most people, seemingly, have to meet much that would claim to disturb their peace, but I can assure you that no matter what assails I find life satisfying and enriching— because unharmony of any kind compels one to seek and find the reality of being, the Life which is Spirit. That is the Life-time job of every 'mortal'. In the past we have discussed the question, and you have tried to find what we have found; so far, without success, but try again, darling, putting away every preconceived idea of so-called 'Life' and its unending miseries. And whenever you feel like wanting a real talk on paper write to me— crash, bang, against anything and everthing [Christian] Science included! But let us get somewhere with our long, long friendship; don't let it hang in mid-air.[21]

Stella said that the Goldsteins 'always treated me as a daugther of the house'.[22] They exchanged Christmas gifts and Stella always included a gift for Lizzie. In 1935 it was a handkerchief and Vida kept it for Christmas morning and later wrote to Stella that Lizzie was 'always so excited over the many parcels she receives'. Lizzie was now very lame, but still 'full of beans' and she often surprised their other maid with her capacity for work. Vida told Stella the maid was a young deserted wife with a seven-month-old baby 'whom we all love'.[23] That year Stella sent Vida a handbag. Vida wrote that it was a 'charming and acceptable bag', adding 'I can never have too many bags ... I always think Sydney gifts and Sydney clothes have an air of distinction that those of Melbourne do not have'.[24]

When 'our most beloved' Lizzie died in January 1941, Vida wrote to Stella:

> We can never forget her lifelong friendship, her unselfed devotion to us. She seemed to give every thought and act to us, and our love and gratitude are undying. She was so happy at Christmas time and treasured your recollection of her.[25]

Vida still followed current affairs and in 1936 asked Stella how the New South Wales public men and newspapers were 'preparing thought' for compulsory military training. The Returned Soldiers had voted in favour of it the day before.[26] In 1936 she wrote an article which appeared in the *Australian Woman's World*. She praised King Edward VIII for being aware of the suffering caused by war and poverty and his aim to work for world peace and full employment. Vida said her ambition to enter Parliament 'to further my ideals for a new social, economic and world order' had long since ceased, but her ideals had not. They had become 'stronger, deeper, more comprehensive' and now she sought to achieve them in another way. When she had read the King's speech, she wished she could have been Prime Minister for a day so she could draw the world's attention to it.

In this article Vida also supported Maurice Blackburn who had been expelled from the Labor Party for his association with the Movement Against War and Fascism. Vida said she had always opposed the Australian Labor Party's pledge system because it excluded worthy people who could not rigidly subscribe to all the platform. She wrote, 'Character is greater than any Party, and our country cannot afford to lose the services of one such man'.[27]

In October 1938, as war loomed once more, only twenty years after the end of the Great War, Vida wrote 'Shall we Organise to Defend Democracy?' for the One Way Club. Christian Scientists believed in self-organisation, 'the organisation of disciplined, reflected spiritual thinking', but as citizens of the Commonwealth they had to fulfil public duty, including submission to compulsory military service. Vida questioned the use of compulsion to defend democracy and advocated defence being organised voluntarily, but she acknowledged that 'We Democrats must face up to the fact that Dictatorial countries have all their resources organised to perfection'. She admired Chamberlain for being the first to use the new method of negotiation and reason.[28]

When the war began in 1939, Robert Menzies' United Australia Party Government introduced conscription for service within Australia without consulting the people by referendum. Maurice Blackburn presided over the No Conscription Campaign in Victoria and was the only member of Federal Parliament to vote against the Curtin Labor Government's Bill which introduced limited overseas conscription in 1943. (Curtin had been an anti-conscriptionist in World War I.) Blackburn was defeated at the 1943 election and died the following year.[29]

Vida responded to the war by campaigning for peace through prayer and exhorting the nation's leaders to return society to godliness as the only sure way of winning victory. In August 1942 she wrote to Prime Minister John Curtin calling on the Australian Government to lead the crusade against the 'Goliath of Drink'. She argued that when the six o'clock closing laws were enacted against alcohol during World War I, victory soon followed because the 'divine law of right was obeyed'.[30]

In November 1942 she wrote to Keith Murdoch, sending the letter to his home to 'safeguard anonymity'. Convinced that the King's Special Prayers Day on 26 May 1940 had resulted in the 'miracle of Dunkirk', she proposed that the *Herald* should carry a message each day showing that God's word was more important than anything else. Vida asked for the 'privilege of selecting the messages, *under the strictest anonymity*' as they 'could only come from the heart of one who felt inspired with a special mission'. She said it 'would require consecrated prayer and deep spiritual research to make the messages a living force, showing suitable sequence when necessary and an intelligent appreciation of the applicability of God's Word to the event of the day'. She said it must have the heading 'GOD FIRST'. She called her suggestion 'The War and National Life from a New Angle—GOD'.[31] Murdoch replied politely:

> I read [the letter] with great interest, but I felt at once that it was impossible for us to carry out your idea. It is brilliantly done, but it is simply not newspaper matter, particularly in these days of spacelessness.[32]

Vida and her sisters also provided practical aid by sending food parcels overseas every month. They were still sending them at the end of 1948. According to Vida their dining room resembled a grocer's store. She thought it was shocking that the Australian Government was not doing more. They sent the parcels to friends in England, as well as to poor districts which had been bombed and to old-age pensioners. Their friends wrote that the parcels tasted 'so very pre-war'. Emmeline Pethick-Lawrence wrote that she felt a 'quite childish' pleasure in receiving them. The sisters also contributed tins of dripping for Britain to the Lord Mayor's Fund, the 'first they had received'.[33]

◆ ◆ ◆

A feature article on Vida appeared in the *Australian Women's Digest* in 1945. It described Vida at the age of seventy-six:

> Here is a woman whose vital and charming personality would still make of her an invaluable leader, whose mind is trained and experienced, whose insight is deep and revealing. But it is with the blessing of all for whom she has fought that she now enjoys the rest and freedom so richly earned through the years of splendid endeavour.[34]

This was not entirely accurate because Vida continued to pursue her lifetime concerns. She was a member of a deputation to Parliament in 1944 regarding the treatment of women with venereal disease and the proposed divorce legislation. She was still interested in social questions and in particular the 'tragic effect' of drink on young people. She believed that women must take an active part in combating this. She still firmly advocated that women should be educated in civic responsibility: 'an active interest in politics is a duty which every woman owes to the community, to herself, and to the home'.[35] She addressed the first meeting of the Women for Canberra Movement, which was established in 1942 to increase the number of women being elected to Parliament. Women had been elected to State parliaments (the first being Edith Cowan in 1921 in Western Australia), but not one woman had been elected to Federal Parliament. The Women for Canberra Movement raised money to help female candidates and adopted Vida's ideas of women's parliaments and sending questionnaires to candidates.[36]

For the 1943 election, Vida sent her own questionnaire to candidates asking if they would support the complete freedom of Christian Scientists to exercise their religion in relying on prayer in sickness, provided they obeyed the law in relation to contagious and infectious diseases. She also called for the reduction of the alcoholic content of liquor; the use of the term 'mistress', not 'female dependent' to describe de facto relationships in the services (a 'complete degradation of marriage'); equal treatment of the sexes (if women with venereal disease were to be gaoled, then the men, their 'paymasters', should be too); revision of the Protection Tariff and White Australia policy; an education system which made the 'training of character the first essential' and a financial system which made 'Money the Servant and not the Master of the people'.[37]

One sadness of Vida's old age was that many of her former colleagues had either settled overseas (including Mary Fullerton, Mabel Singleton and Cecilia John) or had died. One special friend was Edith How Martyn, an English science graduate and the first graduate to be imprisoned in the suffragette campaigns. In 1944 Vida told Edith how much she valued their friendship:

> I told you once that I know no one here, no woman I mean, with whom I can discuss the questions in which you and I are interested. No woman at all to whom the moral and legal status of women, their spiritual value in human affairs, the welfare and rights of the so-called 'common man', and the interdependence of nations, is really vital. What is going to rouse the women of Australia, indeed the women of the world, to such devotion to and sacrifice for freedom, as inspired the Suffragettes?

She asked if Edith had met Stella and added:

> We are great personal friends—we have known her since she was a girl— but we do not always see things alike. Entre nous, she is an unhappy woman, without any spiritual convictions, and always struggling with a sense of frustration, but when she lets herself go, she is witty and amusing.

Edith had asked if Vida had thought of writing of the pioneer days. Vida wished she could, but her Christian Science work took all her time and meant very late hours, 'but what does that matter when one is helping others to live?'. She had thought of doing radio talks, but did not have the time even for that.[38] Four years later, Vida did make the time to contribute an article to *Pioneer Pathways* for the WCTU's jubilee in 1948. She outlined the history of the struggle for the suffrage and summarised its achievements:

> The result has been exactly what the suffrage pioneers of Australia contemplated. Woman Suffrage has worked as leaven in both spheres; the woman's point of view has found expression in special legislation affecting the interests of women and children, but it was never expected that in any country governed by party politics, and the political machine methods used to secure the domination of party interests, women would, as a body, prove themselves to be different from men in regard to party affiliations.[39]

She acknowledged here that she had lost the fight to make non-party politics a force in Australia and to convince women to vote for a woman and not a party.

Vida followed the careers of women in Parliament with interest, although she wrote she was 'so ignorant of their doings ... my work keeps me tied'.[40] She said Dorothy Tangney (the first woman senator, elected in 1943, forty years after Vida's first campaign) had 'valiantly' raised the question of uniform divorce laws but had failed to urge equality of men and women in the legislation. Vida added with a sense of frustration, 'Perhaps she was not fully reported, but she *was* reported as repeating her previous emphatic statement that she is not a feminist!'.[41] In 1946 when Doris Blackburn was elected to her husband's former seat as an Independent Labor member, Vida hoped her former campaign secretary would 'accomplish something worthwhile, although she seems to lack driving force'.[42] Two years later Vida was disappointed in Doris Blackburn's performance because on several occasions her vote had been 'absolutely subservient' to Labor and she showed 'no evidence of independence'.[43]

Vida thought it 'tragic' that the Federation of Women Voters had asked for 75 per cent of men's pay in the hope of obtaining equal pay later. She wrote, 'One would think they were better tacticians than that!'.[44] The Federal Public Service Act of 1902, which Vida had campaigned for, had enshrined the principle of equal pay, but the provision was removed in 1916, with little resistance from women or unions. The Commonwealth did not again accept the principle of equal pay for equal work until 1969.

◆ ◆ ◆

Vida could see little of good in the post–World War II world. She was appalled by the atom bomb

> and still more appalled at the comparative silence of the churches, and the apparent total silence of the women of the world.
> Surely one might reasonably look for the spirit of the Suffragettes to be re-born in women against the inventions of Science being centred on weapons of destruction; and the renewed, frenzied talk of the next war, and preparation for it, by our 'Statesmen'.

She believed bacteriological warfare was 'more horrible and terrible than the atom bomb!' and that women needed moral courage to prevent war.[45] She saw some hope for the future in the women's meeting of Protest against Use of Atomic Energy for Destructive Ends in August 1946. She was ill and unable to attend, so Aileen read her message, which said:

> Protests, to be effective, must be followed by resolute action, and, at this crisis in world history when materialistic energy aims at overthrowing spiritual energy and moral values, action needs to develop into a *World Crusade for the Spiritual Economic Well-being of Humanity.*[46]

Publicly Vida continued to promote her convictions, but privately she admitted to feeling frustration, even despair. Writing to Stella for Christmas 1947 (including some coloured cotton dishcloths she had made herself because 'White dish cloths always get such an abominable colour') she asked:

> Well, what do you think of our post war world? Doesn't Hitler seem to have won the war? He said something to the effect that if he didn't win it, he would bring civilization down with him. As you know, I have not a fraction of sex antagonism in me, but one is almost driven to think that men are absolutely unfit to govern. They seem incapable of thinking and acting on other than belligerent lines. War, war, war—either fighting wars or trade wars. Humanity is their last consideration. The Atomic Bomb doesn't kill off enough human beings quickly enough, so now they turn their attention to bacteria to accomplish their devilish ends.
> But what about women also? I feel they, too, have failed humanity in two world wars. They proved their ability to help their country in a time of national crisis, but have done nothing to prevent crises recurring. Where are the women's demands and organisations for a practical humanitarian programme, a 'fighting' programme to make the world a fit place to

live in? I marvel at the silence and inaction of women. Why don't they rise and war against war, call it by its right name, *mass murder*, strip it of its 'glory', expose the vice, the political and economic and financial corruption that go with it; above all the trade policies that make war inevitable? Sometimes I wish I were thirty years younger, and could have a say and do again on behalf of the common people![47]

In Vida's next letter to Stella she suggested Stella and Alice Henry could organise a 'Women's Crusade' to 'rouse people to the necessity for a radical change in our social system'. It should be educative, not propagandist. 'Not accusation, not distrust — just understanding is needed'. Meetings would be held where different remedies could be debated. 'Anything, anything that will set people thinking!' She added that she had not thought of the proposal until she had started writing to Stella, but that she would write to Bessie Rischbieth about it. She concluded, 'Do you think I am mad!'.[48] Vida wrote to Edith:

> If I did not have an absolute faith that the government of good is pursuing its way to the ultimate recognition by mankind that it is the only law for nations and individuals, I would seek some retreat from the madding crowd, read nothing but the classics, and knit for 'the poor'.[49]

She returned to this theme in a subsequent letter to Edith:

> Such a world! Such men! Such women! Failure 'seems' to stalk triumphantly everywhere. I say 'seems', because I *know* that good, though unseen, is actually triumphing ... God is on the field when most He seems invisible ... I am nevertheless still bewailing the colossal failure, on the surface though it be, of women ... no one organized protest against the Atom Bomb, against Bacteriological Warfare preparations, against the resumption of the methods that produce war, shortages ... 'Time provides the man'—or woman. Does it?[50]

She was inspired by the visit of Dr de Lange, a Dutch metaphysician, in 1948. She told Edith he

> has lifted us on to the mountain top, and now we have to come down to earth again and apply what he has given us ... The future belongs to youth but I would dearly love to see the women leaders of today giving them a lead based on their wide experience. The trouble is they seem to have no vision of a new world.

She wondered why the great religious teachers and founders had been men, when she believed women were more spiritual, and suggested an answer to her own question: 'Motherhood? Domesticity? and a dozen other feminine shackles perhaps'.[51]

She asked if there were any young people of real promise and which group had 'a programme that young people would live and die for?'. The only promising youngsters were in the Communist Party because 'Communists, old and young, promise them the world and all that is therein'. The state of Australian politics was 'absolutely demoralising'; she had 'no respect' for Labor's programme and methods and the Liberal Party had 'neither a worthwhile programme, nor leaders, nor followers'.[52]

◆ ◆ ◆

Vida kept in touch with some friends from the old days, although she forgot to attend one meeting of 'The Group'. When Helen Archdale, a Christian Scientist Vida had met in England, visited Australia the 'Suffragette clan' had tea together, 'small body as they are'. Usually only about four came, but on this occasion eleven 'rolled up' to meet the woman who had been one of the mainstays of the Pankhursts during the hunger strikes.[53] Vida was still in correspondence with the Pethick-Lawrences and in touch with Jennie Baines. Vida said the 84-year-old Jennie was 'a marvel in appearance; doesn't look more than seventy. Although still a militant at heart, the methods of the Labour Party have sobered her a lot. As a member of the local branch she has seen and heard much that revolts her'.[54] Vida and Adela had lost contact. Adela and Tom Walsh had left the socialists and coverted to the extreme right of politics. They campaigned against strikes and Adela ran the anti-union Women's Guild of Empire. In 1940 they visited Japan as guests of the Japanese Government and returned full of praise of Japan. In 1941 Adela joined the Australia First Movement and in 1942 she was interned, accused of espionage. Vida, writing to Edith in 1949, commented, 'Poor Adela Pankhurst—what a miserable life she has led. She has had no vital principle to guide her. I wonder what her politics are these days'.[55]

Vida and Aileen continued to correspond with Stella. When Stella's *My Career Goes Bung* was published in 1946, Aileen read it and wrote forthrightly to Stella that she could not say she enjoyed it 'because sexy things never attract me' and then asked Stella if she thought her 'very old fashioned or prudish'. She found the book 'very clever and amusing but where do you get some of your words from?'.[56] Stella replied in joking vein, obliquely agreeing that they were prudish. She asked if the soap and washing powder Vida and Aileen had sent her was to wash away her sins and accused Aileen of living in a nunnery. Stella found it amusing that in the 'nubile decades' men had called her sexless—a mind not a woman. She believed women had not advanced since Vida and Rose Scott's time because 'women are more freed to ape men's vices and amours'.[57] In 1948 she asked Aileen to tell Vida that her work was 'not without fruit'. She had seen a 'traffic copess'. Commenting on modern dress she recalled that in 1904 a trottoir skirt reaching the ankle bone was considered 'fast'. She concluded, 'The world has progressed but not in the way we hoped!'.[58]

◆ ◆ ◆

Vida was now eighty years old and had been suffering from cancer for some time. One of her last public statements was to the League of Women Voters for its silver jubilee in 1949. She called on the members to work to increase the spiritual stature of average men and women.[59] As her life neared its end, the spiritual became increasingly important to her.

Vida died on 15 August 1949 at her home in South Yarra. She was cremated at a private service at the Springvale Crematorium two days later. Her ashes were scattered.

Aileen wrote to Stella that Vida had remained 'mentally vigorous'. Her death was not unexpected, 'although we hoped to the end'. Vida had lived 'a very full eighty years'.[60] Writing to Edith, Aileen affirmed their faith that 'my sister [Elsie] and I feel that Vida must still be active in the work she loved, so we cannot grieve for her'.[61] Her letter to Stella echoed this belief:

> ... we are so confident that Vida has only passed on to a further interesting experience, continuing in the work she loved—with a greater sense of freedom, having awakened to find the nothingness of death ... If it were *not* so what would be the meaning of this existence![62]

Afterword

♦

Vida's most outstanding traits were her strength of character, her commitment to alleviating suffering and her deep spirituality, traits all fostered by her upbringing. She was the favoured eldest child who was perceived to be special by her parents and teachers. She came from a privileged class that enjoyed a sense of stability and wide horizons of opportunity. From a young age, Vida had a sense of destiny. She wrote her own history at the age of ten. (It is a pity for her biographer and readers that she did not heed her childish advice and go on writing bigger and better autobiographies.)

This belief in herself gave Vida the strength to persevere despite ridicule in the press and five electoral defeats. But it was a belief that did not brook opposition and from this stems the main criticisms of her from contemporaries. Some WPA members rightly resented her high-handed manner when she made the WPA non-militaristic; in this case her behaviour was close to the 'Prussian' methods she later objected to in the NCW.

She was an inspiration to many—women even named their babies after her. Madeleine Westwood wrote that Vida had a great influence on her when she was growing up:

> I never saw her ruffled, always calm but firm, and in command as she was with interjectors at meetings ... I loved Vida and respected her as I did no one else. She was of course highly intelligent, spoke fluently and logically, was quietly dignified and assured, but sympathetic and

understanding, as some of the others were not. She patiently and fully answered all my teenage questions, which added much to my own confidence at the time. She sometimes introduced me as 'our future woman MP', and never rebuked me later for failing so dismally to do anything to carry on her work.[1]

Occasionally Vida's concern for younger people could be resented as interference. Her overriding sense of rightness would not have alerted her to the fact that Doris Hordern did not appreciate her involvement in her private life.

Vida was a warm, loyal and caring friend. She kept helping Adela Pankhurst even though the WPA women felt a sense of betrayal when Adela left and later married Tom Walsh. Men and women enjoyed Vida's company, her appreciation of life and her inner serenity. In many ways, however, Vida found fulfilment through work rather than relationships. She tended to operate on a cerebral rather than an emotional level with most of her friends. Bella Lavender noted how she looked ever sternly to the cause and Madeleine Westwood remarked on this aspect of the friendship between her mother, Edith Gardiner, and Vida.

> I realise now that Vida and my mother's relationship was unusual, in that though they were so close for nearly forty years, I don't remember their ever discussing personal matters to any extent in my hearing. Always it concerned current events, social problems especially for women or children or church affairs or interesting doings of mutual friends.[2]

Vida's overseas trips brought her into contact with the most eminent suffrage workers in the United States and Britain. She revelled in this experience of communing with like minds, appreciating the courage of these women and feeling a sense of sisterhood and camaraderie of equals that she never quite attained in Australia. It is one reason why these trips meant so much to her. It is also significant that many of her WPA stalwarts were not Australian-born. She was increasingly focused internationally and these women (many of whom had been suffragettes) helped fulfil her need. It is one reason why the WPA never became large; it was influenced by the non-party politics of many international suffragists, but in Australia she found few women who shared her political philosophy.

Her principal satisfaction was in the company of her mother, sisters and Hyde Champion. She did seek other intellectual stimulation, often unsuccessfully. Her 'sensible club' for men and women never eventuated. For a time her friendship with Cecilia John provided a special companionship, but the women went their separate ways after the war and Vida became more reliant on her sisters.

It has been noted that in assessing Vida's life 'a personal note is curiously absent'.[3] Vida did not leave extensive diaries, notes or correspondence. She was largely self-sufficient; she had her faith to sustain her in difficult times and her mother and sisters for confidantes and did not generally need to release her doubts in private writing. Only to her 'inner circle' of friends and family did she sometimes commit to paper her private doubts and frustrations. Some of Vida's personal correspondence to friends has survived in other people's collections and these letters have helped to elucidate the more private aspects of her personality. Letters to Stella Miles Franklin, Rose Scott and Edith How Martyn show that she had times of doubt and frustration and was hampered by financial worries. In her letters to Stella, Vida admits to going through 'deep waters' and reveals her financial anxieties about the *Woman's Sphere*. In later years the evidence for her disillusionment with the modern world comes through and, in her letters to Edith, a sadness at the increasing isolation and loneliness of old age. This differed from the public view she always presented of optimism and progress. The letters also reveal new aspects of Vida's character: in the midst of her hectic first election campaign Vida nursed a friend who was 'lying at death's door with pleurisy and pneumonia' night and day. For a fortnight she stayed fully dressed 'except for a bath'.[4] This shows her as a warm, caring person, not just a public persona. It also highlights the problem for women entering the public sphere, that the call of the private is still so demanding. Would a male political candidate have volunteered for or been expected to fulfil such a task?

One jarring note comes from Edith How Martyn. After Vida's death, Aileen sent some of Vida's papers to Edith, who wrote on the Sidelights on Peace manuscript before handing them to the Fawcett Library:

> I have managed to finish this—and find it well—ill-balanced, prejudiced, unchristian... unhistorical, insufficient knowledge of the factors... Why the cold civil war of strikes is to be condoned while international war is a crime seems quite illogical to me.

It is a surprisingly virulent annotation from a friend; Vida ended her letters to Edith with 'Always lovingly yours'. The two had remained close correspondents until Vida's death, so it was obviously the content of the material Edith objected to. It is odd that Vida told Edith she was one of the few women she could really talk to, if they had not realised that they differed so dramatically in political philosophy. The letters Vida wrote to Edith which have been preserved date from after World War II. They express disillusion with all political parties; perhaps it came as a shock to Edith, in the midst of the Cold War, to read of Vida's support of socialism and of Russia, 'the eighth wonder of the world', thirty years before. Edith's criticism of illogicality echoes the earlier criticism of Vida's support for the militant suffragettes and pacificism. The underlying theme in Vida's thinking was choice: workers could go on strike but had no control over war. Of course other people suffered materially because of strikes and the suffragettes' militancy, but the working classes suffered most in war and many died.

As Vida grew older she tended not to move with the times in friendships or new ideas. She kept in contact with many of her friends from her time as a public figure—the 'suffragette circle' and WPA friends like Edith Gardiner—but there is little evidence of new friends after this time.

This lack of input which comes from meeting different people contributed to an increased rigidity of thinking as she got older. Her ill-advised last election campaign shows she was obstinately pursuing a course doomed to failure and which could have harmed the very causes she was supporting by splitting the anti-conscription vote. As a young woman many of her ideas were progressive, but she was also a product of her times, failing to break free of the Victorian sexual mores of her youth, which make her ideas on sexuality and marriage look antiquated and prudish now.

But this is only one side of Vida Goldstein: she won enduring respect because of her sincerity, her pleasant manner and sheer hard work. She had compassion and empathy and managed to help people without being seen as a patronising 'do-gooder'. She was courageous in the face of physical danger. She bravely ventured beyond the private sphere and established two successful newspapers, travelled extensively and made history by standing for Parliament.

Vida enjoyed much of the publicity she attracted, being fêted overseas, being a candidate, even confronting the censor. She was an accomplished public speaker and could 'play' an audience. She did not like lobbying—she called it a distasteful occupation—because she was asking for change from a subordinate position and Vida never accepted that.

Vida saw what needed to be done and set about doing it. This often meant that her energies were dissipated. She learnt the lesson of concentrating solely on the campaign for the suffrage in 1908 by retiring from all public activity and told the British women that this was one of the strengths of the Australian push for the suffrage, but often her energies were directed to myriad causes, which overstretched her physical and financial resources and so reduced her effectiveness.

She was uncompromising and forced people to choose between their allegiance to their sex or to their pacifism, and to a political party. She was absolute in her convictions, but also at times her thinking had apparent contradictions. She made pointed remarks about society ladies knitting to help Belgians while Australians were suffering, yet she supported the suffragettes to the detriment of the WPA and Australian issues.

Her methods and perceived priorities changed over the years and her focus became increasingly an international rather than an Australian one, but the fundamental strands of her life—her spirituality and her desire to help the weak—never changed. Her retreat into spirituality did not please her supporters, and many found it hard to accept or understand, but Vida believed she would achieve the same goals in a different way. In later life she expressed both disappointment at the weakness of the women's movement and dislike of many aspects of modern society, but what impressed those who knew her in these later years was the serenity that came from her spiritual belief in the 'eternal "coming right of right things"'.

◆ ◆ ◆

As an early feminist, Vida represented the new generation of the movement in Australia and was the 'greatest of the Victorians, and perhaps of the Australian suffragists'.[5] Pioneers such as Spence, Scott, Lowe and Dugdale were considerably older than Vida. She had energy and commitment and the drive to consolidate the Victorian suffrage societies. There were the inevitable antagonisms and politicking within the United Council for Women's Suffrage and the WPA, but generally her leadership was accepted and respected and Lowe at least was happy to hand on the mantle—and the workload.

Vida was the first Australian suffragist to receive international recognition, especially in America and Britain, where she enjoyed considerable personal success. The English suffragettes in particular acknowledged her uniqueness, her dedication and her skills as a speaker and campaigner. This international recognition also helped her standing in Australia, as did her role as editor of the *Woman's Sphere*. (The *Dawn* had similarly brought Louisa Lawson to the forefront of the New South Wales movement.)

Vida brought new elements into the battle for the suffrage in Victoria. Other refined, middle-class women were associated with the formation and membership of the movement, but the ones who spoke publicly were often deliberately eccentric in their dress; for example, Henrietta Dugdale wore divided skirts, her own home-spun creations. Others were not always blessed with all the skills required for public speaking and dealing with hecklers. Even Annette Bear-Crawford's voice was 'hardly so strong as her opinions'.[6] Very much a part of the mainstream middle-class, well-educated and stylishly dressed, Vida threatened the status quo because she could not be discounted or ridiculed as many of her courageous predecessors had been and yet her ideas were progressive, even radical. Vida was seen as a threat by conservative forces and posed a dilemma for the popular press, which did not know how to depict her. Operating in a male-dominated world, she showed she was 'as good as a man', but there was no place for this articulate, non-emotional, efficient woman. As one diehard put it, Vida was 'one of those dangerous, persuasive women'.[7]

Her campaign for the suffrage was based on her fundamental belief in equality of opportunity for both sexes. Vida refused to be limited by her sex. She travelled unaccompanied and made lecture tours when it was still unusual for women to speak in public. She was, nevertheless, hampered by external societal constraints because she was a woman. During her first electoral campaign, male and female reporters spent as much time describing her physical appearance as her policies. (Eighty-seven years later, Australia's two female premiers had to contend with the media focusing on their physical appearance and cartoons associating them with domestic activities.) Her lack of a large support network equivalent to a political party was also a major handicap, compounded by the lack of reporting of her campaigns, especially the third, by the daily papers.

Vida won a place for herself in Australian history by standing for Parliament in 1902. Her five nominations for Parliament created the precedent for women to enter the political arena. In 1903 the press feared that she would be contaminated by being exposed to so many unsavoury male politicians and that she would not have the physical strength to stay up for an all-night sitting. The objections have changed, but this problem remains unresolved: many female parliamentarians still sense they are 'intruders' in a men's club.[8] There will be reform as greater numbers of women are elected, but the process of change will necessarily be slow. Vida helped to start this process. Her nominations provoked the question of how women could share political power, in a system which was and is male-oriented and male-dominated. She chose to form a separate women's party rather than work within the existing political parties. The question of whether to seek reform by working from within a system (and therefore having to make compromises) or by being an autonomous group (which has independence but limited power) is still debated today.

Like many suffragists of the period Vida adopted non-party politics because she could see that party politics subsumed the interests of women. Yet ironically, one major reason for her failure to win a seat was her non-party politics. Even today it is difficult for Independents to be elected. Vida grossly underestimated party loyalties and failed to take into account the reality that Australia was becoming increasingly party-political. This decision meant that she was left with no heartland of support. Her WPA would remain weak, always scratching for funds, with the work falling on the few, while the two major political groups flourished. Vida's desire to convince women of all political persuasions to vote for what she considered was the 'higher loyalty' of their sex, was at best optimistic. She could understand that men would have to be re-educated to accept women entering the public sphere, but found it disappointing that women did not support her ahead of party politics.

Vida never reconciled the contradictory notions that women would contribute special qualities to the public sphere and that men and women were equal and should be treated equally. There is always the sense that she thought 'men and women are equal, but women are a bit more equal because they have finer qualities of spirituality and higher-mindedness than men'. It is an appealing philosophy—for women—which is still propounded today: that women will bring the special qualities of nurturing, gentleness and respect for life into the public sphere.

Her conviction that she could best represent all women because she was a woman was resented, especially by AWNL members. Second-wave feminists also went through the process of embracing the communality of woman. Only recently has the debate moved to addressing and accommodating the diversity of women, in terms of ethnicity, class, political allegiance and sexual preference.[9]

While she condemned the patriarchial system for its iniquitous treatment of women and children, Vida dealt with people as individuals, not stereotypes. She became more outspoken after her time in England, and Maurice Blackburn noted her increasing 'sex antagonism', but she did not blame individuals for the oppression of women; rather she blamed poor education and lack of social awareness. Her emphasis on the importance of environmental factors such as education and opportunity was humane and perceptive in a period where the importance of heredity was being emphasised by eugenists who advocated selective breeding and racial hygiene. In contrast Vida argued for improvements in the health and well-being of the mother and that well-adjusted children were the product of happy, secure parenting in a situation where men and women operated as equals and had the same chances to develop and be educated.

Well-educated and intelligent, Vida was a teacher at heart. She always stressed that her campaigns were for educating and increasing awareness. She was prepared to accept other women's political education groups because she wanted people to be thinking about the issues. This 'consciousness-raising' was not unique to Vida, but her emphasis on it was especially strong.

Her work for social reform and later as a foremost pacifist also warrant recognition in Australian history. In many ways her thinking was very modern. She fought for the right of women to earn an income, pursue a career and receive fair working conditions, including equal pay for equal work. She wanted improvements in health, especially the eradication of VD, and safer and planned child-bearing.

She faced opprobrium by talking about sexual matters, going beyond the realm of 'virtuous' women because she could see the terrible effects of VD on women and babies, yet she was a product of her times and did not significantly challenge the importance of the family and women's traditional maternal role.

One of the earliest sociologists, she was an accepted authority who sought to tackle the causes of poverty and unemployment through scientific analysis rather than with handouts. Her commissions from the Victorian Government and the Trades Hall Council to investigate these issues in America also show that she was respected in this field. The Women's Labour Bureau and the women's farm were successful means of creating work for women, rather than handing out charity. Her support of women in the courts was brave and visionary. She is credited with important reform to the Children's Courts Act (1906) and helping to bring the cost of living of a working man into the consideration of the Harvester case. She brought a clear-headed and far-seeing approach to social issues in Australia.

Suffragist, social reformer, pacifist — Vida will always be remembered for bringing her talents to bear on such a variety of causes to improve the quality of people's lives; she will also be remembered for extending the boundaries of female endeavour, refusing to be restricted by the stereotypical views of her contemporaries and living her philosophy that 'I am a human being, and there is nothing human beyond my sphere'.

Appendix 1

Disposal of Vida's papers

◆

Vida sent her 1908 diary (which records the winning of the suffrage in Victoria but has only a few personal entries) to the Fawcett Library in London in 1947. She chose this library because it was a suffrage library named after Millicent Garrett Fawcett, the president of the non-militant National Union of Women's Suffrage Societies. After Vida's death, Aileen sent what was left of Vida's papers to Edith How Martyn, who also deposited them in the Fawcett. These holdings constitute the major primary source material relating to Vida, namely the 1903 Senate Campaign Scrapbook, the two autograph albums from the American and English trips, the 1919 Sidelights on Peace: a Warning and an Appeal series of letters, and a few other manuscripts of lectures. Until the microfilm of this material became available in Australia, material on Vida was limited.

Most of the Australian material is in the Bessie Rischbieth collection in the National Library of Australia. Vida left a brown-paper package addressed to Bessie Rischbieth which presumably contained these papers. Bessie had the foresight to realise the importance of preserving the suffrage primary sources and sought material from Vida, but as early as 1933 Vida wrote that she had disposed of the WPA badges and colours 'long ago'. She did not value such memorabilia. The material she sent to London was all she considered of historical interest. She was concerned with the now, and the future; she was too busy to write about the past or even record her story for radio. It is history's loss.

Appendix 2

Chronology of memorials

◆

1949 Daily papers publish a short obituary by Vida's niece Leslie Henderson. Aileen Goldstein writes to Stella Miles Franklin that she and her sister Elsie have received 'scores and scores of letters telling us what a wonderful woman she [Vida] was. A pity more appreciation was not shown when she was here ... very few of this generation have any idea of what she accomplished'.[1]

1950 The Vida Goldstein Memorial Committee is formed to collect funds to establish a 'memorial in perpetuity'[2] to Vida: a prize for an essay on the history of the woman suffrage movement and the 'evolution of women as citizens.' The prize is abandoned after a few years. The League of Women Voters takes responsibility for the fund.

1967 The Vida Goldstein Memorial Fund presents a portrait of Vida to the National Library of Australia. It was painted by Phyl Waterhouse in 1944 from the 1902 photograph of Vida as delegate to the International Suffrage Conference in the USA. The National Library of Australia also has a Goldstein collection of books on women's issues.[3]

1973 The League of Women Voters closes the fund by presenting a glass showcase to the State Library of Victoria, to be used for displays commemorating Vida. On it, a small plaque reads, 'Vida Goldstein: Pioneer of freedom and justice for women'.

1974   Vida is one of only two Australians among the 999 women commemorated in Judy Chicago's *Dinner Party*. She is grouped with American suffragist Susan Anthony whom she greatly admired. Vida is described as a 'Suffragist, journalist, publisher and political figure'.[4]

1984   The Federal Government honours Vida for the first time when it names eleven electorates after women (there were four already). Then sitting member and Opposition Spokesman for the Status of Women Ian Macphee said Vida was 'recognised as one of the most respected and best known pioneers of feminism'.[5]

1985   The first in a series of Victorian 150th Anniversary plaques to honour women is unveiled in the grounds of Parliament House, Melbourne. It records that Vida was the first woman to nominate for the Australian Parliament.

1988   Historian Manning Clark selects eighty-eight prominent Australians to mark Australia's Bicentenary. He includes Vida for 'advocating the equality of women'.[6] Later in the year the Heritage 200 Committee selects Vida as one of the 200 entries in its book *The People Who Made Australia Great*.

Notes

◆

Abbreviations

AAB	Australian Archives, Brighton
AAC	Australian Archives, Canberra
ADB	*Australian Dictionary of Biography*
AG	Aileen Goldstein
BR	Bessie Rischbieth
EHM	Edith How Martyn
FL	Fawcett Library, City of London Polytechnic
IG	Isabella Goldstein
ML	Mitchell Library
NLA	National Library of Australia
RS	Rose Scott
SLV	State Library of Victoria (La Trobe Collection)
SMF	Stella Miles Franklin
VG	Vida Goldstein
WS	*Woman's Sphere*
WV	*Woman Voter*

Preface

1 Franklin papers, 364/10/127, VG to SMF.

1 Childhood

1. *Life and Work of Miss Vida Goldstein*, Australasian Authors' Agency, n.d.; L. M. Henderson, *The Goldstein Story*, Stockland Press, North Melbourne, 1973; ADB, vol. 9, pp. 43–5.
2. Samuel Hawkins's estate was valued at £64 000. Isabella's marriage settlement: Lawson Family Letters, James Hawkins to D. MacPherson, 23 February 1871 and James Hawkins to Penelope Lawson, 9 April 1873.
3. Henderson, *Goldstein Story*, p. 42.
4. 'The Dignity of Labor' n.d., Henderson papers, 10797, MSB 322.
5. *Life and Work*, p. 3.
6. Ibid., p. 4.
7. Henderson, *Goldstein Story*, p. 31.
8. Y. Smith, *Taking Time*, Union of Australian Women, Fitzroy, c. 1989.
9. *Life and Work*, p. 3.
10. VG, Autobiography, 21 September 1879.
11. Rapke papers, pp. 1–2.
12. Elsie Goldstein, Autobiography, 21 September 1879.
13. J. Sutherland, Report for Second Half Year, n.d.
14. *Life and Work*, p. 3.
15. Letter, J. Sutherland to IG, 12 August 1884.
16. *Prospectus*, PLC, 1886.
17. *Patchwork*, December 1885, pp. 306–7; June 1886, pp. 345–6.
18. Ibid., October 1885, p. 296.
19. Ibid., April 1885, p. 266.
20. *Annual Report*, PLC, 1886.
21. *Life and Work*, p. 3.
22. *Annual Report*, PLC, 1886.
23. ADB, vol. 6, pp. 208–9.
24. C. Strong, *A Memoir*, 1958, p. 5, in Strong papers, 2882/1/1.
25. *History of the Scots' Church Case*, Mason, Firth and M'Cutcheon, n.d., in Strong papers, 2882/1/2.
26. Monash papers, Diary, 12 October 1887, in G. Serle, *John Monash*, Melbourne University Press, Carlton, 1982, p. 71.
27. Serle, *John Monash*, p. 513.
28. Rapke papers, p. 18.
29. *Life and Work*, p. 3.

2 The New Woman

1. Letter, VG to Penelope Lawson, n.d.
2. F. Kelly, The 'Woman Question' in Melbourne 1880–1914, PhD thesis, Monash, 1983, pp. 171–2.

3 Rapke papers, p. 15.
4 L. Henderson, VG: Biographical Notes, typescript, pre-1949, Rischbieth papers, 2004/4/191.
5 John Holroyd, interview with author, 28 March 1988.
6 *Life and Work*, p. 5.
7 Ibid., p. 4.
8 *Herald*, 30 April 1891.
9 *Charity Reviews*.
10 *Proceedings of the Australasian Conference on Charity*, 1890.
11 Ibid. For COS philosophy, see *The Citizens' Welfare Service of Victoria 1887–1987*, 100th Annual Report 1986–1987, in particular, Paul Anderson, 'A Centenary Review'.
12 Not a new idea, see M. Wollstonecraft, *A Vindication of the Rights of Women*, Dent, London, 1982, p. 187.
13 *The Citizens' Welfare Service*.
14 S. Swain, The Victorian Charity Network in the 1890s, PhD thesis, Melbourne, 1976, p. 272.
15 *Charity Review*, September 1900.
16 M. Maxwell, *Herald*, 8 June 1974.
17 Henderson, *Goldstein Story*, pp. 49–68 and *Charity Review*.
18 *Tocsin*, 17 August 1899.
19 *Charity Review*, March 1903.
20 Henderson, *Goldstein Story*, pp. 66–7.
21 M. Lake and F. Kelly, *Double Time: Women in Victoria—150 Years*, Penguin, Ringwood, 1985, p. 154.
22 Vida would have used 'suffragist'. The term 'suffragette' was first used to deride the militant suffragists in England, but the Pankhursts adopted the term.
23 Rapke papers, p. 1.
24 VG, 'The Struggle for Woman Suffrage', in I. McCorkindale (ed.), *Pioneer Pathways*, Morris Walker, Melbourne, 1948, p. 117.
25 Rischbieth papers, 2004/4/233.
26 McCorkindale, *Pioneer Pathways*, p. 115.
27 Rapke papers, p. 1.
28 Ibid.
29 Kelly, 'Woman Question', p. 85.
30 C. Strong, 'Concerning Women', *Australian Herald*, No. 7, Melbourne, 1895, in Scott papers, 38/61.
31 H. H. Champion, 'The Claim of Women', *Cosmos*, 31 May 1895.
32 Henderson, *Goldstein Story*, p. 149.
33 Scott papers, A2272/562–5, VG to RS.
34 R. Reid, 1899, in *WS*, September 1900.
35 Ibid.
36 J. C. Campbell, MLC, 1896, ibid.
37 Staughton, ibid.

38 J. Brownfoot and D. Scott, *The Unequal Half*, Reed Education, Sydney, 1977, p. 60.
39 Scott papers, A2272/562-5, VG to RS.
40 *Tocsin*, 22 September 1898, in N. MacKenzie, *Women in Australia*, Cheshire, Melbourne, 1962, p. 48.
41 VG and A. Bear-Crawford, *Reply to Speech against Women's Suffrage*, Rischbieth papers, 2004/4/142.
42 Ibid.
43 *ADB*, vol. 12, pp. 98–100.
44 Rischbieth papers, 2004/4/20, letter by VG. Note: Elsie or Hyde Champion may also have been at this meeting. Vida credits Hyde Champion with the idea of the Shilling Fund in ibid., 2004/4/240.
45 Scott papers, A2272/550, VG to RS.
46 J. Menadue, *A Centenary History of the Australian Natives' Association 1871–1971*, Horticultural Press, Melbourne, 1971, p. 394.
47 Attorney-General's Department, Intelligence Records 1914–1923, AAB, MP 16/1, 15/3/1371.
48 *Charity Review*, June 1900.
49 Try papers, 9910, box 1, *Annual Report*, 1899, brought to my attention by Dr David Maunders. For more information on the Try Society see D. Maunders, Keeping Them off the Streets, PhD thesis, La Trobe, 1987.
50 *WV*, 8 September 1910; *WS*, March 1902.
51 *Argus*, 15 August 1899.
52 *Life and Work*, p. 6.
53 Rapke papers, p. 1.
54 Minutes, Trades Hall Council, 6 October 1899, University of Melbourne Archives.
55 Scott papers, A2272/562-5, VG to RS.
56 Henderson, *Goldstein Story*, p. 149.
57 Scott papers, A2272/615-6, VG to RS.
58 Ibid., 38/39.
59 *WS*, September 1900.
60 Ibid.
61 Ibid., October 1901.
62 Ibid., November 1901.
63 Ibid., January 1902.
64 Ibid., October 1900.
65 Ibid., February 1901. Also see: C. Bacchi, 'Evolution, Eugenics and Women'.
66 F. Kelly, 'Woman Question', p. 58.
67 *WV*, 23 May 1918.
68 C. Bacchi, 'First-wave Feminism: History's Judgement', p. 166.
69 Lake and Kelly, *Double Time*, p. 156.
70 *WS*, December 1900.
71 *Argus*, 24 July 1900.

72 Ibid., 4 August 1900.
73 Ibid., 26 September 1900.
74 Scott papers, A2272/562–5, VG to RS.
75 Lawson Family Letters, item 39, Georgina Nicholls to Penelope Lawson.
76 WS, September 1900.
77 VG, 'Should Women Enter Parliament?', *Review of Reviews*, vol. 23, no. 2, 20 August 1903.
78 WS, July 1901.
79 Ibid., December 1901.

3 To America and back

1 WS, December 1901.
2 Minutes, Trades Hall Council, 12 December 1901, University of Melbourne Archives.
3 WS, January 1902.
4 *Daily Telegraph*, 6 January 1902.
5 VG papers, 'To America and Back', FL. Copy: SLV, MS 7865, MF 118.
6 WS, March 1902.
7 VG papers, 'To America'.
8 Ibid.
9 WS, April 1902.
10 Ibid.
11 VG papers, 'To America'.
12 WS, April 1902.
13 Ibid.
14 *Woman's Journal*, Boston, 1 March 1902, p. 66, Gerritsen Collection, SLV, MF 130.
15 WS, April 1902.
16 Ibid.
17 Ibid., December 1902.
18 Ibid., April 1902.
19 Ibid., May 1902.
20 Ibid., April 1902.
21 *Woman's Journal*, Boston, 22 February 1902, p. 60.
22 WS, April 1902.
23 *Woman's Journal*, Boston, 1 March 1902.
24 VG papers, Autograph Album, 1902, FL. Copy: SLV, MS 7865, MF 118.
25 VG papers, 'To America'.
26 WS, May 1902.
27 VG papers, Senate Campaign Scrapbook, 1903, FL. Copy: SLV, MS 11956.
28 WS, July 1902.

29 Ibid., August 1902.
30 Ibid., July 1902.
31 Ibid.
32 Ibid., August 1902.
33 Ibid.
34 VG papers, 'To America.'
35 WS, August 1902.
36 Ibid.
37 VG papers, 'To America.'
38 WS, April 1902.
39 Ibid.
40 Scott papers, 38/61/123, clipping from the *Star*, August 1902.
41 WS, September 1902.
42 Scott papers, 38/62/7.
43 The idea of trial by peers was not new, see Wollstonecraft, *Vindication*, p. 188.
44 VG papers, The George Junior Republic, FL. Copy: SLV, MS 7865, MF 118.
45 WS, October 1902.
46 *New Idea*, 1 October 1902.
47 VG papers, 'To America'.
48 VG, *Report to the National Council of Women*, Melbourne, 1902.
49 E. M. Ramsay, *Christian Science and its Discoverer*, Christian Science Publishing Society, Boston, 1955, p. 119.
50 M. Baker Eddy, *Key to the Scriptures*, Riverside Press, Cambridge, 1934, p. 517.
51 Ramsay, *Christian Science*; *Encyclopaedia Britannica, Macropaedia*, vol. 4, Benton, Chicago, 1974, pp. 562–4.
52 Rapke papers, p. 4.

4 The lady candidate

1 Scott papers, A2273/806–8, VG to RS.
2 Ibid., A2273/816a, VG to RS.
3 Ibid., A2273/806–8.
4 Ibid., A2273/816a.
5 WS, March 1903.
6 Ibid., June 1903.
7 Scott papers, A2273/832.
8 Ibid.
9 WS, June 1903.
10 Rischbieth papers, 2004/4/98. For analysis of membership, see Kelly, 'Woman Question', ch. 9.

11 *WS*, June 1903.
12 Ibid., July 1903.
13 Ibid.
14 VG, 'Should Women Enter Parliament?', pp. 135–6.
15 A. Steinbach, 'Women politicians may not be kinder, gentler', *Age*, 25 November 1992.
16 VG, 'The Political Woman in Australia', *Nineteenth Century*, vol. 59, July 1904.
17 Rischbieth papers, 2004/4/2.
18 Newspapers referred to in chapter 3 appear in VG papers, Scrapbook. *Australian Star*, 11 August 1903.
19 *Bulletin*, 20 August 1903.
20 *Punch*, 13 August 1903.
21 Ibid.
22 *Argus*, 5 August 1903.
23 *Truth*, 8 August 1903.
24 *Argus*, 8 August 1903.
25 *Punch*, 13 August 1903.
26 *Bulletin*, 13 August 1903.
27 *Punch*, August 1903.
28 South Australian State Archives, D2475, Catherine Spence to Alice Henry, in K. Daniels and M. Murnane, *Uphill All the Way*, University of Queensland Press, St Lucia, 1980, p. 280.
29 *White Ribbon Signal*, 1 September 1903.
30 *WS*, September 1903.
31 VG papers, Scrapbook.
32 *Age*, 22 August 1903.
33 VG papers, Scrapbook.
34 *Weekly Courier*, 28 November 1903.
35 *Weekly Times*, 19 September 1903.
36 *Adelaide Advertiser*, 23 September 1903.
37 *Age*, 8 October 1903.
38 *Portland Guardian*, n.d.
39 *Portland Guardian*, 14 October 1903.
40 *Portland Observer*, 15 October 1903.
41 *Portland Guardian*, 14 October 1903.
42 *Hamilton Spectator*, 17 and 22 October 1903.
43 *Ararat Advertiser*, n.d.
44 *Western Star*, 23 October 1903.
45 *Horsham Times*, 23 October 1903.
46 *Ararat Advertiser* in *Avoca Mail*, 27 October 1903.
47 *Yarrawonga Chronicle*, 20 October 1903.
48 *Age*, 14 November 1903.
49 *Age*, 17, 24 and 25 November 1903.
50 Ibid., 18 November 1903.
51 *WS*, November 1903.

52 Scott papers, A2273/879, IG to RS.
53 *Bairnsdale Courier*, 20 November 1903.
54 *Bairnsdale Advertiser*, 17 November 1903.
55 VG papers, Scrapbook, n.d.
56 *Benalla Standard* in *West Gippsland Gazette*, 1 December 1903.
57 *Ballarat Courier*, 8 December 1903.
58 Ibid., 18 December 1903.
59 *Ovens and Murray Advertiser*, 12 December 1903.
60 *Bulletin*, 3 December 1903.
61 *Argus*, 12 December 1903; *Age*, 12 December 1903.
62 VG papers, Scrapbook, n.d.
63 Ibid.
64 *Brisbane Worker* in *Tocsin*, 26 November 1903, cited in Kelly, 'Woman Question', p. 275.
65 *Labour Ticket*, 9 December 1903.
66 Scott papers, A2273/879 IG to RS.
67 VG, 'The Australian Woman in Politics', *Review of Reviews*, vol. 24, no. 1, 20 January 1904.
68 *Argus*, 11 December 1903.
69 *Ballarat Courier*, 11 December 1903.
70 Scott papers, A2273/872 VG to RS.
71 Letter, John Holroyd to author, 22 November 1987.
72 *WS*, 15 January 1904.
73 *Age*, 17 December 1903; also *Argus*, 17 December 1903.
74 *Bulletin*, 24 December 1903.
75 Ibid.
76 *Age*, 17 December 1903.
77 *Bulletin*, 21 January 1904.
78 Ibid., 24 December 1903.
79 *Age*, 18 December 1903.
80 *WS*, March 1904.
81 Counting may have been incomplete, hence the discrepancy in the voting tally.
82 *Argus*, 24 December 1903; *WS*, 15 January 1904.
83 *Bairnsdale Courier*, 25 November 1903; *Morwell Advertiser*, 27 November 1903; *Avoca Free Press*, 28 November 1903; *West Gippsland Gazette*, 1 December 1903.
84 *Bulletin*, 24 December 1903.
85 Ibid., 7 January 1904.
86 VG, 'The Australian Woman in Politics'.
87 *WS*, 15 January 1904.
88 *Worker*, 9 January 1904.
89 *Age*, 28 December 1984.
90 VG, 'The Australian Woman in Politics'.
91 Ibid.
92 M. J. J. Pawsey, *WS*, January 1904.

93 VG papers, Scrapbook.
94 VG, 'The Australian Woman in Politics'.

5 Deep waters

1 J. Brownfoot and D. Scott, *The Unequal Half*, Reed Education, Sydney, 1970, p. 33.
2 WS, March 1904.
3 Franklin papers, 364/10/105–6, VG to SMF.
4 Ibid., 364/10, IG to SMF, 2 May 1904.
5 Ibid.
6 Ibid., 364/10/105–6, VG to SMF.
7 Ibid., 364/10, IG to SMF, 2 May 1904.
8 WS, November 1904.
9 Franklin papers, 364/10, IG to SMF, 28 July 1904.
10 Ibid., IG to SMF, 2 May 1904.
11 L. M. Henderson, VG: Biographical Notes, typescript, 1961.
12 Scott papers, A2273/969, VG to RS.
13 Newscuttings, ML, Vol. III, p. 38.
14 WS, November 1904.
15 Scott papers, A2273/974, VG to RS.
16 Ibid., A2273/969, VG to RS.
17 Franklin papers, 364/10/109, VG to SMF.
18 Ibid.
19 Ibid., 364/10/17, IG to SMF.
20 Ibid., 2 May 1904, IG to SMF.
21 Ibid., 28 July 1904, IG to SMF.
22 E. Stanford-Thomas, 'Workers for Women's Rights'.
23 Franklin papers, 364/10/109, VG to SMF.
24 Ibid., IG to SMF, 26 November 1904.
25 WS, January 1905.
26 VG, *Woman Suffrage in Australia*, Woman's Press, London, 1911.
27 WS, January 1905.
28 Ibid., February 1905.
29 Ibid.
30 *Argus*, 4 July 1905.
31 *Age*, 29 May 1905.
32 Ibid., 12 September 1905.
33 *Liberty and Progress*, 25 November 1905.
34 Ibid., 21 December 1905.
35 Ibid., 25 November 1905.
36 Ibid., 21 December 1905.

37 VG, 'Socialism of Today—an Australian View', *Nineteenth Century*, vol. 62, September 1907, pp. 406–16.
38 Henderson, *Goldstein Story*, p. 86.
39 E. Ryan and A. Conlon, *Gentle Invaders*, Penguin, Ringwood, 1989, p. 91.
40 *Charity Review*, September 1906.
41 *WS*, April 1904.
42 *Argus*, 26 July 1906.
43 Charity Organisation Society records, Box 1/19, University of Melbourne Archives, drawn to my attention by Dr David Maunders.
44 Vida is credited with drafting the manifesto in Brownfoot and Scott, *Unequal Half*, p. 58.
45 *Life and Work*, p. 15.
46 Photographs of fifty-six of the first group (including VG) in *Weekly Times*, 17 August 1907.
47 Deakin papers, 1540/15/618, folder 9, VG to Alfred Deakin.
48 Scott papers, A2273/989, VG to RS.
49 Rischbieth papers, 2004/4/229.
50 *Argus*, 15 November 1907.
51 VG papers, Diary, 1908, FL. Copy: VG papers, SLV, MS 7865, MF 118.
52 Ibid.
53 Northcote papers, VG to Lady Northcote.
54 VG papers, Diary, 1908, from *Woman's Journal*, 4 January 1908.
55 VG papers, Diary, 1908.
56 Ibid. Probably a quote from a Miss Cobden.
57 Ibid.
58 Ibid.
59 *ADB*, vol. 10, pp. 16–18.
60 VG papers, Diary, 1908.
61 Ibid.; *Herald*, 19 August 1908.
62 VG papers, Diary, 1908.
63 Scott papers, A2273/1009, VG to RS.
64 VG papers, Diary, 1908.
65 Ibid. Note: 'old Pitt' refers to William Pitt who was elected to the Legislative Council in 1891.
66 *Argus*, 8 October 1908.
67 D. Scott, 'Woman Suffrage: the Movement in Australia', *Journal of the Royal Australian Historical Society*, vol. 53, part 4, December 1967, p. 315.
68 VG papers, Diary, 1908.
69 Scott papers, 38/39/131, VG to RS.
70 *WV*, May 1910.
71 Palmer papers, 1174/1/4, VG to Vance Palmer.
72 VG papers, Diary, 1908.
73 F. Biskup, The Suffrage Movement in Australia, BA thesis, Western Australia, 1959.

74 VG, *Woman Suffrage in Australia*.
75 Ibid.; Rapke papers, p. 9; VG, 'The Struggle for Woman Suffrage', p. 116. Quotes from the first mentioned.
76 Rapke papers, p. 9.
77 *Socialist*, 27 November 1908, in Kelly, 'Woman Question', p. 535.
78 VG, *Woman Suffrage in Australia*.
79 Scott papers, A2273/1019, VG to RS.

6 Women voters

1 Scott papers, A2273/1043, Champion to RS.
2 *Argus*, 12 February 1910.
3 *WV*, December 1909.
4 Scott papers, 38/20X, VG to RS.
5 *WV*, February 1910.
6 Ibid.
7 *Age*, 1 December 1909.
8 *WV*, February 1910.
9 Ibid.
10 *Argus*, 25 February 1910.
11 Ibid., 8 March 1910.
12 Rischbieth papers, 2004/4/225.
13 *Liberty and Progress*, 25 February 1910, in *WV*, March 1910.
14 *Life and Work*, pp. 8-9.
15 For examples of other women being heckled, see *Argus*, 24 February 1910, 10, 11, 24 March 1910 and 5 April 1910.
16 *Argus*, 16 March 1910.
17 Ibid., 6 April 1910.
18 B. Collins in *WV*, June 1910.
19 Ibid., May 1910.
20 *Argus*, 8 April 1910.
21 Ibid., 12 April 1910.
22 E. Jeffreys, 'What is "Difference" in Feminist Theory and Practice?'.
23 *Argus*, 13 April 1910.
24 Ibid.
25 *WV*, May 1910.
26 *Weekly Times*, 23 April 1910.
27 *WV*, May 1910.
28 J. F. Young, *C. H. Spence*, Lothian, Melbourne, 1937, p. 100.
29 Ibid., p. 176.
30 J. Ackermann, *Australia from a Woman's Point of View*, Cassell, London, 1913, pp. 240-2.
31 Scott papers, A2273/1025, VG to RS.

32 *ADB*, vol. 10, pp. 445–6; *Southern Sphere*, 1 July 1910.
33 *Argus*, 16 August 1910.
34 *WV*, September 1910.
35 Ibid.
36 *Patchwork*, December 1911, pp. 123–4.

7 Face to the dawn

1 *WV*, March 1911.
2 Ibid., April 1911.
3 Rischbieth papers, 2004/4/232.
4 Ibid.
5 Ibid.
6 *WV*, June 1911 and May 1911.
7 *Votes for Women*, 31 March 1911.
8 Rischbieth papers, 2004/4/16.
9 Letter, M. Westwood to author, 2 May 1987.
10 *WV*, June 1911.
11 Ibid.
12 Ibid.
13 Ibid., July 1911.
14 Ibid.
15 Ibid.
16 Ibid.
17 Ibid.
18 Ibid.
19 Ibid.
20 VG papers, Autograph Album, 1911, FL. Copy: SLV, MS 7865, MF 118.
21 *WV*, July 1911.
22 Rischbieth papers, 2004/4/232.
23 Interview with I. Creightmore, 22 August 1988.
24 *WV*, 1 July 1911.
25 Letter, George Bernard Shaw to VG, 15 June 1911.
26 M. Mackenzie, *Shoulder to Shoulder*, Penguin, Harmondsworth, 1975, p. 158.
27 *Votes for Women*, vol. 4, June 1911, p. 631.
28 VG papers, Sidelights on Peace: a Warning and an Appeal, FL. Copy: SLV, MS 7865, MF 118.
29 Rischbieth papers, 2004/4/232.
30 *WV*, August 1911.
31 VG, *Woman Suffrage in Australia*.
32 *WV*, September 1911.
33 Ibid.

34 Ibid.
35 Ibid., August 1911.
36 Mackenzie, *Shoulder to Shoulder*, p.170.
37 *WV*, September 1911.
38 Henderson, *Goldstein Story*, p. 39.
39 Rischbieth papers, 2004/4/4, Emmeline Pethick-Lawrence to IG.
40 VG papers, Autograph Album, 1911, SMF to IG.
41 Mackenzie, *Shoulder to Shoulder*, pp. 179–80.
42 VG papers, Autograph Album, 1911, entry by Ella Gilliland McLean.
43 Mackenzie, *Shoulder to Shoulder*, pp. 218, 180
44 VG papers, Autograph Album, 1911.
45 *WV*, March 1912.
46 Ibid., May 1912.
47 *Herald*, 6 August 1912.
48 *WV*, May 1912.
49 Ibid., June 1912.
50 Ibid., August 1912; *Herald*, 6 August 1912.
51 *Herald*, 8 June 1974.
52 *WV*, June 1912.
53 Deakin papers, 1540/16/761.
54 *WV*, August 1912.
55 Ibid., September 1912.
56 MacKenzie, *Women in Australia*, p. 48.

8 Campaigns for Kooyong

1 *WV*, July 1912.
2 Ibid., October 1912.
3 Ibid., 10 March 1913, also includes examples.
4 *Argus*, 1 March 1913.
5 *WV*, 10 March 1913.
6 Ibid., 25 March 1913.
7 Ibid., 8 April 1913.
8 Ibid., 22 April 1913.
9 Ibid.
10 Ibid., 29 April 1913.
11 *Age*, 23 April 1913.
12 *WV*, 13 May 1913.
13 Ibid., 20 May 1913.
14 *Age*, 28 May 1913.
15 *WV*, 22 April 1913.
16 Ibid., 3 June 1913.
17 Ibid.

18 *Age*, 2 June 1913.
19 *WV*, 24 June 1913.
20 Ibid., 10 June 1913.
21 Ibid.
22 Ibid., 17 June 1913.
23 Ibid., 12 August 1913.
24 Ibid., 5 August 1913.
25 Rischbieth papers, 2004/4/237.
26 E. Pankhurst in Mackenzie, *Shoulder to Shoulder*, p. 241.
27 *WV*, 17 June 1913.
28 Ibid., 14 October 1913.
29 Ibid., 2 September 1913.
30 Ibid.
31 Ibid., 23 September 1913.
32 Ibid.
33 *Argus*, 29 November 1913.
34 *WV*, 2 December 1913.
35 Ibid.
36 Blackburn papers 11749, box 73A. Subsequent references same unless specified.
37 *WV*, 28 October 1913.
38 Ibid., 18 November 1913.
39 Ibid.
40 Ibid., 9 October 1912.
41 Ibid., 10 February 1914.
42 Blackburn papers.
43 Ibid.
44 Ibid.
45 Ibid.
46 *WV*, 3 February 1914.
47 Blackburn papers.
48 *WV*, 10 February 1914.
49 Pankhurst Walsh papers, 2123/2/17; see also A. Summers, 'The Unwritten History of Adela Pankhurst Walsh'.
50 Tom Barker, in D. Mitchell, *The Fighting Pankhursts*, Baylis, London, 1967.
51 F. Sternberg, 'The Militant Suffragettes', *Lone Hand*, 1 July 1914, pp. 96–7.
52 *WV*, 18 August 1914.
53 *Argus*, 17 July 1914.
54 *WV*, 28 July 1914.
55 Preference to unionists was not mentioned in Vida's 1913 platform, although in her speeches she advocated it.
56 Ibid., 30 June 1914.
57 *Age*, 25 July 1914.
58 *WV*, 18 August 1914.
59 *Socialist*, 4 September 1914, in Kelly, 'Woman Question', p. 535.
60 *WV*, 25 August 1914.

61 Ibid.
62 Ibid., 2 September 1914.
63 Ibid., 9 September 1914.
64 Ibid., 15 September 1914.
65 Ibid., 22 September 1914.
66 *Age*, 21 September 1914.
67 Earlier allegations of disenfranchisement, ibid., 18 September 1914.

9 Casualties of war

1 *WV*, 11 August 1914.
2 Ibid., 29 September 1914.
3 VG, 'Open Letter to Members of Parliament', 21 September 1916, in *WV*, 5 October 1916; uncensored in L. C. Jauncey, *The Story of Conscription in Australia*, Macmillan, South Melbourne, 1968, pp. 175–80.
4 Attorney-General's Department, General Correspondence Files 1914–38, AAB, MP 707/1 V287.
5 Censor's Reports, AAB, 3 MD 15/1/15.
6 Attorney-General, Intelligence Reports, 1914–23, AAB, MP 16/1, item 14/3/682.
7 Ibid.
8 Ibid., MF 95 SI B9, 29 January 1916.
9 Ibid., MP 95, 10 February 1917; Censor's Reports, 3 MD, MF 814; MF 778; MF 786.
10 M. Brodney, 'The Militant Propagandists in Action', *Labour History*, no. 5, 1963, p. 13. in J. Sendy, 'Women's Peace Army', *This Australia*, summer edition, 1987, pp. 9–10.
11 *WV*, 5 October 1914.
12 Ibid., 17 November 1914.
13 Ibid., 10 November 1914.
14 Blackburn papers.
15 *WV*, 17 November 1914.
16 Ibid., 5 January 1915.
17 Ibid., 10 November 1914.
18 Ibid., 15 July 1915; see also P. Gowland, 'The Women's Peace Army'.
19 *WV*, 22 July 1915.
20 E. M. Moore, *The Quest for Peace*, Wilke, Melbourne, 1950, pp. 28–9.
21 *WV*, 15 December 1914.
22 Ibid., 12 January 1915.
23 Ibid., 8 December 1914.
24 Ibid., 16 February 1915.
25 Ibid., 2 March 1915.

26 Ibid., 23 February 1915.
27 Ibid., 27 May 1915 and 1 July 1915.
28 Ibid., 27 May 1915.
29 Ibid., 17 June 1915.
30 Letter, Westwood to author, 2 May 1987.
31 WV, 3 June 1915.
32 Ibid., 8 July 1915.
33 Ibid., 9 March 1915.
34 *Socialist*, in WV, 1 June 1916.
35 Letter, Westwood, 2 May 1987.
36 *Argus*, 21 October 1914 and WV, 27 October 1914.
37 21 July 1915 and 25 December 1915.
38 *Argus*, 21 July 1915.
39 WV, 12 August 1915.
40 Ibid., 23 September 1915.
41 Ibid., 30 September 1915.
42 *Argus*, 24 Septembr 1915.
43 WV, 30 September 1915.
44 Blackburn papers.
45 WV, 27 January 1916.
46 Ibid., 23 September 1915.
47 Ibid., 9 September 1915.
48 Ibid., 30 September 1915.
49 *Argus*, 2 August 1916.
50 WV, 8 June 1916.
51 *Argus*, 23 August 1916.
52 Ibid., 2 August 1916.
53 Ibid., 3 August 1916.
54 WV, 14 June 1917.

10 Battles for peace

1 Ibid., 7 October 1915.
2 Ibid., 24 February 1916.
3 Ibid., 7 October 1915.
4 Ibid., 3 February 1916 and 9 March 1916.
5 Attorney-General, Correspondence, AA, War Series, 'Press Articles and News' 1915–17, CRS A456, WI/6/-, from *Patriot*, n.d.
6 Ibid., from *Daily Standard*, 12 November 1915; WV, 2 December 1915.
7 Attorney-General, CRS A456, WI/6/-, from advertisement in *Daily Standard*, 13 November 1915.
8 Ibid., folio D.
9 WV, 15 July 1915.

10 Ibid., 25 November 1915.
11 Attorney-General, CRS A456, WI/6/-.
12 *WV*, 2 December 1915.
13 Ibid.
14 Ibid., 12 August 1915.
15 Ibid., 23 December 1915; *Argus*, 20 December 1915.
16 *WV*, 23 December 1915.
17 Ibid., 6 January 1916.
18 *Argus*, 25 December 1915.
19 *WV*, 6 January 1916.
20 Ibid.
21 Ibid., 10 February 1916.
22 Ibid., 20 January 1916.
23 Ramsay, *Christian Science*, p. 89.
24 *WV*, 2 March 1916.
25 Ibid., 24 February 1916.
26 Ibid., 18 May 1916 and 13 April 1916.
27 Ibid., 16 March 1916.
28 C. Honig, as related to her by her aunt, Eileen McLoughlin, interview with author, 21 August 1988. Also mentioned in B. Walker, *Solidarity Forever*, National Press, Melbourne, 1972, p. 115.
29 *WV*, 30 March 1916; *Argus*, 27 March 1916.
30 *WV*, 30 March 1916; *Argus*, 28 March 1916.
31 *WV*, 30 March 1916.

11 Conscription, strikes and spies

1 *Age*, in *WV*, 16 March 1916.
2 Promise made by Andrew Fisher, 31 July 1914.
3 *Walker, Solidarity Forever*, p. 105.
4 VG, 'Open Letter to Members of Parliament'; uncensored: Jauncey, *Story of Conscription*.
5 Letter, Cecilia John to R. S. Ross, NLA, MS 3516.
6 *WV*, 5 October 1916.
7 Ibid., 26 October 1916.
8 Ibid., 12 October 1916.
9 *Argus*, 20 October 1916, in J. Bassett, *The Home Front 1914–1918*, Oxford University Press, Melbourne, 1983, p. 57.
10 Scott papers, 38/62, item 3.8.
11 *WV*, 26 October 1916; *Argus*, 23 October 1916.
12 Letter, Westwood to author, 2 May 1987.
13 *WV*, 26 October 1916.
14 Letter, Westwood, 2 May 1987.

15 WV, 26 October 1916.
16 B. Walker, *How to Defeat Conscription*, Merrifield collection, SLV, Women's Political Association file, folder no. 14.
17 Honig, interview with author.
18 WV, 2 November 1916.
19 Ibid., 30 November 1916.
20 Ibid., 18 January 1917.
21 Pankhurst Walsh papers, 2123/7, Adela Pankhurst to R. S. Ross.
22 WV, 5 April 1917.
23 *Christian Science Monitor*, 4 December 1918, in Rischbieth papers, 2004/4/144.
24 WV, 29 March 1917.
25 Ibid., 18 July 1918.
26 Scott papers, 38/62, item 3.
27 WV, 19 April 1917.
28 Scott papers, 38/55, newspaper cutting, n.d.
29 WV, 5 April 1917.
30 *Bendigo Advertiser*, 30 March 1917.
31 WV, 3 May 1917.
32 Ibid., 26 July 1917.
33 Ibid., 3 May 1917.
34 Ibid., 14 June 1917.
35 *Argus*, 16 August 1917. See also J. Smart, Feminists and Food.
36 *Age*, 16 August 1917.
37 Ibid., 21 September 1917.
38 WV, 30 August 1917; *Age*, 23 August 1917.
39 *Age*, 25 September 1917.
40 Murdoch papers, NLA, William Hughes to Keith Murdoch, quoted in Smart, Feminists and Food, p. 15.
41 Pankhurst Walsh papers, 2123/7/618.
42 Attorney-General, AAC, A456, W26/148/212.
43 WV, 6 September 1917.
44 Ibid., 30 August 1917.
45 VG, 'Open Letter to Workers, Unarmed Australia', ibid., 18 April 1918.
46 Ibid., 6 September 1917.
47 Ibid., 13 September 1917.
48 Ibid., 20 September 1917.
49 Ibid., 25 October 1917.
50 Ibid., 8 November 1917.
51 Attorney-General, Intelligence, AAB, MP 16/1, 15/3/1371.
52 WV, 18 April 1918.
53 *Mercury*, 19 December 1917, in M. Lake, *The Divided Society*, Melbourne University Press, Carlton, 1975, pp. 127–8.
54 WV, 13 December 1917.
55 Attorney-General, AAB, MP 16/1, 17/2150.
56 *Argus*, 17 December 1917.

57 Walker, Merrifield collection, SLV.
58 Moore, *Quest for Peace*, p. 37.
59 WV, 22 March 1917.
60 Ibid., 25 April 1918.
61 Censor, AAB, 3MD, MF 1228.
62 Ibid., MF 1402.
63 Ibid., 169/26–34.
64 Ibid., MF 2083.
65 Ibid., MF 2340.
66 Ibid., MF 430; MF 2054.
67 P. F. McDonald, *Marriage in Australia, 1860–1971*, ANU, Canberra, 1975, p. 160.
68 WV, 15 August 1918.
69 Ibid., 26 September 1918.
70 Blackburn papers, box 51.
71 WV, 24 October 1918.
72 Ibid.
73 Walker, *Solidarity Forever*, p. 124.

12 The world moves

1 WV, 30 January 1919.
2 Censor, AAB, 3MD, MF 2592.
3 WV, 27 March 1919.
4 VG papers, Letters During her Voyage from Australia to London, FL. Copy: SLV, MS 7865, MF 118, 29 March 1919.
5 Ibid., 8 April 1919.
6 Ibid., 11 April 1919.
7 Ibid., 19 April 1919.
8 Ibid., 28 April 1919.
9 Ibid., 4 May 1919.
10 Ibid., 13 May 1919.
11 Ibid., 23 May 1919.
12 *Report of the International Congress of Women, Zurich, May 12–17, 1919*, p. 131.
13 Ibid.
14 Ibid., p. 235.
15 Moore, *Quest for Peace*, p. 54.
16 WV, 1 September 1919.
17 Ibid.
18 VG papers, Letters, 17 June 1919.
19 WV, 6 November 1919.
20 VG papers, Letters, 8 July 1919.

21 *WV*, 18 December 1919.
22 Rischbieth papers, 2004/4/243.
23 *WV*, 18 December 1919.
24 Rapke papers, p. 13A.
25 *WV*, 18 December 1919.
26 Blackburn papers, box 51.
27 Pankhurst Walsh papers, 2123/7, VG to Adela Pankhurst.
28 VG papers, Sidelights.
29 Rischbieth papers, 2004/4/231.
30 Ibid.
31 Ibid.
32 Ibid.
33 Ibid.
34 Ibid.
35 Ibid.
36 Rapke papers, p. 14.

13 A spiritual woman

1 Henderson, VG: Biographical Notes, NLA, MS 1444.
2 Letter, John Holroyd to author, 22 November 1987.
3 Ibid.; Henderson, *Goldstein Story*, pp. 175–6.
4 Ibid., p. 176.
5 Franklin papers, 364/10/131, SMF to VG.
6 Henderson, *Goldstein Story*, p. 178.
7 *Herald*, 11 January 1930, in Rischbieth papers, 2004/4/219(a).
8 Rischbieth papers, 2004/5/1589, BR to VG.
9 Ibid., 2004/5/2173, VG to BR.
10 Ibid., 2004/5/1585, VG to BR.
11 Draft in ibid., 2004/4/101.
12 F. Fraser and N. Palmer (eds), *Centenary Gift Book*, Robertson & Mullens, Melbourne, 1934.
13 Rischbieth papers, 2004/4/211.
14 Ibid., 2004/4/242, VG to Ellinor Walker.
15 Ibid.
16 Ibid., 2004/4/243.
17 Rapke papers, p. 14.
18 Franklin papers, 364/10/133, VG to SMF.
19 Letter, M. Elizabeth Pratt to author, 27 October 1987.
20 Rapke papers, p. 19.
21 Franklin papers, 364/10/133, VG to SMF.
22 Ibid., 364/10, SMF to AG, 5 December 1953.
23 Ibid., 364/10/133b, VG to SMF.

24 Ibid., 364/10/121–2, VG to SMF.
25 Ibid., 364/10/133c, VG to SMF.
26 Ibid., 364/10/127, VG to SMF.
27 VG, 'Notes by the Way', *Australian Woman's World*, 1 July 1936, p. 7 and p. 37, in Rischbieth papers, 2004/4/141.
28 Rischbieth papers, 2004/4/247.
29 *ADB*, vol. 7, pp. 310–12.
30 Rischbieth papers, 2004/4/23, VG to John Curtin.
31 Ibid., 2004/4/246, VG to Keith Murdoch.
32 Ibid., 2004/4/245, Keith Murdoch to VG.
33 Ibid., 2004/4/26, VG to EHM.
34 *Australian Women's Digest*, vol. 1, no. 11, June 1945, p. 34.
35 Ibid.
36 M. Sawyer and M. Simms, *A Woman's Place*, Allen & Unwin, Sydney, 1984, p. 68.
37 United Associations of Women papers, ML MSS 2160 in Daniels and Murnane, *Uphill All the Way*, pp. 309–10.
38 Letter, FL, VG to EHM, 26 January 1944.
39 VG, 'The Struggle for Woman Suffrage', p. 117.
40 Rischbieth papers, 2004/4/30, VG to EHM.
41 Letter, FL, VG to EHM, 26 January 1944.
42 Rischbieth papers, 2004/4/27, VG to EHM.
43 Ibid., 2004/4/30, VG to EHM.
44 Ibid., 2004/4/27, VG to EHM.
45 Ibid., 2004/4/26, VG to EHM.
46 Ibid., 2004/4/244.
47 Franklin papers, 364/10/139, VG to SMF.
48 Ibid., 364/10/145, VG to SMF.
49 Rischbieth papers, 2004/4/27, VG to EHM.
50 Ibid., 2004/4/28, VG to EHM.
51 Ibid., 2004/4/30, VG to EHM.
52 Ibid., 2004/4/32, VG to EHM.
53 Ibid., 2004/4/28. For Vida's previous acquaintance with her, see Pankhurst Walsh papers, 2123/61, VG to Adela Pankhurst.
54 Rischbieth papers, 2004/4/28.
55 Ibid., 2004/4/32.
56 Franklin papers, 364/10, AG to SMF, 23 February 1947.
57 Ibid., 364/10/51, SMF to AG.
58 Ibid., 364/10/61, SMF to AG.
59 M. Clarke, 'VG', *ABC Weekly*, 10 March 1951, p. 21.
60 Franklin papers, 364/10/69, AG to SMF.
61 Rischbieth papers, 2004/4/35, AG to EHM.
62 Franklin papers, 364/10/69, AG to SMF.

Afterword

1 Letter, Westwood, 2 May 1987.
2 Ibid., 9 July 1987.
3 Lake and Kelly, *Double Time*, p. 177.
4 Scott papers, A2273/872, VG to RS.
5 A. Oldfield, *Woman Suffrage in Australia*, Cambridge University Press, Cambridge, 1992.
6 *Bulletin*, 25 August 1894, in Kelly, 'Woman Question', p. 72.
7 *WV*, 18 November 1913.
8 *Age*, 'Good Weekend', 26 November 1988.
9 Jeffreys, 'What is "Difference"'.

Chronology

1 Franklin papers, 364/10/69–71, AG to SMF.
2 *VG Pioneer of Freedom and Justice for Women*, pamphlet for the VG Memorial Fund, Rischbieth papers, 2004/4/224.
3 Information from Bill Tully.
4 *Dinner Party*, Melbourne 1988 programme.
5 *Hansard*, 16 May 1985, p. 2539.
6 *Age*, 1 January 1988.

Bibliography

◆

Vida Goldstein — Personal Papers

Unpublished

The Vida Goldstein papers in the National Library of Australia contain a number of typescripts by other people about Vida. These are listed separately by author under Primary Sources.

Goldstein papers, NLA, MS 1444.
Goldstein papers, SLV, MF 77/4.
Autobiography, 21 September 1987. (Copy in author's possession.)
Autograph Album, 1902, FL. (Copy of all FL material in SLV, MS 7865, MF 118.)
Autograph Album, 1911, FL.
A Bird's Eye View, 1902–1920, Rischbieth papers, NLA, MS 2004/4/231.
Diary, 1908, FL.
The George Junior Republic, FL.
Letters During her Voyage from Australia to London, FL.
Senate Campaign Scrapbook, 1903 FL. (Copy: SLV, MS 11956.)
Sidelights on Peace: a Warning and an Appeal, FL.
Shall we Organise to Defend Democracy?, Rischbieth papers, NLA, MS 2004/4/247.
'To America and Back', FL.
Towards a New Social Order, Rischbieth papers, NLA, MS 2004/4/211.

Published

'The Australian Woman in Politics', *Review of Reviews*, 20 January 1904.
'Notes by the Way', *Australian Woman's World*, 1 July 1936, pp. 7, 37.
'Open Letter to Members of Parliament', *WV*, 5 October 1916.
'Open Letter to Workers, Unarmed Australia', *WV*, 18 April 1918.
'The Political Woman in Australia', *Nineteenth Century*, vol. 59, July 1904, pp. 105–12.
'Report to the National Council of Women of New South Wales of an Informal Conference with Mrs M. W. Sewell', Melbourne, 1902.
'Should Women Enter Parliament?', *Review of Reviews*, vol. 23, no. 2, 20 August 1903.
'Socialism of Today—an Australian View', *Nineteenth Century*, vol. 62, September 1907, pp. 406–16.
'The Struggle for Woman Suffrage', in I. McCorkindale (ed.), *Pioneer Pathways*, Morris Walker, Melbourne, 1948, pp. 115–17.
'Women Can Help Australia More', *Herald*, 11 January 1930.
Woman Suffrage in Australia, Women's Press, London, 1911.

Goldstein, Vida and A. Bear-Crawford, *Reply to Speech against Women's Suffrage by Sir Henry Wrixon, K.C.M.G., M.L.C.*, Melbourne, 1898.
Goldstein, Vida and A. Lowe, *Women's Appeal to the Men of Victoria*, Melbourne, 1907.

Primary sources

Attorney-General's Department, Intelligence Records 1914–23, AAB, MP 16/1 and MP 95/1; General Correspondence Files 1914–38, AAB, MP 707; AA, War Series, 1915–17, CRS A456, WI/6/- and W26/148/212.
Australian Women's Political Association file, Merrifield collection, SLV.
Baker papers, NLA, MS 2022/2/103.
Blackburn papers, SLV, MS 11749, boxes 51 and 73A.
Censor's Reports, AAB, 3MD 169/1–73.
Charity Organisation Society records, Box 1/19, University of Melbourne Archives.
Deakin papers, NLA, MS 1540/15/618; NLA, MS 1540/16/761 and 796.
Franklin papers, ML, MSS 364/10/1–145.
Fullerton, M., *Memoirs*, Moir Collection, SLV, MF 77/4.
Goldstein, E., Autobiography, 21 September 1879.
Henderson papers, NLA, MS 1637; SLV, MS 10797, MSB 322; VG:

Biographical Notes, typescript, pre-1949, Rischbieth papers, NLA, MS 2004/4/191; typescript, 1961, in VG papers, NLA, MS 1444; typescript, 1966.
Lawson Family Letters.
Monash papers, NLA, MS 1884/5, Diary, 12 October 1887.
Newscuttings, ML, vol. VIII.
Northcote papers, NLA, MS 590.
Palmer papers, NLA, MS 1174/1/4; NLA, MS 1174/28/193–199.
Pankhurst Walsh papers, NLA, MS 2123/2/17; NLA, MS 2123/7.
Presbyterian Ladies' College Archives: *Prospectus and Annual Report*, 1884–1886; *Patchwork*, 1884–1887 and 1911.
Rapke papers, NLA, MS 842/12.
Rischbieth papers, NLA, MS 2004/4; NLA, MS 2004/5.
Scott papers, ML, MSS 38/20X; ML, MSS 38/39; ML, MSS 38/55; ML, MSS 38/61–2; ML, A2272–3.
Strong papers, NLA, MS 2882/1/1–2.
Sutherland, J., Report for Second Half Year, n.d.
Trades Hall Council papers, University of Melbourne Archives.
Try papers, SLV, MS 9910, box 1.

Secondary sources

Ackermann, J., *Australia from a Woman's Point of View*, Cassell, London, 1913.
Amery, K. L., *Hidden Women: Locating Information on Significant Women*, Melbourne College of Advanced Education, 1986.
'Ancient Briton', 'The Discriminators', *Petherick Pamphlets*, vol. 186, nos 3604–15, Thompson, 1906.
Australian Dictionary of Biography, vols 1–12, Melbourne University Press, Carlton.
Bacchi, C., 'Evolution, Eugenics and Women', in E. Windschuttle (ed.), *Women, Class and History*, Fontana, Melbourne, 1980.
―――, 'First-wave Feminism: History's Judgement', in N. Grieve and P. Grimshaw (eds), *Australian Women: Feminist Perspectives*, Oxford University Press, Melbourne, 1985.
Baker Eddy, M., *Key to the Scriptures*, Riverside Press, Cambridge, 1934.
Bassett, J., *The Concise Oxford Dictionary of Australian History*, Oxford University Press, Melbourne, 1986.
―――, *The Home Front 1914–1918*, Oxford University Press, Melbourne, 1983.

Brownfoot, J. and Scott, D., *The Unequal Half*, Reed Education, Sydney, 1977.
Champion, H. H., 'The Claim of Women', *Cosmos*, 31 May 1895.
The Citizens' Welfare Service of Victoria 1887–1987, 100th Annual Report 1986–87.
Clark, C. M. H., *A History of Australia*, vols V and VI, Melbourne University Press, Carlton, 1981, 1987.
Clarke, M., 'Vida Goldstein', *ABC Weekly*, 10 March 1951.
Cookson, R., The Role of Certain Women and Organisations in Politics in New South Wales and Victoria, 1900–1920, B.A. (Hons) thesis, Sydney, 1959.
Daniels, K. and M. Murnane, *Uphill All the Way*, University of Queensland Press, St Lucia, 1980.
Fabian, S. and M. Loh, *The Changemakers*, Jacaranda, Milton, 1983.
Fitzpatrick, K., *Presbyterian Ladies' College — The First Century*, Burwood, 1975.
Fraser, F. and N. Palmer (eds), *Centenary Gift Book*, Robertson & Mullens, Melbourne, 1934.
Gowland, P., 'The Women's Peace Army', in E. Windschuttle (ed.), *Women, Class and History*, Fontana, Melbourne, 1980.
Grieve, N. and A. Burns (eds), *Australian Women: New Feminist Perspectives*, Oxford University Press, New York, 1986.
Henderson, L. M., *The Goldstein Story*, Stockland Press, North Melbourne, 1973.
Jauncey, L. C., *The Story of Conscription in Australia*, Macmillan, South Melbourne, 1968.
Jeffreys E., 'What is "Difference" in Feminist Theory and Practice?', *Australian Feminist Studies*, no. 14, summer 1991.
Kelly, F., The 'Woman Question' in Melbourne 1880–1914, PhD thesis, Monash, 1983.
Lake, M., *The Divided Society*, Melbourne University Press, Carlton, 1975.
Lake, M., and F. Kelly, (eds), *Double Time: Women in Victoria — 150 Years*, Penguin, Ringwood, 1985.
Lewis, B., *Australia During World War One*, Melbourne University Press, Carlton, 1980.
Life and Work of Miss Vida Goldstein, Australasian Authors' Agency, Melbourne, 1913.
McDonald, P. F., *Marriage in Australia, 1860–1971*, ANU, Canberra, 1975.
Mackenzie, M., *Shoulder to Shoulder*, Penguin, Harmondsworth, 1975.
MacKenzie, N., 'Vida Goldstein: the Australian Suffragette', *Australian Journal of Politics and History* 1959–60, pp. 190–204.
———, *Women in Australia*, Cheshire, Melbourne, 1962.
Maunders, D., Keeping Them off the Streets, PhD thesis, La Trobe, 1987.
Mitchell, D., *The Fighting Pankhursts*, Baylis, London, 1967.
Moore, E. M., *The Quest for Peace*, Wilke, Melbourne, 1950.

Oldfield, A., *Woman Suffrage in Australia*, Cambridge University Press, Cambridge, 1992.
Pankhurst, A., *Put Up the Sword*, Women's Peace Army, Melbourne, 1915.
Proceedings of the Australasian Conference on Charity, 1890.
Ramsay, E. M., *Christian Science and its Discoverer*, Christian Science Publishing Society, Boston, 1955.
Reed, J., and K. Oakes, *Women in Australian Society*, Canberra, 1977.
Report of the International Congress of Women, Zurich, May 12–17, 1919.
Ryan, E., and A. Conlon, *Gentle Invaders*, Penguin, Ringwood, 1989.
Scott, D., 'Woman Suffrage: the Movement in Australia', *Journal of the Royal Australian Historical Society*, vol. 53, part 4, December 1967.
Sendy, J., 'Women's Peace Army', *This Australia*, summer edition, 1987, pp. 6–10.
Serle, G., *John Monash*, Melbourne University Press, Carlton, 1982.
Sherrard, K., 'The Political History of Women in Australia', *Australian Quarterly*, vol. 15, no. 4, December 1943.
Smart, J., Feminists and Food: The Cost of Living Demonstrations in Melbourne August–September 1917, paper presented to the Australian Historical Association Conference, Melbourne 1984.
Standford-Thomas, E., 'Workers for Women's Rights', *Treasures of the Mitchell*, ABC broadcast, 20 January 1966, ML, MSS 1855.
Steinbach, A., 'Women politicians may not be kinder, gentler', *Age*, 25 November 1992.
Sternberg, F., 'The Militant Suffragettes', *Lone Hand*, 1 July 1914.
Summers, A., 'The Unwritten History of Adela Pankhurst Walsh', in E. Windschuttle (ed.), *Women, Class and History*, Fontana, Melbourne, 1980.
Swain, S., The Victorian Charity Network in the 1890s, PhD thesis, University of Melbourne, 1976.
'Vida Goldstein', *Australian Women's Digest*, vol. 1, no. 11, June 1945.
'Vida Goldstein', *Imperial Review*, no. 39, 1904, vol. l, pp. 4–5.
Walker, B., *How to Defeat Conscription*, Merrifield collection, SLV, Women's Political Association file.
_____, *Solidarity Forever*, National Press, Melbourne, 1972.
White, A. J., *Advance Australia*, Sydney, 1908.
Wollstonecraft, M., *A Vindication of the Rights of Women*, Dent, London, 1982.
Young, J. F., *C. H. Spence*, Lothian, Melbourne, 1937.

Index

♦

Abbott, Edith, 187
Aborigines, 139
Ackermann, Jessie, 100–1
Addams, Jane, 196, 197
age of consent, 37, 101, 110, 132–3, 146, 165, 166; *see also* Vigilant Society
age of marriage, 123, 138
Allen, Stella ('Vesta'), 96, 99
America, *see* Goldstein, Vida: travels
Anderson, Selina, 55
Anthony, Susan, 38, 40, 229
Anti-Suffrage movement, 29–30
Anti-Sweating League, 16
Archdale, Helen, 216
Asquith, Herbert Henry, 101, 109, 113
Austral Salon, 34, 57
Australia First Movement, 216
Australian Church, 10, 49, 148, 150
Australian Labor Party, 53, 70, 96, 98, 114, 123, 124, 126, 128, 139, 169, 174, 176, 187, 190, 209; in government, 76, 141, 144, 170, 173, 210; Victorian ALP, 88, 90
Australian Natives' Association, 23, 53
Australian Peace Alliance, 147, 161, 168, 176
Australian Women's Association, 23
Australian Women's National League, 53, 73, 81, 88, 97, 98, 102, 122, 125, 139, 141, 145, 225

Baines, Jennie, 136, 138, 177, 178–9, 190, 216
Balfour, Lord and Lady, 108
Barrett, Dr James, 28, 132
Bear-Crawford, Annette, 17, 18, 20, 22–3, 24, 27, 32, 54, 78, 101, 166, 223
Bent, Sir Thomas, 76, 80, 85, 88–92
Best, Sir Robert, 123, 125, 126, 138, 139, 141, 142
Bijou Theatre riot, 162–3, 164, 167
birth rate, 28, 132, 166, 188, 192
Blach, Emily, 197
Blackburn, Doris, 129, 133, 135, 146, 213, 219
Blackburn, Maurice, 124, 133, 135, 136, 209, 210, 213, 225
Book Lovers' Library, 28, 204, 205
Britain, *see* Goldstein, Vida: travels
British Dominions' Women's Citizens' Union, 109, 200
Brodney, May, 146
Butler, Cuthbert, 160

Campbell, J.C., 89, 232
canvassing, 17–18, 97, 128, 140

Catt, Carrie Chapman, 35, 36, 38, 40, 41, 79, 202
Catt, George, 40, 41
censorship, 144–5, 148, 170, 197, 222; see also World War I
Champion, Elsie Belle (née Goldstein), 1, 4, 5, 6, 10, 13, 20, 28, 30, 31, 49, 204–5, 217, 219, 228, 233
Champion, Henry Hyde, 16, 18, 19–20, 26, 28, 30, 31, 71, 201, 204–5, 220, 223
Charity Organisation Society, 14–16, 83, 149, 151
Chicago, Judy, 229
children, delinquent or neglected, 24, 32, 33, 41, 45, 83; see also George Junior Republic
children's courts, 32, 36, 40, 83–4, 97, 226
Children's Peace Army, 164
Christian Science, 10, 49–50, 66, 74, 76, 77, 86, 165, 200, 203, 204, 206, 208, 209, 212; see also First Church of Christ, Scientist; religion
Clark, Manning, 229
Clarke, Mary, 111
Clarke, Lady Janet, 32
Clopton, Miss, 37
Colley, Miss, 117
Collingwood Free Kindergarten, 86
Commonwealth Franchise Act (1902), 39, 68
Communist Party, 201, 216
compulsory military training, 130, 139, 141, 169, 196, 209; see also conscription
Conciliation Bill, 107, 111, 113, 115
Connolly, Mrs, 13
conscription, 146, 174, 175, 176, 184, 210; referenda, 145, 169–73, 180, 184–6; see also compulsory military training; World War I
conservatives, 67, 73, 128
contraception, 28–9
cost of living, 81–3, 153, 178, 180, 226
court friends, 154, 165, 226

Cowan, Edith, 211
Criminology Society, 16, 33, 86
Curtin, John, 210
Cuthbertson, Margaret, 32, 150

Davison, Emily Wilding, 130
Deakin, Alfred, 25, 47, 71, 84, 87, 96, 118
deputations, 22, 79, 88, 89, 113, 117, 144, 152–3, 178, 180, 211
Derham, Freda, 29
Despard, Charlotte, 107
domestic servants, 32, 102
Duffy, Ella Gavan, 139
Dugdale, Henrietta, 3, 17, 57, 222, 223
Duval, Victor, 114

Eddy, Mary Baker, 50, 208
election campaigns, 54–68, 93–9, 120, 136, 138–41, 174, 221, 223–4; analysis of, 69–72, 99–100, 126–9, 141–2, 223–4; campaign meetings, (Albury) 58, (Ararat) 60, (Avoca) 62, (Ballarat) 65, (Bairnsdale) 64, (Benalla) 65, (Bendigo) 176, (Bridgewater) 59, (Brunswick) 97, (Camberwell) 120, 123, (Carlton) 95, (Casterton) 93, (Essendon) 98, (Fitzroy) 67, 70 (Hawthorn) 98, 124, 126, 138, (Hamilton) 60, (Horsham) 61, (Kew) 124, (Korumburra) 59, 65, (Malvern) 95–6, (Melbourne Town Hall) 97, (Portland) 59–60, (Prahran) 63, 97 (Stawell) 61, (Wangaratta) 58, (Warragul) 65; policies, 58, 60, 94, 120, 123, 138–9, 176; results, 69, 99, 126, 141, 177; women and, 56–7, 67, 70, 95, 98, 99–100, 128, 140, 141, 224
equal pay, 17, 31–2, 52, 62, 83, 101, 106, 110, 123, 134–5, 146, 148, 213, 225

Factories and Shops Act (1896), 16, 33
Fawcett, Millicent Garrett, 107, 227
Federal Public Service Act (1902), 31–2, 213
Fenshaw, Florence, 40

INDEX ◆ 259

First Church of Christ, Scientist, Melbourne, 49, 207–8; *see also* Christian Science
Fisher, Andrew, 108, 117, 118, 144
Fisher, Margaret, 108, 109
Flynn, Kate, 124, 138, 189
food adulteration, 52
foot riots, 178–80, 183; *see also* World War I
forcible feeding, 94 104, 114, 115, 118, 136–7; *see also* suffragettes
Franklin, Hugh, 114
Franklin, Stella Miles, 74–5, 77, 102, 112–13, 205, 208–9, 212, 214–15, 216–17, 220, 228
free love, 63, 66, 81, 177, 190
free trade, *see* protection
friendly visitors, 14, 15
Fullerton, Mary, 95, 102, 133, 177, 181, 186, 189–90, 212
Fusion Party, 96, 98, 99

Gallipoli, 152, 194
Gardiner, Connie, 153
Gardiner, Edith, 106, 151, 153–4, 219, 221
Gardiner, Madeleine, *see* Westwood, Madeleine
George Junior Republic, 45–6, 83; *see also* children; United States of America
George, W. R., 46
Golding, Annie, 77
Goldstein, Aileen, 1–2, 5, 10, 13, 30, 31, 34, 49, 75–6, 77, 135, 204, 205, 214, 216–17, 219, 220, 227, 228
Goldstein, Isabella (née Hawkins), 1, 2, 7, 9, 10, 12, 16, 23, 27, 28, 30–1, 49, 83, 112–13, 165, 219; correspondence, 64, 66, 74–6, 77; philanthropic work, 3, 10, 13, 14–15, 17, 18
Goldstein, Jacob Robert, Yannasch, 1–5 *passim*, 12, 14–16, 30–1, 153; opposes woman suffrage, 17, 29–30
Goldstein, Selwyn, 1, 5, 6, 108–9, 183, 193, 200
Goldstein, Vida: education, 3–9 *passim*; homes and offices, 1, 5, 13, 23, 30–1, 46, 75, 102, 120, 150, 170–1, 181–4, 207; internationalism, 49, 115, 130, 173, 175, 196, 198, 200, 202, 206, 219, 222; interviewed, 34, 41, 44, 46–7, 58, 211; male and working-class support, 17–18, 44, 46, 67, 71, 92, 103; newspaper coverage, 39, 41, 54, 55–8, 60–6, 68–9, 76–7, 80–1, 92, 96, 97, 98, 99, 106, 124, 134, 138, 140, 143, 149, 155, 157, 159, 164, 167, 178, 183, 185, 223; non-party, 48, 52, 60, 70, 100, 110, 116, 123, 124, 125, 129, 140, 174–5, 199, 209, 213, 219, 224; opinions, (of education) 13, 19, 28, 42, 47, 49, 52, 59, 67, 74, 82, 92, 131, 146, 166, 207, 212, 215, 225, (of next generation) 205–6, 212, 213, 214–15, (of post-World War II world) 214–15, 220, 222, (of royalty) 23, 108, 109, 200, 209, 210, (of science) 2–3, 9–10, 14, 49–50, 214, 226; opposition to alcohol, 3, 27, 210, 211, 212; pacifism, 23, 49, 89, 123, 127, 131, 141, 143, 146–7, 155, 156, 175, 176–7, 186, 190, 198, 214–15, 221, 225; philanthropic work, 10, 13, 15, 16–17, 149–50; physical appearance, 25, 46, 58, 62, 65, 206, 223; public recognition, xiii, 33, 45, 50, 105, 119, 129, 223, 228–9; public speaking, 25, 30, 31, 35, 37, 39, 41, 43, 44, 47, 50, 52, 54, 55, 57, 59, 76–7, 79, 80–1, 84, 94, 106, 109, 110, 114, 130, 134, 183, 200, 222; 'sex antagonism', 97, 118–19, 128, 132, 135, 136, 225; social life, 10–11, 31, 129, 208, 219; spiritually, 9, 19, 29, 49–50, 70, 197, 200, 205–6, 207, 210, 212, 214–16, 217, 222, 224–5; teaching career, 13, 23, 24, 225; travels (Adelaide) 58, 134, (Bombay) 193, (Brisbane) 186–7, (Britain) 105–15, 194–5, 199–203, 204–5, 219, (Colombo) 104–5, 192–3, 204, (France) 196, 198, (Honolulu) 35, (New Zealand) 34–5, (Samoa) 35,

(Switzerland) 196–8, 202, (Suez) 194, (Sydney) 34, 44, 76–7, 184–5, (Tasmania) 185, (United States of America) 35–6, 40–4, 47–8, 205, 219; writings, 22, 46, 54, 69–71, 81–2, 85, 88, 89, 109, 110, 118, 125, 174–5, 181, 201, 202, 205–6, 207, 209, 213, 214; see also Christian Science; election campaigns; wharf labourers; Women's Labour Bureau; Yarra Bank meetings
Guerin, Bella, see Lavender, Bella

Hagelthorn, Frederick, 151–2
Hardy, Keir, 105
Harper, Andrew, 7–9
Harris, Lillian, 123
Harvester Judgment, 83, 226
Hawkins, Samuel, 1, 3, 13, 231
Heagney, Muriel, 173
Heffernan, Maggie, 29
Helsy, Rachel, 146
Henderson, Leslie, 76, 86, 204, 205, 228
Henderson, Lina (née Goldstein), 1, 6, 10, 75
Henry, Alice, 207, 215
Heymann, Fraulein, 197
Higgins, Henry, 83
Higgins, Ina, 24, 49, 153
Hills, Mr, 188
Hillyar, Mrs, 77
Hodge, Margaret, 124
Hordern, Doris, see Blackburn, Doris
Hordern, Mollie, 154
Hotson, Kathleen, 166, 174, 182
Household Economic Association, 32
How Martyn, Edith, 212, 215, 216, 217, 220–1, 227
Hughes, Eva, 98, 99
Hughes, William Morris, 169, 170, 171, 173, 176, 179, 180, 184, 186, 194

Imperial Conference, 109
International Committee of Women for Permanent Peace, 148–9, 187
International Conference on the Suffrage Question, see International Women Suffrage Conference
International Council of Women, 32, 34, 40, 48–9, 58
International Woman Suffrage Alliance, 129
International Woman Suffrage Committee, 37–8
International Women Suffrage Conference, 33, 37–8 45, 86, 202, 228

Jeffries, Cr, 68
John, Cecilia, 129, 134, 135, 136, 144, 145, 147, 150, 153, 154, 159–65 passim, 168, 172–87 passim, 191–8, 212, 220
Johnson, Henrietta, see Dugdale, Henrietta

Katz, Fred, 163–4, 176
Kavanagh, Lizzie, 2, 31, 196, 208–9
Kenney, Annie, 89, 111, 114, 138
Kerr, Doris, 129, 136, 146
Kilkelly, Catherine, 117
King, Private G. A., 161
Kirby, Rica, 153
Knorr, Frances, 17

Labour Party (UK), 105, 107, 108, 114
Ladies' Benevolent Society, 151, 154, 155, 157, 183
Lambrick, Miss, 95
Lavender, Bella, 123, 129, 136, 138, 175, 219
Lawson, Sir Henry, 88
Lawson, Louisa, 77, 223
Lawson, Penelope (Aunt Appie), 12
League of Nations, 196, 197, 198, 200, 201, 202–3
League of Women Voters, 206, 213, 217, 228
Leongatha Labour Colony, 15–16, 153
Liberal Party, 88, 123, 125, 126, 128, 138, 142, 216

Liberal Party (UK), 130
lobbying, 20, 32, 222
Locke, Lilian, 49, 53, 66
Lowe, Annie, 17, 25, 45, 85, 91, 100, 222, 223
Lyne, Sir William, 44, 55

McInerney, Major, 162–3
McInerny, Mrs, 155, 157
Macky, Annie, 187
McLaren, Rev. S. G., 121–2
McLoughlin, Eileen (née McMahon), xiv, 177
Macphee, Ian, 229
Madden, Frank, 21
Magpie Club, 7
Malcolm, Mary, 57
Maloney, Dr William, 17, 45
Manifold, Walter, 132
Mann, Tom, 63
Mannix, Dr Daniel, 166, 170
Marion, James, 88
Markino, Yoshio, 108
marriage and divorce laws, 37, 52, 84, 94, 110, 123, 211, 213
Martel, Nellie, 55
Matters, Muriel, 101, 105, 112
Maxwell, May, 15, 117
Melin, Madame, 197
Men's League for Woman Suffrage, 88, 89, 92; UK, 107
Miles, W. J., 188
military police, 145, 162–3, 164, 183
Miller, Emma, 166
Miller, Florence Fenwick, 38
Monash, Sir John, 10–11
Moody, Hilda, 146, 171
Moore, Beatrice, 57
Moore, Eleanor, 148, 186, 196, 197
Moore, Mary Ann, 55
Morice, Lucy, 134
Mormons, 35
Murdoch, Keith, 204, 210
Murphy, Agnes, 94, 112–13
Murray, John, 152

National American Woman Suffrage Association, 35, 36–40
National Council of Women, 32, 34, 40, 48–9, 58, 76, 86, 90, 154–6, 200, 218
National Union of Women's Suffrage Societies, 227
naturalisation, 74, 109, 123
Newcombe, Harriet, 124
Nicholls, Mr, 182
No-Conscription Fellowship, UK, 200
Northcliffe, Lord, 109
Northcote, Lady, 86
Northcote, Lord, 75

Old Franchise League, 160
One Woman One Recruit League, 178

Paling, Lucy, 123, 124, 129, 136, 138, 145, 148, 154–5
Pankhurst, Adela, 137–8, 141, 145, 147, 150, 152, 154–5, 159, 160–1, 162–3, 165, 168, 171, 173–4, 178–80, 200, 216, 219
Pankhurst, Christabel, 89, 107, 110, 113, 114, 131, 137, 147, 200,
Pankhurst, Emmeline, 87, 105, 107, 110, 111, 113–14, 118, 137, 147, 171, 200
Pankhurst, Sylvia, 200
Pankhurst family, 86, 103–4, 122, 129, 131, 138, 216, 232
paper selling, 116–17, 146
peace conference: Powers, 191, 194, 196, 197; women's, 191, 194–5, 196–8
peace marches, 171–3, 185–6, 200
peace mission, 160–1
Peddie, Mr, 182
penal reform, 16, 32, 33, 35, 36, 41, 52
pensions, 52, 74, 207
People's Conservatorium, 187, 198, 199
People's Proclamation Day, 171
Pethick-Lawrence, Emmeline, 103, 105, 107, 112, 113, 114, 118, 138, 211, 216
Phelps, Editha, 112–13
Piddington, Marion, 189
Pitt, William, 90, 239

Political Labor Council, 53, 66, 166, 179, 182
Political Labor Leagues, 52
Political League, Auckland, 34
Prendergast, George, 88
Presbyterian Ladies' College, 6–9, 13, 90, 103, 121
press boycott, 89, 121–2, 125, 128
probation officers, 84
prostitution, 74, 123, 132, 138, 165, 167
protection, 57, 60, 61, 63, 71, 94, 123, 206, 212
Public Service Association, 31
Put Up the Sword, 160

Queen Victoria Hospital, 23, 66

race suicide, *see* birth rate
Rankin, Florence, 106
Rapke, Julia, 208
Red Plague, *see* venereal disease
Rede, Geraldine, 31
Reid, Carrie, 29–30
religion, *see* Christian Science; Mormons; Society of Friends
Religious Science Club, 10
Rennick, Mrs, 17
Reverchon, Blanche, 196
Richardson, Mary, 136
Riley, Fred, 168, 172, 176
Rischbieth, Bessie, xiv, 206, 215, 227
Roosevelt, Theodore, 39
Ross, R. S. (Bob), 173, 188, 190
Russia, 181, 187, 201, 221

St Paul, 49, 79
Sargood, Sir Frederick, 20
Save the Children fund, 198
Schreiner, Olive, 108, 177
Scientific Motherhood, 188–90
Scott, Ernest, 122
Scott, Rose, xiv, 23, 26, 28, 34, 44, 51, 52, 57, 76–7, 85, 86, 89, 92, 93, 130, 217, 220, 222
Sewell, May Wright, 20

Shaw, George Bernard, 108, 109, 204–5
Shilling Fund, 23, 233
Simonoff, Peter, 188
Singleton, Mabel, 95, 138, 162, 174, 176, 183, 190, 200, 212
Sisterhood of Peace, 148–9, 196
Skurrie, Joseph, 165
Smith, Mr, 182
Smyth, Dame Ethel, 105, 123
Social Improvement, Friendly Help and Children's Aid Society, 10, 150
social reform, *see* age of consent; children's courts; equal pay; marriage and divorce laws; suffrage
Socialist Party, Victoria, 140, 162–3, 165, 173–4, 187, 190
Society of Friends, 166, 200–1
Speddy, Theresa, 43
Spence, Catherine, 28, 56, 100, 134, 222
Squire, William, 16
Stanton, Elizabeth Cady, 41–2
Stapleton, Mr, 182
Stone, Dr Constance, 23
strikes, *see* unions; wharf labourers
Strong, Rev. Charles, 9, 10, 13, 18–19, 25, 32, 49, 86, 88, 148
Strong, Janet, 154
suffrage, woman, 32, 50, 51, 55, 109; bills, 17, 18, 20–1, 22, 30, 37, 39, 51, 76, 85, 88, 90–1; campaign for, Victoria, 59, 60, 64, 75, 78–80, 85, 86–92, 223; debated, 8, 19–23, 25, 106–7, (in America) 38–9, 42, 46–7, (in New Zealand) 37; petitions, 17–18, 88, 91, 117; pioneers, 3, 17, 94, 112, 222; results of, 101, 110, 114, 132–3, 206, 213; won, 3, 18, 31, 35, 37, 39, 51, 76, 78, 85, 90–2, 202; *see also*, Goldstein, Vida, writings; deputations; National American Woman Suffrage Association; United Council for Woman Suffrage
suffragettes, 134–41 *passim*, 146, 179, 207, 212, 214, 216, 219, 221; origin of term, 232; Vida's support of, 87, 89, 94,

101, 115–18, 121–2, 125, 129–31, 147; Vida works with in Britain, 106–14; *see also* forcible feeding; Pankhurst, Adela; Pankhurst, Christabel; Pankhurst, Emmeline; Pankhurst, Sylvia; Pankhurst family; Women's Social and Political Union
Sutherland, Julia, 5–7

Tangney, Dorothy, 213
tariffs, *see* protection
Terry, E. W., 138, 141
Thorpe, Margaret, 160
Tillard, Violet, 112
Trades Hall Council, 25–6, 33–4, 52, 65, 190, 226
Try Society, 24
Tybjerg, Clara, 187

unemployment, 14, 15–16, 83, 149–52, 156–8, 207, 209; *see also* Women's Labour Bureau; women's farm
unions, 33, 45, 139, 141, 151, 166, 171, 181, 183, 187, 203, 243
United Council for Woman Suffrage (United Council for Women's Suffrage, United Council for State Suffrage), 18, 23, 24–7, 29, 31, 78, 85, 223
United Kingdom, *see* Goldstein, Vida: travels
United States of America, *see* Goldstein, Vida: travels
United Women's No-Conscription Committee, 171–2

venereal disease, 119, 131–3, 165, 166–7, 211, 212, 225, 226
'Vesta', *see* Allen, Stella
Victorian Employers' Federation, 80
Victorian Lady Teachers' Association, 31, 166
Victorian Temperance Alliance, 17
Victorian Women's Suffrage Society, 17
Vigilant Society, 101, 166

Wallace, Lizzie, 172, 178
Walsh, Tom, 179–80, 200, 216, 219
War Precautions Act, 144–5, 161, 165 178, 179, 180, 185, 190; *see also* World War I
Warawee Club, 19
Waterhouse, Phyl, 228
Westwood, Madeleine, 153–4, 172–3, 218–19
wharf labourers, 172; strike, 178, 180–4
White Australia policy, 60, 105, 172, 212
White Slave Traffic, *see* prostitution
Williams, Henria H. L., 111
Woman Suffrage League, Prahran, 19, 30
Woman Suffrage Declaration Committee, 85–8 *passim*, 91
Woman Voter, xiv, 93, 97, 98, 101, 102, 104, 115, 118, 122–36 *passim*, 140–51 *passim*, 154, 156–60 *passim*, 163, 165, 170–81 *passim*, 187, 188, 190, 199; founded, 92–3; publication ceased, 199; *see also* paper selling; press boycott
Womanhood Suffrage League of New South Wales, 34, 44
Woman's Christian Temperance Union, 17, 32, 56–7, 74, 100, 201, 213
Woman's Sphere, xiv, 8, 26–9, 30–4 *passim*, 51–3, 57, 63, 67, 73–5, 77–9, 83, 93, 132, 220, 223; founded 26–7; publication ceased, 79
women, condition of, 3, 19–20, 45; higher education, 8; parliamentarians, 201, 211, 213, 224; police, 152, 153, 186; prison officers, 16, 101, 206; scrutineers, 126; teachers, 134–5; *see also* birth rate; contraception; suffrage; unemployment; working conditions
Women for Canberra Movement, 211
Women's Club, Sydney, 76
Women's Congress (1899), 24
women's farm, 16, 153, 226
Women's Federal Political Association, *see* Women's Political Association
Women's Franchise League, 18, 25–6, 56

Women's Freedom League, 107
Women's Guild of Empire, 216
Women's Labour Bureau, 150–2, 155, 156–8, 226
Women's No-Conscription demonstration, 171–3, 184
women's parliament, 74, 102, 186, 211
Women's Peace Army, 147–9, 160–1, 167–8, 171, 174, 176, 177, 178, 184, 187, 190, 191
Women's Peace League, 178–9
Women's Political Association, 52–3, 57, 66, 70, 73–4, 78–9, 99, 101, 116, 128, 131, 132, 141, 142, 164, 169, 218–24 passim; activities, 93, 102, 120–2, 133–4, 149–53, 156–9, 165, 169–91 passim; disbands, 199–200; loses support, 115, 130, 135–8 passim, 146–7, 154–5; members, 95, 106, 123–4, 129, 145, 174; supports Vida's election campaigns, 54–5, 67, 93, 95, 96, 120, 123–4, 126, 138–9, 174–5; see also Women's Progressive League; Yarra Bank meetings

Women's Political Education League, 77
Women's Progressive Association, 77
Women's Progressive League, 23, 45, 52; see also Women's Political Association
Women's Rural Industries Co. Ltd, see women's farm
Women's Social and Political Union, 86–7, 93, 104–10 passim, 113, 114, 116, 130, 136, 147; see also suffragettes
Women's Union, 183
Women's Writers' Club, 86
Woodhull, Victoria, 63
working conditions, 16, 28, 32, 45, 52, 82, 111, 112, 181, 192; see also equal pay
World War I, 139, 143, 190; see also censorship; conscription; food riots; War Precautions Act; Yarra Bank meetings
Writers' Suffrage League, 108
Wrixon, Sir Henry, 22

Yarra Bank meetings, 164–5, 167, 171–3, 177, 179, 181, 182, 184, 186; see also World War I